Invitation to Read:

More Children's Literature in the Reading Program

Bernice E. Cullinan
Editor

International Reading Association
Newark, Delaware 19714, USA

The International Reading Association attempts, through its publications, to provide a forum for a wide spectrum of opinions on reading. This policy permits divergent viewpoints without assuming the endorsement of the Association.

The poems "The Reader Voice" and "The Night I Caught the Burglars" by Brod Bagert are reproduced by permission of the author. "Always Be Polite When You Boss an Allosaurus," "Skinny Minnie," and "Dr. Womback's Needle" by Brod Bagert appear in *Let Me Be the Boss* and are reproduced here by permission of the publisher, Wordsong (an imprint of Boyds Mills Press), and the author.

The illustrations from children's books that appear in this volume are reproduced by permission. Acknowledgments of the sources from which they are taken appear separately, on pages 185-186.

Cover art by Tomie dePaola

Copyright 1992 by the
International Reading Association, Inc.
All rights reserved.

Library of Congress Cataloging in Publication Data

Invitation to read: more children's literature in the reading program/Bernice Cullinan, editor.
  p. cm.
Includes bibliographical references and index.
  1. Reading (Elementary)—United States—Language experience approach. 2. Children's literature—Study and teaching—United States. 3. English language—Study and teaching (Elementary)—United States.
I. Cullinan, Bernice E.   II. International Reading Association.
LB1573.33.I58   1992   92-4587
372.4—dc20   CIP
ISBN 0-87207-371-8
Second Printing, February 1994

*To the memory of Ron Mitchell
and his enduring vision that every child
will learn to read and will love reading.*

Ron Mitchell joined the staff of the International Reading Association in 1966 and served as Executive Director from 1984 until his death in 1989. His vision was shaped by visits with many colleagues—the teachers, reading specialists, librarians, and teacher educators who make up the membership of the Association. From his conversations with these professionals, Ron recognized early the growing role literature would play in the teaching of reading. His insight led him to ask a group of us to write *Children's Literature in the Reading Program*, a book he nurtured and launched with a great deal of personal pride.

This book is dedicated with humility and love to him.

CONTENTS

SECTION THREE: Putting It All Together

CONTRIBUTORS

Ira E. Aaron
University of Georgia (Emeritus)
Athens, Georgia

Francie Alexander
California State Department of Education
(on leave)
Sacramento, California

Brod Bagert
New Orleans, Louisiana

Rudine Sims Bishop
The Ohio State University
Columbus, Ohio

Bernice E. Cullinan
New York University
New York, New York

Linda DeGroff
University of Georgia
Athens, Georgia

Lee Galda
University of Georgia
Athens, Georgia

M. Jean Greenlaw
University of North Texas
Denton, Texas

Charlotte S. Huck
The Ohio State University (Emeritus)
Columbus, Ohio

Sylvia M. Hutchinson
University of Georgia
Athens, Georgia

Roselmina Indrisano
Boston University
Boston, Massachusetts

Joanne Lionetti
Marion Street School, Lynbrook Public Schools
Lynbrook, New York

Dianne L. Monson
University of Minnesota
Minneapolis, Minnesota

Jeanne R. Paratore
Boston University
Boston, Massachusetts

Arlene M. Pillar
USBBY *Newsletter*
Long Beach, New York

Sam Leaton Sebesta
University of Washington
Seattle, Washington

Dorothy S. Strickland
Rutgers University
New Brunswick, New Jersey

Deborah A. Wooten
P.S. 11, New York Public Schools
New York, New York

Foreword

Tomie dePaola

Looking back at my early school years, I can say thankfully that three of the teachers I had (or who had me) were wonderful. They were islands of understanding and patience, and were more than happy to challenge, with creativity and gentleness, my mind and my desire to learn everything about everything. Their names are Mildred Kinivey, "Miss" Bailey, and Rose Mulligan. These teachers also listened and knew I was serious when I said I wanted to be an artist when I grew up. First, third, and fifth grades were highpoints in my school career.

Of course, there were other, adjunct grown-ups who affected my educational well-being. There was Mrs. Beulah Bowers, the art supervisor, who came to school every two or three months so we could have ART. I celebrated my love for Mrs. Bowers in my book *The Art Lesson*. There was Mr. Conklin, who was the music supervisor. He also came to school every two or three months, to teach music appreciation and, more important, SINGING. (I was also good at that!) And then there was Mrs. Cowing, who was the "liberry" lady. Every Friday morning, Mrs. Cowing would pull up in front of Samuel Huntington Elementary School....

But more on this a bit later. First, I want to introduce one of the not-so-wonderful adults in my life—the children's librarian at the public library. Now, I don't mean to be cruel or to point fingers, just to report what my experience was. Miss X was rather formidable. She sat at a large desk smack in the middle of the charming children's room at the Curtis Memorial Library in Meriden, Connecticut. She wielded a large, wooden ruler to maintain silence, banging it on her desk if you so much as whispered—and I *did* do a lot of talking! But one of the most negative things she did was to label all the bookshelves with grades. Woe to the child who was only in second grade (me) but tried to sneak out a book on the shelf marked "FIVE." The reaction I experienced—and which I have never forgotten—was akin to what I would have faced if I'd tried to steal the crown jewels from the Tower of London. The other thing was that the small patrons of the children's room were allowed to check out only *one book per week*. I'm sure there were reasons for both these rules, but for young Tomie this was a disaster.

You see, reading was just about the most important thing in the world to me. (My art was *the* most important.) I couldn't get enough books in my hands. Books were in short supply at home; the Second World War was on, there was a paper shortage, and besides, the array of books for children available now just didn't exist in the early forties.

"But why," I hear you ask, "didn't your mother help you take out more books from the library?"

She tried. Miss X zapped her, too!

But, aha—when there is a child who must have a "book fix," that child will figure something out. And I did. It took some time, but here's what I came up with.

Friday morning was "liberry" day at school, when the liberry lady came. I was aware of this when I was in kindergarten even though I went only in the afternoon. I heard about it from the older kids. In first grade, we were excluded—because we were just learning to read, I guess. But I had a plan. Every Friday, I hung around and waited for Mrs. Cowing to drive up and park in the reserved spot in front of the school. Older kids who were liberry monitors would line up, Mrs. Cowing would unload boxes of books from her old car, and they would carry them up to the almost-always-locked library room on the second floor of the school. I quickly got the picture. If

I endeared myself to Mrs. Cowing, perhaps I could be a liberry monitor (whatever that was) too!

After several weeks, I started saying hello to Mrs. Cowing. Then, after making sure she recognized me, I said, "Can I help carry in books, too? I'm only in the first grade, but I love to read."

"Why, isn't that nice," Mrs. Cowing cooed. It was working.

By this time, the school year was coming to an end. I gave Mrs. Cowing a drawing I'd done. "I can't wait to see you next year," I said with a brave smile concealing just the hint of a tear, "and maybe I'll be lucky enough to be a liberry monitor." And even though my second grade teacher and I didn't get off on the right foot, Mrs. Cowing *requested* that I be one of the second grade library monitors.

Our jobs were very clear. First of all, we had to help unload the car of the boxes of books. Next, under Mrs. Cowing's supervision we would set the book out on the large tables. This was done one grade at a time. Then one of us (there were two or three monitors for each grade) would go to the classroom and let the teacher know that it was time for "the second grade to come to the library." Once the second graders had browsed through the books and had each checked *one* out, we monitors cleared off the tables, reboxed the left-over books, and the next grade monitors would arrive to repeat the process.

It was time now for me to put my full plan into effect. I began to look in the boxes intended for other grades. I would be wistful about having to wait for a whole year before I could take out one of the books from an upper grade box. I would be downright depressed at the existence of another one-book rule. Mrs. Cowing nibbled the bait and she was hooked. Or so I thought.

Before too long, I was taking home books from the other grades' boxes. I was taking home two and three books a week. I was a library monitor from grade 2 on. By the time I was in fourth, fifth, and sixth grade, Mrs. Cowing was bringing in books especially for me. I was her pet, and boy, did I have books to read. It was wonderful! Meanwhile, the public library opened its West Side Branch, and one of my dancing school colleagues' *mother* was the school librarian. She had no rules about grade levels or the number of books we could take home each week. The war was over and books literally poured into our house. But Mrs. Cowing was still one of several fairy godmothers who made sure my reading habit was served.

But that's not the end of the story. Years later when I hit high school, lo and behold, Mrs. Cowing was in charge of the bookroom where the textbooks for the various classes were handed out. I liked to stop by during breaks between classes and just chat with my old friend. One day, I decided to come clean and tell Mrs. Cowing about my earlier calculated behavior.

She listened to my confession very patiently. Then she smiled at me and said, "Oh Tomie, I knew that all along. I just had to make sure that I could help your love of reading stay alive."

Well, Mrs. Cowing, you certainly did!

PROLOGUE

Leading with Literature

The Reader Voice

She took me to the forest
And showed me fairies, elves, and trolls.
We watched a hunter's firewood
Burn low to the glow of coals.

We met a boy who was just like me,
He tried to win each race
And cried alone in his room at home
When he finished second place.

I listened as she read each tale
And made each tale my own,
And now...I still hear her magic voice,
Even though I'm old and grown.

Brod Bagert
November 30, 1991

Bernice E. Cullinan

When I began teaching I was very young and very scared. I was 17—almost a child myself. I knew I had enough lessons planned to keep my first graders busy for the first two days of school, but then what would I do? I was afraid those 27 six-year-olds were going to rise up against me and get out of hand. I soon learned, though, that I was good at two things: recess and read-aloud. On the playground, I knew exactly what to do. When Hank chased Elmer and Butch across the top of the jungle gym at full speed, I shook my head and they stopped the rough-housing. When Nedra jumped off the teeter-totter so she could watch Dolores crash to the ground, I reminded her about fair play. I felt confident and spoke with authority because on the playground I knew I was in charge.

I also knew I was in charge when I had the power of a good story in my hands. All I needed to do was pick up a storybook and walk slowly to the carpeted corner; 27 children followed me as if I were the Pied Piper. There I sat down regally on a low chair, solemnly opened the book, and looked expectantly into the children's faces to affirm the unspoken promise that no one among us would break the spell of the story. Before I read the first word, 27 pairs of eyes were focused on me and my book. I dropped my voice a register and turned my shoulders to add a bit of drama and mystery to my theatrical moment. I began to read aloud, investing each character with a distinct voice. Requests for encores were blurted out as orders—"Read it again!"—but I honored them nonetheless. Needless to say, we had lots of recess and read-aloud while I earned my wings as a teacher.

I've kept track of that special group, the very first children I ever taught. They're grown now with children of their own. Last summer at a school reunion, I ran into Hank, one of those former students. If it hadn't been for the same gentle, warm, brown eyes that had stared at me trustingly from a six-year-old's face, I might not have recognized the stocky six-foot man who stood before me. We pulled our lawn chairs into the shade so we could catch up on each other's news. He has four young ones, all but one already in school. As we sipped lukewarm iced tea, he looked at me and said, "I can still hear your voice when I read." Hank reads stories to his own children now, but the voice of his first grade teacher still echoes in his ear.

That legacy may not seem like a great one to some people, but teachers will know what it means to me. We teachers know that we leave something behind that lives on after us. For me, the legacy is a child who discovered the magic of reading through the sound of my voice and who as an adult still hears my voice when he reads to his own children. That's what draws us into teaching; that's what teaching is all about. That's why we continue to teach—we know that we help shape the next generation.

Brod Bagert's poem "The Reader Voice" touches the heart of the read-aloud experience—the child who hears the reader voice. That voice is created by a teacher, librarian, or parent; children hear it and internalize it and eventually use it to give sound to their own voices. This is the same process authors describe when they say that they try on other people's styles when they are learning to write and finding their own voices. Children, too, imitate the voices around them—whether it's the crisp monotone of the TV newscaster or the stylized voice of a Teenage Mutant Ninja Turtle.

By reading aloud, teachers and librarians give children a rich, expressive voice they can hear in their heads to help them develop their own voice. We know that the voice children hear in their heads guides their writing voice. In that way, the reader voice nurtures the child's voice—a voice that grows courageous and strong as a child expresses it in writing and reading.

In this book, you hear the voices of people who have given the sound of stories and poems to thousands of children and to teachers to pass along to their own students. I invite you to join the chorus. It can be your voice children remember; you can help them find their own voices as readers and writers. It is a legacy worth leaving.

In what follows, I describe some aspects of whole language programs at work, relate research findings that underlie the whole language philosophy, and present scenes of teachers actively using literature in their classrooms. The entire book, written by specialists in our field, is filled with practical, theoretically sound guidance about using literature to develop literacy. We all invite you to use the information presented here to introduce more children's literature into your own reading programs. An RSVP from you means that you will Respond, Stretch, Venture, and Pass on the love of literacy to another generation.

Whole Language Programs at Work

The whole language movement is a grassroots effort led by those who work directly with children: librarians and teachers who see children learning to read—and to love reading—through literature. The movement is grounded in three basic beliefs: children learn to read by actually reading and not by doing exercises, reading is a part of language and is learned in the same way as are other forms of language, and learning in any one area of language helps learning in other areas. Good literature, clearly the foundation of an effective language program, is central to reading and writing in whole language classrooms.

Whole language teachers work from a philosophy that guides their practice; they meet with support groups to clarify ways to translate theory into practice. They base classroom strategies on what they know about teaching and integrating literature across the curriculum, and about how children learn language. They use trade books extensively. They develop a personal teaching style. They observe how students learn best and they create supportive, collaborative learning environments. They surround students with literature and share their own delight in well-crafted fiction and nonfiction. The whole language reforms sweeping across schools in the United States and other countries are based on the beliefs of many educators that the use of quality materials will encourage students to read and to enjoy reading (Cullinan, 1989a).

Whole language teachers engage students in reading and writing workshops. They develop thematic units, genre studies, and author studies, and integrate reading, writing, and literature with social studies, science, art, and other content areas. Observant teachers and librarians are drawn to literature-based programs because they see the effects of exposure to stories and informational books on children's reading comprehension, writing abilities, and overall learning.

What Research Says

A large and growing body of research supports the use of literature in reading and writing programs. (For a comprehensive review of this research, see Galda & Cullinan, 1991.) We have known for some time that the children who become fluent readers are those who were read to early on (Durkin, 1966; Wells, 1986). Reading to children lays the groundwork for their liking to read, getting hooked on good stories, and choosing to read on their own frequently.

Today we know a great deal about *why* this happens (Clay, 1991). We now know that children can learn to read in much the same way they learn to talk (Cambourne, 1987; Holdaway, 1979). Being surrounded by trade books and supportive adults helps children in their active search for literacy, much as being surrounded by oral language is necessary for learning speech (Goodman, 1990). It happens this way: When children are born, we immerse them in language, surrounding them with talk and constantly demonstrating what language can accomplish. If we do the same thing with reading, children will learn to read in the same natural way (Strickland & Morrow, 1989). Frequent and positive contact with books creates interest in reading; increased interest results in more reading; more reading results in better reading. It's as simple as that.

Literature and Language Development

The language children hear and read forms the language they use in speaking and writing. More important, language shapes thought just as thought shapes language. The language children learn is not just the core of their future language possibilities; it is the wellspring from which their understanding and expression will flow.

Teachers enrich children's vocabulary and knowledge of syntax through extensive use of trade books, by reading books aloud to children and by having them read or pretend to read them on their own. This is so because the language of literature differs from the language of daily conversation: literature contains a richer vocabulary and more complex sentence structures. Furthermore, the language used in trade books is more varied than that found in traditional reading texts and workbooks. Literary language is often lyrical, poetic, and stylized; the ordinary language of conversation pales in comparison.

The language of literature sometimes calls attention to itself and causes a reader to pause and think about not only *what* is said but *how* it is said. We go back to reread a phrase and ponder it just to savor the language. For example, when I first read Cynthia Rylant's *A Couple of Kooks and Other Stories about Love* I stopped to reread a passage in which an older man reflects on his long-suffering sister-in-law: "Will you, on your death bed, mourn the life you never cared to savor because you were too busy counting your losses?" I also stopped to reread one of Rylant's sentences in *Appalachia: The Voices of Sleeping Birds*: "Many of them [Appalachians] are coal miners because the mountains in Appalachia are full of coal which people want and if you are brave enough to travel two miles down into solid dark earth to get it, somebody will pay you money for your trouble." Such language does more than accomplish the business of the day; it causes us to think about the world in a new way. It is the kind of language we want young learners to know about.

The Effect of Instructional Materials on Literacy Learning

DeFord (1981) demonstrated vividly that students' writing is influenced by the language they read. She observed a number of first grade classrooms where different types of reading programs were in place and found that children in phonics and skills-based classrooms believed that they had to know how to read a word before they could write it. The language they wrote was an imitation of the language in their reading textbooks. Children in whole language classrooms wrote richer and more well-formed texts, using invented spellings when they wanted to write a word they had not yet learned to read. These children read from a wide variety of trade books, newspapers, and other print materials; the language of their reading material was reflected in their writing.

We used to think that children must learn to read before they can learn to write; we now know that it doesn't have to be that way (Chomsky, 1971; Henderson & Beers, 1980; Read, 1971; Teale, 1989). In fact, the development of reading and writing skills in young children is interrelated: children learn to read by writing; they also learn to write by reading. They figure out letter-sound correspondences by encoding words into print as much as by decoding words from print (Calkins, 1986; Calkins & Harwayne, 1991; Graves, 1989).

Numerous studies have been undertaken in this area of emergent literacy. For example, Eckhoff (1983) studied second graders' writing in relation to their basic reading texts. She found that children who read from texts written with the style and complexity of literary prose used more elaborate linguistic structures in their own writing than did children who read from more traditional texts with their simplified sentence structures.

The variety of narrative structures children see in trade books helps them become better writers by adding to their storehouse of writing possibilities. King and Rentel (1983), for example, found that many children have a basic understanding of folktale structure by the time they enter school. When the researchers asked children to tell and write original stories, the children drew freely on the folktales they had already encountered as rhetorical models for their own creations. They had absorbed the structures along with the stories.

Blackburn (1985) refers to children's use of other people's stories in their own writing as "borrowings." She observes a borrowing cycle: children read and discuss trade books; they weave bits of stories they have read or heard into the stories they write; they share their compositions; and then bits of these compositions make their way into their classmates' compositions. Graves (1983) and Hansen (1987) among others believe that reading and discussing trade books helps children become more critical readers and increases their awareness of choices they make as writers. It undoubtedly gives them more alternatives from which to choose.

Many researchers embrace the use of literature to show young writers what other writers do (see, for example, Atwell, 1987; Calkins, 1986; Calkins & Harwayne, 1991; Graves, 1991; Hansen, 1987; Harste, Short, & Burke, 1988; and Harwayne, 1992). Writing teachers in whole language classrooms have turned this research into practice: they use literature with their students in part to illustrate the many forms writing can take—personal narrative, exposition, poetry, fantasy, persuasion, and so on (Cullinan, 1989b). Young writers can then borrow from models in literature as they shape their own pieces, adapting story structures to their own needs and imitating patterns other writers create. Whole language teachers show students that adult writers use personal experiences as a basis for writing;

this example encourages young writers to value and use their own experiences as the substance or inspiration for their writing. Teachers also talk about the kinds of research writers conduct before they write; they show children that finding out background information can help with their own creations. In essence, children's book authors serve as mentors to their readers who are learning the craft of writing.

Schema Theory and the Power of Stories

When students have a framework, or schema, on which to hang facts, they remember the facts more easily and retain them longer. For example, Anderson et al. (1985) showed that people are more likely to remember things on a 30-item grocery list if they are told they are shopping for a given dinner-party menu than if the list seems only to be a haphazard grouping. Further, Smith (1979) found that people remember more items from a list of concepts when they group the concepts into categories than when they study them as random items. The menu and the categories serve as meaningful frameworks. Stories provide a comparable sort of framework for remembering; because of this trait, and because good stories are intrinsically interesting, they make events memorable.

Literature speaks to our elemental need for story and our search for meaning. Bruner (1986, 1990) calls for using literature as a way into literacy because literature encompasses the wide range of human experience and shapes events into some kind of meaning. Literature, he says, is the driving force in language learning. Hardy (1978) says literature is compelling because "narrative is a primary act of mind." She illustrates the concept by describing how we dream in story form and remember the past and plan the future as stories. In fact, she says, story is the way in which we organize our minds. Britton (1970) and Rosen and Rosen (1973) established a strong research base in this area by recording thousands of hours of children's speech to determine the impact of story on children's language development. They saw numerous reflections of stories—such as the use of particular turns of phrase or certain story conventions—in children's language. Their ground-breaking work guides literacy research today.

Literature's Emotional Appeal

The emotional impact of literature is a major reason it serves us so well in handing down the magic of reading. Because literature deals with the range of human emotions, it portrays feelings we all experience. When we read about characters who suffer shame or feel joy we have compassion for them and understand their pain or happiness because we, too, have experienced these feelings. Sometimes we clarify our own emotions when we read about another's experiences in a book.

Good writers are able to express feelings in words; sometimes they pinpoint feelings we didn't know we had until we read about them. Kafka once said, "A book is an ax to break up the frozen sea within us." This is precisely what books do for children; they melt the unformed, frozen sea of feelings and help young readers express what they know. Stories help children realize that they are not alone in facing whatever problems they meet. They give children the courage to be strong in the presence of difficult circumstances. They hold out hope to every child who needs to know that one day he or she will be competent, successful, a winner.

I walk through lots of airports in my travels but now I don't walk through them in quite the same way I did before I read Eve Bunting's *Fly Away Home*. Now I watch for homeless people who might be living there. Bunting tells the gripping story of Andrew and his father, who live at the airport because the only other home for them is the street. Andrew and his father move from terminal to terminal trying not to be noticed. One day Andrew sees a little brown bird trapped inside the airport terminal and recognizes himself in the bird. The bird tries to escape; it injures its wing flying so hard against skylights and windows, but it keeps on trying. Andrew thinks, ''It took a while, but a door opened. And when the bird left, when it flew free, I know it was singing.''

I watched one teacher read this book to her first grade students in a suburban middle-class community. The children had heard about homeless people and had seen some on the TV news; a few had seen homeless people first-hand on an infrequent trip to the city. Bunting's book stunned them, however. Suddenly an author gave a face to what had previously been an abstract concept for these children. Bunting showed them a real person behind that nameless mass of ''the homeless.'' When the children met Andrew, a child whose hopes and fears matched their own, they put a face to homelessness. They began to ask questions about Andrew, they worried, they wanted to help. (Paula Fox takes a compassionate look at and evokes similar feelings about a homeless child in her book for intermediate-grade students, *Monkey Island*.) Because the experiences found in literature have this power to touch our deepest emotions, they also have the power to create profound and lasting impressions.

How Children Spend Their Time

Another group of researchers who support increased use of trade books in the reading program looked at the amount of time students spend reading. In Allington's (1983) study, the students who were slower readers tended to read for much shorter periods than those with greater ability, in part because their teachers tired and cut the reading period short when students labored and proceeded at a snail's pace. In short, students who needed the most practice received the fewest opportunities.

Dishaw (1977) found that children in general spend little time reading in the average classroom. In this study, primary-grade students typically read connected text for 7 minutes a day; intermediate-grade students averaged 10 to 15 minutes a day. Of course, students spend more time than this on the subject we call reading, but it is often time spent filling in blanks, matching pictures and words, or drawing.

Children don't seem to spend much time reading outside of school either. In a study by Fielding, Wilson, and Anderson (1986), the majority of students read from books for at most 1 percent of their free time. They frequently watched television for more than two hours a day, but they read for only five to ten minutes, if at all.

Whole language teachers and librarians try to counter such troubling statistics by giving children appealing books to read on their own. They know that students will not read independently unless the material is inherently interesting. These librarians and teachers also provide uninterrupted time for silent reading in school; they know that if students read good literature in school they are more likely to read outside of school. Administrators today do not say, as one once said to me on entering my classroom and seeing every child with his or her nose stuck in a book, "Oh, I'll come back when you're doing something." We know that silent reading *is* doing something.

Whole Language Teachers in Action

Whole language teachers differ markedly in the ways they work with students, but they share a common appreciation for literature and recognize its centrality in their programs. What follows are brief descriptions of some of the ways whole language teachers communicate this appreciation to their students. They may choose to introduce a single new book, focus on a particular genre, integrate literature with other areas of learning, or guide an author study. Whatever the approach, they build on the natural appeal of literature to draw students into literacy.

Introduce a New Book

Dawn discovered Mary Hoffman's book *Amazing Grace* at a children's literature conference and stopped to purchase a copy on the way home; it was one of those books she felt she could not live without a moment longer. She read the book about Grace, a girl who loves stories, to her fourth grade class the next morning. The students smiled in recognition as they learned that Grace likes to act out stories and always gives herself the best parts. They predicted she would want to be Peter Pan when her teacher announces that the class will present that story as a school play. When they heard the part where classmate Raj says that Grace can't be Peter Pan because she's a girl and Natalie says she can't because she's black, the tension in the classroom became electric. Dawn's students gave a collective sigh of relief when they heard that Grace gets the part and made I-told-you-so smiles when Grace plays it well. In a satisfying ending, Grace says, "I feel as if I could fly all the way home!" Her Ma replies, "You probably could," and Nana says, "If Grace put her mind to it, she can do anything she want." The listeners were pleased to the point of smugness to know that when the book ends, justice has been served and all's right with the world.

Dawn allowed her students to relish the pleasure of lingering in the spell of a good book for a while, but later, during writers workshop, she asked them to think about how the author had structured the story. Her intent was to help the students discover the techniques writers use so they could adopt some of them in their own writing. After they talked about the book, she asked, "What did the author do to tell the story?" Dawn wrote their comments on a chart:

1. She told us about Grace: what she likes, what she does.
2. She told us about a problem: Grace couldn't be Peter Pan.
3. She made a happy ending.

Dawn may eventually recast their ideas into more literary terms—such as "establishing character," "identifying a problem," and "creating a resolution"—but right now she is pleased that her students understand the concepts. She knows that the concepts are far more important than the labels.

Grace plays the part of
Anansi the Spider in
Amazing Grace.

Genre Study

Lorraine, a graduate student, works as a student teacher with a third grade class. Before beginning a study of biography, she and the cooperating teacher invited a colleague in to be interviewed by their students. The stu-

dents' questions were supposed to be "important" and pertain to "milestones" in that person's life. After a period of freewheeling questions, the group stopped to evaluate the information they had obtained. The teachers guided the students to ask themselves these questions:

- Can you put the events into sequential order?
- Have you discovered milestones? If not, why not?
- Which pieces of information should you include in a biography?
- What else do you need to know?

The teachers were modeling criteria to evaluate information; the students would eventually apply these criteria to select information for their autobiographies.

A Halloween celebration in October led to reading a biography of Harry Houdini and a nonfiction book on trickery. After reading, the students brainstormed about magic, illusion, and tricks. They discussed Houdini's mastery of illusion, the difficulty of writing instructions for performing tricks, and the importance of following directions. Some students performed their own tricks in front of the class; they discussed self-confidence and what to do if a trick fails. The students then saw videotapes about the lives of Harry Houdini and the modern magician David Copperfield; they talked about how the questions who, what, when, where, and why are answered in biographies.

All of these activities were undertaken before the students wrote their autobiographies. Through them, the class learned important background information for their task, which undoubtedly led to higher quality writing. The teachers integrated authentic practice in reading, writing, listening, and speaking with their study of biography.

Integrating Literature, Social Studies, and Writing

Deborah, a fifth and sixth grade teacher, has successfully incorporated literature into her social studies program in the past. When students were studying the Revolutionary War period in American history, she used James and Christopher Collier's *My Brother Sam Is Dead* and *Who Is Carrie?* along with Elizabeth George Speare's *The Sign of the Beaver* to enrich the social studies textbook's depiction of life during that time (Wooten, 1992). More recently, she incorporated Katherine Paterson's historical novel *Lyddie* into teaching about the Industrial Revolution.

Deborah launched the social studies unit by reading aloud from *Lyddie*. At the end of the first chapter, her students wanted to talk:

"It reminds me of *Sarah, Plain and Tall* because of what you told us about the letters."

"No, I think it's more like *Little House on the Prairie* because of the part about the bear."

"I say *Witch of Blackbird Pond*."

"Well, what about *Trouble River*? It's like that, too."

Deborah's students were making connections to other books they had read. As they became more involved in Paterson's novel, their comments focused on elements inside the story and their growing knowledge about the life Lyddie leads. They were developing a context for understanding the impact of industrialization on people's lives.

As a writing teacher, Deborah tells her students about the kinds of research writers conduct to prepare for writing. She told them, for example, that before Paterson began writing *Lyddie*, she interviewed experts from the Museum of American Textile History, studied how weaving looms work, and read letters written by girls who worked in the textile mills of Lowell, Massachusetts, between 1826 and 1860. Paterson, a masterful storyteller, grounded her superb novel about a farm girl turned factory worker in the 1840s in authentic information. Young writers develop respect for Paterson's care as a researcher as they research and prepare to write their own stories.

Deborah says that students respond positively to novels set in the historical period they are studying because "a story provides a framework for students to house the facts." She observes that historical novels pull readers into the period they depict and allow students to personalize the information they learn from history lessons. Deborah notes that students go back and forth between the historical facts they read about in their social studies textbooks and the facts of a related novel: "They relax into the story and absorb the factual information about the historical period. It works because the story is nonthreatening." Deborah's students also make connections between historical periods and modern times. For example, they commiserated with Lyddie, who had to work in a lint-filled room surrounded by the pounding noise of weaving looms, and compared the environmental conditions she lived under with those in a region in Russia they had read about in a current magazine. In short, Deborah's students were drawing on the drama of historical fiction and incorporating factual information from nonfiction to integrate what they were learning with what they already knew.

An Author Study

Charlotte, a student teacher, proposed a study of Chris Van Allsburg when she noticed how enthusiastically her third graders responded when she read one of his books aloud. Charlotte was intrigued by the fact that Van Allsburg's dog, Fritz, appears in every book and thought the search for Fritz would appeal to the students. Charlotte created a soft sculpture of Fritz's head and attached a five-foot piece of muslin to it. Sewn to the muslin were pockets, and into each of these Charlotte put projects and task cards related to a particular Van Allsburg book. When the students found Fritz in one of the books, they wrote the page number and attached it to the appropriate pocket on the sculpture.

Charlotte introduced the unit with a minilesson on Van Allsburg. She pasted a photograph of the author on a large piece of paper and wrote down his date and place of birth along with a three-line biography highlighting his childhood and his art career. Above and below the picture she wrote out quotes from Van Allsburg: "I've got a sketchbook in my head with thousands of pieces of sculpture and enough descriptions for ten books. But I let those things sit in the back of my mind whereby the weaker ideas settle out by themselves."

Charlotte asked the students to focus on Van Allsburg's statement that "the reader has to resolve the book after he has read it. The book itself is merely chapter one." The students accepted the challenge to participate actively in Van Allsburg's storytelling; they easily understood the implied ending to *Jumanji* and enjoyed imagining what might happen after the story's close.

They were not as quick to see the layers of meaning in all of Van Allsburg's books, however. Charlotte read aloud *The Wretched Stone*, a story about people who watch a grey stone until they turn into apes. The children laughed at the final line about the crew having acquired a taste for bananas. But when the teacher asked about the possible meaning of the grey stone, they guessed it was a magic stone. Only after she reread the description and suggested that they probably had one at home did the children venture that the stone might represent television or technology.

Once they sensed the possibility of a larger meaning, however, the children embarked on a lively discussion of Van Allsburg's message, the apes, and the use of exaggeration to make a point. What began as an author study ended up including reading for different levels of meaning and developing an understanding of symbolism.

An Invitation

This prologue is an invitation to join the growing group of whole language teachers who incorporate literature in their programs. It is an invitation to add your voice to the chorus of teachers and librarians who give children "the reader voice" that lingers in their heads. The research underlying whole language supports the idea that children's writing is influenced by what they read; reading trade books increases children's vocabulary and knowledge of narrative structures. Further, reading trade books helps to increase the amount of time children want to read on their own.

The preceding vignettes of practicing teachers suggest a variety of ways whole language teachers put these ideas into practice. In what follows, you'll be introduced to more teachers and more practices. And so this prologue is also an invitation to you to keep reading. I hope you will find much to encourage and inspire you in this volume.

References

Allington, R.L. (1983). The reading instruction provided readers of differing ability. *Elementary School Journal, 83,* 255-265.

Anderson, R., Hiebert, E.H., Scott, J.A., & Wilkinson, I.A.G. (1985). *Becoming a nation of readers: The report of the Commission on Reading.* Washington, DC: National Institute of Education, U.S. Department of Education.

Atwell, N. (1987). *In the middle: Writing, reading, and learning with adolescents.* Portsmouth, NH: Heinemann.

Blackburn, E. (1985). Stories never end. In J. Hansen, T. Newkirk, & D. Graves (Eds.), *Breaking ground: Teachers relate reading and writing in the elementary school.* Portsmouth, NH: Heinemann.

Britton, J. (1970). *Language and learning.* New York: Penguin.

Bruner, J. (1986). *Actual minds, possible worlds.* Cambridge, MA: Harvard University Press.

Bruner, J. (1990). *Acts of meaning.* Cambridge, MA: Harvard University Press.

Calkins, L.M. (1986). *The art of teaching writing.* Portsmouth, NH: Heinemann.

Calkins, L.M., & Harwayne, S. (1991). *Living between the lines.* Portsmouth, NH: Heinemann.

Cambourne, B. (1987). Language, learning and literacy. In A. Butler & J. Turbill (Eds.), *Towards a reading-writing classroom.* Portsmouth, NH: Heinemann.

Chomsky, C. (1971). Write first, read later. *Childhood Education, 46,* 296-299.

Clay, M. (1991). *Becoming literate: The construction of inner control.* Portsmouth, NH: Heinemann.

Cullinan, B.E. (1989a). Latching on to literature: Reading initiatives take hold. *School Library Journal, 35,* 27-31.

Cullinan, B.E. (1989b). *Literature and the child* (2nd ed.). Orlando, FL: Harcourt Brace Jovanovich.

DeFord, D. (1981). Literacy: Reading, writing, and other essentials. *Language Arts, 58*(6), 652-658.

Dishaw, M. (1977). Descriptions of allocated time to content areas for A-B period. In *Beginning teacher evaluation study* (Technical Note IV-11a). San Francisco, CA: Far West Regional Laboratory for Educational Research and Development.

Durkin, D. (1966). *Children who read early.* New York: Teachers College Press.

Eckhoff, B. (1983). How reading affects children's writing. *Language Arts, 60,* 607-616.

Fielding, L.G., Wilson, P.T., & Anderson, R.C. (1986). A new focus on free reading: The role of trade books in reading instruction. In T.E. Raphael (Ed.), *The contexts of school-based literacy* (pp. 149-160). New York: Random House.

Galda, L., & Cullinan, B.E. (1991). Literature for literacy: What research says about the benefits of using trade books in the classroom. In J. Flood, J.

Jensen, D. Lapp, & J.R. Squire (Eds.), *Handbook of research on teaching the English language arts*. New York: Macmillan.

Goodman, Y. (Ed.). (1990). *How children construct literacy: Piagetian perspectives*. Newark, DE: International Reading Association.

Graves, D.H. (1983). *Writing: Teachers and children at work*. Portsmouth, NH: Heinemann.

Graves, D.H. (1989). *The reading/writing teacher's companion: Experiment with fiction*. Portsmouth, NH: Heinemann.

Graves, D.H. (1991). *Building a literate classroom*. Portsmouth, NH: Heinemann.

Hansen, J. (1987). *When writers read*. Portsmouth, NH: Heinemann.

Hardy, B. (1978). Narrative as a primary act of mind. In M. Meek, A. Warlow, & G. Barton (Eds.), *The cool web: The pattern of children's reading* (pp. 12-23). New York: Atheneum.

Harste, J.C., Short, K., & Burke, C. (1988). *Creating classrooms for authors: The reading-writing connection*. Portsmouth, NH: Heinemann.

Harwayne, S. (1992). *Lasting impressions*. Portsmouth, NH: Heinemann.

Henderson, E.H., & Beers, J. (Eds.). (1980). *Developmental and cognitive aspects of learning to spell*. Newark, DE: International Reading Association.

Holdaway, D. (1979). *Foundations of literacy*. New York: Ashton Scholastic.

King, M.L., & Rentel, V.M. (1983). *A longitudinal study of coherence in children's written narratives* (Final Report; NIE-G-8-0063). Columbus, OH: Research Foundation, Ohio State University.

Read, C. (1971). Preschool children's knowledge of English phonology. *Harvard Educational Review*, *41*, 1-4.

Rosen, H., & Rosen, C. (1973). *The language of primary school children*. London: Penguin/Education for the Schools Council.

Smith, F. (1979). *Reading without nonsense*. New York: Teachers College Press.

Strickland, D.S., & Morrow, L.M. (1989). *Emerging literacy: Young children learn to read and write*. Newark, DE: International Reading Association.

Teale, W. (1989). Emergent literacy: New perspectives. In D.S. Strickland & L.M. Morrow (Eds.), *Emerging literacy: Young children learn to read and write*. Newark, DE: International Reading Association.

Wells, G. (1986). *The meaning makers: Children learning language and using language to learn*. Portsmouth, NH: Heinemann.

Wooten, D. (1992). The use of historical fiction trade books in collaboration with a social studies textbook and its relation to learning in the social studies classroom. Unpublished doctoral dissertation, New York University.

Children's Books

Bunting, E. (1991). *Fly away home*. (Ill. by R. Himler.) New York: Clarion.

Collier, J.L., & Collier, C. (1974). *My brother Sam is dead*. New York: Four Winds.

Collier, J.L., & Collier, C. (1984). *Who is Carrie?* New York: Delacorte.

Fox, P. (1991). *Monkey Island*. New York: Orchard.

Hoffman, M. (1991). *Amazing Grace*. (Ill. by C. Binch.) New York: Dial.

Paterson, K. (1991). *Lyddie*. New York: Lodestar/Dutton.

Rylant, C. (1990). *A couple of kooks and other stories about love*. New York: Orchard.

Rylant, C. (1991). *Appalachia: The voices of sleeping birds*. (Ill. by B. Moser.) San Diego, CA: Harcourt Brace Jovanovich.

Speare, E.G. (1983). *The sign of the beaver*. Boston, MA: Houghton Mifflin.

Van Allsburg, C. (1981). *Jumanji*. Boston, MA: Houghton Mifflin.

Van Allsburg, C. (1991). *The wretched stone*. Boston, MA: Houghton Mifflin.

SECTION ONE

Quality children's literature comes in all genres. Whether you are teaching your students poetry appreciation, the structure of novels, where to look for information, or the fundamentals of the craft of writing, countless fine books are available to make your job easier.

This section introduces some of those books, along with teaching ideas and strategies for using them in the classroom. Chapter 1 discusses books for preschool and early elementary students and suggests ways to help young children on their way to becoming enthusiastic and capable readers. Chapter 2 introduces an innovative technique for teaching poetry. The "performance method" invites children to have fun with poetry and at the same time teaches them how this genre of literature works.

Reading realistic fiction, both contemporary and historical, can help students in the upper elementary, middle school, and junior high years understand more about their own worlds. Chapter 3 discusses some examples of outstanding realistic fiction and suggests how such books can be linked to students' lives. Nonfiction, often overlooked when literary genres are being considered, can be a valuable classroom resource. Chapter 4 shows how informational books can be used to further literacy learning as well as to enhance students' knowledge in other content areas.

Genre Studies

CHAPTER 1

Books for Emergent Readers

Charlotte S. Huck

Emergent Reading at Home

Emily was just four and a half when I first visited her home. She loved books. In fact there were books all over her house—her own books on her own shelves in her room, books in the family room, books in the living room. There were even books mixed in with her toys. Emily and her two-year-old brother, Andrew, heard about six stories a day. They connected stories with real life. When the birds came up to the feeder in the winter, Andrew went and found Ashley Wolff's *A Year of Birds* by himself and pointed to an illustration of a feeding station. Emily said that when Andrew lost his teddy bear he was just like the little boy who lost his blanket in John Burningham's *The Blanket*: Andrew had the whole household looking for the bear, just as the family in the story looked for the blanket, and Andrew found his bear in the same place the boy in the story had found his blanket— under his pillow! Emily had her favorite stories; she had memorized Bill Martin's *Brown Bear, Brown Bear, What Do You See?*, she loved to join in reciting large parts of the caterpillar's menu in *The Very Hungry Caterpillar* by Eric Carle, and she sang along with Carol Jones's *Old MacDonald Had a Farm*.

One day, as Emily gave me Cindy Ward's *Cookie's Week* to read for the third time, she whispered confidentially, "You know, Andrew can't read yet." Well, Emily couldn't read yet either, but luckily she didn't know it. Emily was an emergent reader, memorizing books, joining in on refrains, retelling stories to Andrew, linking books to their illustrations, and connecting them to her own life. She was playing at reading on the way to becoming a real reader. When I saw her again a year later, Emily was reading everything on her own.

What made Emily an accomplished reader at five and a half? First of all, she was surrounded by books; they were a natural part of her environment. Second, both her mother and her father read to her frequently, enjoyed reading themselves, and enjoyed reading to the children. By the time Emily entered first grade she had heard more than 12,000 stories! Third, from the time she was a baby her parents had connected books to real life, saying things like "Emily has great big new yellow boots" after they read a line about boots from A.A. Milne's poem "Happiness." The family talked about favorite books, authors, illustrators, and poets. Everyone was thrilled when Emily's mother brought home a new book titled *What Game Shall We Play?* and Emily identified the author as Pat Hutchins after taking one look at the patterned animals. Books were good friends and companions in Emily's life.

It would be wonderful if all children had Emily's literacy background, but of course they don't. So what can we learn from Emily and her family that we can use in school with all children?

Beginning Reading in School

One of the first things we can do is surround children with books, good books with exciting, well-written stories that will help convey the idea that reading is enjoyable. Storybooks shouldn't be something extra that we buy with lottery money. Good books are essential to education and should be at the top of every school's budget. I have tremendous respect for teachers who buy books for children, but I worry about it. Should they be spending their own money for children's books? Do school football coaches pay for the footballs? Something is very wrong with our priorities in schools when we economize on children's books.

One way we can allocate funds for classroom libraries is to use the money ordinarily spent on workbooks and worksheets. For first graders in the United States, this averages about $28 a student, or $700 a class—enough for approximately 70 trade books. In *Becoming a Nation of Readers*, Anderson et al. (1985) decry schools' overreliance on workbooks and worksheets, maintaining that up to 70 percent of U.S. reading instruction in the elementary grades is devoted to this kind of "seatwork." Anderson and his colleagues go on to say that "the amount of time devoted to worksheets is unrelated to year-to-year gains in reading proficiency" (pp. 75-76). Children would be far better off to read literature, write in journals, or create their own stories than to spend their time filling in meaningless blanks in workbook exercises.

The second thing teachers can do is read aloud to children as often as Emily's parents read to her—four to six times a day for children in kindergarten and primary grades. We should also reread stories, just as Emily heard her favorite bedtime stories over and over again. If you do only one thing to improve your reading program, I would urge that it be increasing the time you spend reading aloud to children. Every time you read aloud, you are helping young children learn to read (see, for example, Clark, 1976; Sulzby, 1985; Teale, 1984; Wells, 1986).

What do children gain from listening to an adult read aloud?

- Children learn that reading is pleasurable, that it is something they want to be able to do.

- Children learn about the structure of stories—that stories have beginnings, middles, and endings. They learn that some stories begin the same way ("Once upon a time") and end the same way ("They lived happily ever after") and that the action of certain characters (a fox or wolf, a princess or witch) is predictable.

- Children learn the concepts behind print: that print carries meaning; that printed text remains the same and can be read again in the same way; that print is read in a specific direction; that printed words correspond to spoken words; and that pictures carry clues to meaning and vocabulary.

- Children begin to build a frame of reference for literature and to find out how books work. They learn that books are written by authors and that pictures are done by illustrators (who may also be authors). They also become acquainted with certain genres of literature (rhymes, folktales, picture books, informational books, and longer "chapter books").

- Children learn new words and increase their vocabularies. They become familiar with terms such as title, dedication, author, illustrator, characters, fairy tales, and poetry. They learn about the sounds of language—such things as rhyme, rhythm, and alliteration—as well as believable dialogue. And they learn that every subject has its own vocabulary.

What a lot children can learn by listening to a variety of stories read well by an enthusiastic teacher!

Trade Books or Textbooks?

The line between trade books and textbooks is blurring as more and more textbook publishers scurry to provide literature-based reading programs. Five years ago I could talk about a literature-based reading program and everyone knew I meant teaching children to read with "real" books. This is no longer true. Textbook companies have adopted the term to describe basal readers that contain selections from literature. Now when I want to talk about the kind of reading program I believe in, I try to be very specific and discuss a program that uses trade books.

I suppose we should be pleased with the change in the content of many basal reader series, but we need to remember that even those with lots of literature include only *selections* from books. Reading whole books provides much of the real pleasure of literature. Many teachers complain that frequently the selections include story endings, which makes it nearly impossible to motivate students to read the whole book.

Textbook companies are also producing "little books" as rapidly as they are printing Big Books. These little books have soft covers and contain one simple story. Some are well written and have exciting plots, while others are as dull as preprimers. The new basal series packages often consist of many books: readers with some literature content; little books; Big Books; workbooks; end-of-the-unit tests; teacher guidebooks; and sometimes a collection of trade books. The content and format have changed, but the recommended practices for teachers and the workbooks remain the same. When basal series workbooks assign exercises on Arnold Lobel's *Frog and Toad Are Friends* or use Mother Goose rhymes to study phonics, they defeat the very purpose of using literature—introducing new readers to the joy that literature brings. These new series some-

Frog and Toad wait for the mail in Arnold Lobel's familiar favorite *Frog and Toad Are Friends.*

times succeed only in "basalizing" literature by asking children to respond to it by filling in blanks and answering adult questions, rather than listening to children's responses to it—what pleased them, made them laugh, or confused them.

Choosing Literature

Let me suggest some general guidelines for selecting books for use with emergent readers and then move to some specific recommendations for predictable books. (See Huck, Hepler, & Hickman, 1987, for suggestions about picture books.)

1. Select books that will delight children, make them giggle, surprise them, comfort them, and please them. Do nothing with the story that will destroy that pleasure; read and share the books *as they are* to encourage those responses, and suggest instructional activities that will strengthen children's delight with stories.

Recently I visited a wonderful kindergarten/first grade class in which the students had made a mural of nursery rhyme characters. The children had painted and cut out large figures for Jack and Jill, Humpty Dumpty, Peter Peter Pumpkin Eater, and other favorites. They had written their own "balloons" (in invented spelling) to indicate characters' thoughts: Humpty Dumpty says, "Help, I'm going to fall"; Peter says smugly, "I'm glad I put her in a shell," while his wife plans her escape, saying "I'm going to get out of here." This activity synthesized various elements of the class's study of Mother Goose rhymes. It helped the children develop empathy for certain characters, take their point of view, and have the

emotional response that reading literature is meant to prompt.

2. Evaluate each book for its imaginative qualities. Many little books and some Big Books use a formula like that of predictable books, but they lack real literary quality. They may be easy to read and include repetition, but they're dull. To test for literary merit, examine the language and content of each story.

Listen to the quality of the language in Eric Carle's *The Very Hungry Caterpillar*. It starts, "In the light of the moon / a little egg lay on a leaf." All those soft l's (*light, little, lay, leaf*) create a quiet beginning. The illustration shows a huge moon, a large leaf, and a very tiny egg. Then you come to the patterned part of the book where each day the caterpillar eats more and more. The numbers and the days of the week make it easy for children to join in, but the language is what makes the story stand out.

3. Ask yourself whether the story contains natural language and familiar speech patterns that children can predict, or whether instead it has a contrived, controlled text.

Some of the little books in New Zealand's Ready-to-Read series qualify as real literature. (I particularly love Joy Cowley's *The Greedy Cat* and her *Mrs. Wishy Washy*.) But sometimes even good authors do not succeed in creating books with literary merit. Margaret Mahy, an award-winning author for whom I have a good deal of admiration, wrote these contrived and unnatural lines in her *Going to the Beach*:

Up, up, up
Out, out, out
In, in, in
Off, off, off

I have heard this passage read in very dramatic fashion, but it is still not the way we talk. On the other hand, listen to the wonderful language Mahy uses in a trade book titled *17 Kings and 42 Elephants*:

Seventeen kings and forty-two elephants
Going on a journey on a wild wet night
Baggy ears like big umbrellaphants
Little eyes a-gleaming in the jungle light.

Obviously, such language is not predictable and is too difficult for emergent readers to attempt on their own—but it isn't too difficult for them to enjoy. It is important to read aloud both books like this one that will stretch children's imaginations and predictable books that they can attempt on their own. Just remember that each book must be evaluated on its own merits.

These three questions, then, are essential to keep in mind when choosing trade books to use with emergent readers:

1. Does this book provide delight and pleasure in reading?
2. Does it have the imaginative quality of literature?
3. Is it written in natural, uncontrived language?

Choosing Predictable Books

What makes a book easy for children to read? Bruner uses the term "scaffold" to describe the way a parent helps a child learn language (see Ninio & Bruner, 1973). When a toddler says, "Car, go," the parent responds with "Yes, we're going in the car to Grandma's today."

Language patterns. In many ways patterned books provide a kind of scaffold to help children climb up to real reading. Sometimes it is simply a language pattern repeated frequently. *Brown Bear, Brown Bear, What Do You See?* by Bill Martin Jr has helped many a child into reading.

From Australia comes a similar patterned book, titled *I Went Walking*, written by Sue Williams and illustrated with vivid watercolors by Julie Vivas. The rhythmic text begins every other page with "I went walking. / What did you see?" followed by the answer, "A brown cow [green duck, pink pig, etc.] looking at me." Picture clues show just a part of the animal looking at the young boy. Turn the page and you see a large brown cow or a bright green duck. The pictures also provide a kind of substory as the little boy discards various articles of clothing on his walk. While the text is not cumulative, the pictures are: all the animals the boy sees follow him on his walk. This gives the reader a chance to go back over the pictures and name all the animals and their colors.

Familiar sequences. Eileen Christelow's *Five Little Monkeys Jumping on the Bed* is based on the old rhyme in which five monkeys jumping on the bed fall off one by one, bumping their heads:

The mama called the doctor.
The doctor said,
"No more monkeys jumping on the bed!"

Of course, they continue until there is only one little monkey left. Then you have a wonderful surprise ending: Mama monkey finally gets the little ones tucked in and then she jumps on her own bed! Five- and six-year-olds go into fits of giggles at this point and cry, "Read it again!" And of course you do, and you let them join in the monkey countdown and the doctor's refrain, and in no time this is a book they are reading again and again on their own.

This is also a story that lends itself to creating an alternative text. One kindergarten group was doing a bear unit, so they changed the rhyme to "Five little teddy bears jumping on the bed." They created a page a day, and then the teacher put the pages together as a Big Book with the children's own illustrations.

Cindy Ward's *Cookie's Week* captures children's interest from the very first page. It begins, "On Monday, Cookie fell in the toilet." The rest of the story describes the mischief that Cookie, a little black cat, gets into every day of the week. The ending is an open-ended invitation for boys and girls to discuss what

Cookie does on Sunday. One class changed the setting from home to school and wrote their own book called *Cookie's Week at School*.

Repetitive story patterns. One of the reasons young children so enjoy the old traditional tales is that the stories' familiar format and storyline make them easy to read and retell. Another advantage of using traditional literature is that there are so many versions of each tale. Search for the easiest one to share first. For example, you may want to read Paul Galdone's *The Three Bears* before you share Jan Brett's *Goldilocks and the Three Bears*, which has more complex sentences and pictures. Children love seeing different versions, pointing out similarities and differences.

Some modern stories use the patterns of traditional tales. Nancy Van Laan's *The Big Fat Worm* (illustrated with large, clear pictures by

Mama monkey tends to the first little monkey to bump his head in Eileen Christelow's *Five Little Monkeys Jumping on the Bed.*

A richly detailed illustration from Jan Brett's version of *Goldilocks and the Three Bears.*

Marisabina Russo) is a circular tale. In this story a big fat bird threatens to eat a worm, then a big fat cat finds the bird, a big fat dog sees the cat.... Each of them escapes and the story ends at its beginning with the big fat bird eyeing the big fat worm. After one reading, children join in on the repetitive dialogue.

Cumulative tales. Cumulative stories that repeat and build on an initial image or idea provide another kind of scaffold for children. Many such tales follow the format of the well-known story "The House That Jack Built." One favorite cumulative tale, *The Cake That Mack Ate* by Rose Robart, begins this way:

> This is the cake
> That Mack ate.
> This is the egg
> That went into the cake
> That Mack ate.

Then we go on to hear about the hen that laid the egg, the corn that fed the hen, the farmer who planted the corn, and so on. But only at the end of the story do we discover that Mack is a great big dog who ate a very special birthday cake.

Predictable plots. Children love stories with predictable plots that help them read or retell the story. Probably one of the easiest plots I know is in Brian Wildsmith's *The Cat on the Mat*. In this story, a cat sits serenely alone on his mat until a dog, a goat, and then a cow join him. You see the cat getting angrier and angrier until, when an elephant sits down, the cat spits at them all, and they leave. The last page shows the cat once again sitting alone on his mat. One child was so anxious to get to the "ssppstt" part that he made the sound himself before we turned the page. This is a simple story, but it has a strong plot, a real climax, and superb pictures.

Familiar rhymes and songs. Familiar rhymes and songs also help children begin to read. Boys and girls who already know the words of a song or rhyme can recognize them in print.

Increasingly songs are being published in exciting new formats that in themselves help children read verses. One of these is *I Know an Old Lady Who Swallowed a Fly*, a "lift the flap" book by Colin and Jacqui Hawkins. Small animals provide some of the text in cartoon blurbs, and you can lift the old lady's apron and look into her tummy to see all the animals she's eaten. I know a teacher who made a big old lady out of cardboard and then pinned a large see-through sandwich bag under the old lady's apron. While singing the song, the children lifted the apron and put cutouts of animals in the old lady's plastic bag tummy. Later they made their own book of the song, writing cartoon blurbs for each of the animals.

Carol Jones's *This Old Man* illustrates that song with peep-holes to help children guess where the old man will play nick nack next. Readers have number clues, rhyming clues, and picture clues to help them read and sing along.

Environmental print. Part of the task for new readers is to become aware of all the print that surrounds them at home and at school. We need to call attention to all print in the classroom: the many charts with stories, poems, and songs on them; the numbers and words on the calendar; the "daily news" that the teacher records for the class. Children can read the blurbs on their murals and the captions on their pictures. Give children a part in creating and illustrating the stories you display in the class. Children will then take ownership of them and enjoy reading them.

Environmental print's benefits for literacy learning are well known to many teachers in New Zealand's primary schools. One of the activities engaged in regularly in that country's elementary classrooms is something called "Reading Around the Room." A pair of children take a pointer and walk together around the classroom, pointing out and reading aloud all the print that they can. They read story charts displayed on the walls, the cartoon blurbs they have included in their murals, and class Big Books they have helped to create and illustrate. The large poem cards they read might include favorite Mother Goose rhymes they have illustrated.

Teachers keep in mind the Reading Around the Room activity when working with children on other literacy-related projects. For example, alternative stories for classics such as *Good-Night Moon* by Margaret Wise Brown might be developed during the class's shared reading time, and phrases from the new version can be written out on large strips of paper and displayed on the classroom walls. This way children feel secure in reading "good-night room, good-night plants, good-night chairs, good-night tables, good-night paints" when they're Reading Around the Room because they connect the phrases with their own version of a favorite story. No print appears in the room without the children's talking about its meaning and re-hearsing what it says.

The time and effort put forth by the teacher to make these displays, charts, and class books is rewarded by the children's many readings of them. And children develop fluency in reading because they feel secure about rereading stories they have helped to create and materials whose meaning they understand. Print is changed frequently to keep the classroom activities vibrant. When children are no longer reading a particular chart, the teacher replaces it. In this way, Reading Around the Room continues to capture their interest.

Teaching Idea

Reading Around the Room

Children may take a walking trip outside and see how many of the signs around the school they can read. When they return to the room the teacher can put out Tana Hoban's *I Read Signs* or Ron and Nancy Goor's *Signs* and the children can see how many of the signs they saw. The teacher can also share Donald Crews's *Truck*, which shows the many freeway signs that a truck driver sees on the road.

The Best Advice

Young children need to be exposed to all kinds of books—picture books, storybooks, poetry, songs, informational books—and they need to be able to relate reading to their own lives. In selecting which books to use with the emergent reader, there is no substitute for knowing literature and being familiar with as many children's books as possible. Teachers need to read the books before they share them with children, buy them for their classroom libraries, or borrow them from a public library. Then they can select the best of all these books and share their enthusiasm for high-quality literature with their students. Any activity you do with a book or a group of books should be guided by a desire to help children develop a real love of reading, the kind of joy that Emily feels for books and reading.

References

Anderson, R.C., Hiebert, E.H., Scott, J.A., & Wilkinson, I.A.G. (1985). *Becoming a nation of readers.* Washington, DC: National Institute of Education, U.S. Department of Education.

Clark, M.M. (1976). *Young fluent readers.* Portsmouth, NH: Heinemann.

Huck, C.S., Hepler, S., & Hickman, J. (1987). *Children's literature in the elementary school* (4th ed.). Forth Worth, TX: Holt, Rinehart & Winston.

Ninio, A., & Bruner, J. (1973). The achievement and antecedents of labelling. *Journal of Child Language, 5,* 1-15.

Sulzby, E. (1985). Children's emergent reading of favorite storybooks: A developmental study. *Reading Research Quarterly, 20,* 458-481.

Teale, W.H. (1984). Reading to young children: Its significance for literacy development. In H. Goelman, A. Oberg, & F. Smith (Eds.), *Awakening to literacy.* Portsmouth, NH: Heinemann.

Wells, G. (1986). *The meaning makers.* Portsmouth, NH: Heinemann.

Children's Books

Brett, J. (1987). *Goldilocks and the three bears.* New York: Putnam.

Brown, M.W. (1947). *Good-night moon.* (Ill. by C. Hurd.) New York: HarperCollins.

Burningham, J. (1976). *The blanket.* New York: Crowell.

Carle, E. (1969). *The very hungry caterpillar.* New York: Philomel.

Christelow, E. (1989). *Five little monkeys jumping on the bed.* New York: Clarion.

Cowley, J. (1980). *Mrs. Wishy Washy.* (Ill. by E. Fuller.) San Diego, CA: Wright Group.

Cowley, J. (1983). *The greedy cat* (Ready-to-Read series). Katonah, NY: Richard C. Owen.

Crews, D. (1980). *Truck.* New York: Greenwillow.

Galdone, P. (1985). *The three bears.* New York: Clarion.

Goor, R., & Goor, N. (1983). *Signs.* New York: Crowell.

Hawkins, C., & Hawkins, J. (1987). *I know an old lady who swallowed a fly.* New York: Putnam.

Hoban, T. (1983). *I read signs.* New York: Greenwillow.

Hutchins, P. (1990). *What game shall we play?* New York: Greenwillow.

Jones, C. (1989). *Old MacDonald had a farm.* Boston, MA: Houghton Mifflin.

Jones, C. (1989). *This old man.* Boston, MA: Houghton Mifflin.

Lobel, A. (1970). *Frog and toad are friends.* New York: HarperCollins.

Mahy, M. (1984). *Going to the beach* (Ready-to-Read series). Katonah, NY: Richard C. Owen.

Mahy, M. (1987). *17 kings and 42 elephants*. (Ill. by P. MacCarthy.) New York: Dial.

Martin, B., Jr. (1983). *Brown bear, Brown bear, what do you see?* (Ill. by E. Carle.) New York: Henry Holt.

Robart, R. (1986). *The cake that Mack ate*. (Ill. by M. Kovalski.) Boston, MA: Joy Street/Little, Brown.

Van Laan, N. (1987). *The big fat worm*. (Ill. by M. Russo.) New York: Knopf.

Ward, C. (1988). *Cookie's week*. (Ill. by T. dePaola.) New York: Putnam.

Wildsmith, B. (1983). *The cat on the mat*. New York: Oxford.

Williams, S. (1990). *I went walking*. (Ill. by J. Vivas.) San Diego, CA: Harcourt Brace Jovanovich.

Wolff, A. (1984). *A year of birds*. New York: Putnam.

CHAPTER 2

Act It Out: Making Poetry Come Alive

Brod Bagert

I have a daughter named Colette. She is grown now but when I look into her hazel-brown eyes I remember the little girl for whom I wrote "The Night I Caught the Burglars." She was seven then and ambitious and frightened. There was a program at school in which children were to recite poems. She wanted to participate but she was a little nervous. She wanted to succeed and, like any performer, she wanted good material.

"I want you to write a poem for me, Daddy," she said. "A good one that I can act out and make everybody laugh." I was not then a children's poet, but my little girl, the soul of my joy, wanted a poem that she could act out and make everybody laugh. I decided to do my best to give her what she wanted. This is the poem I wrote for her.

The Night I Caught the Burglars

Last night I heard a funny noise
While I was in my bed
And thought, should I get up and take a peek
Or go back to sleep instead.

Up I got, feet on the floor
As quiet as a mouse
And made my way from room to room
Throughout the darkened house.

Then I saw them, tall and mean
In the middle of the night
Two men were stuffing all my toys
Into a sack and out of sight.

I jumped right out and shouted STOP!
I pushed them to the floor.
I held them till the policemen came
And led them out the door.

It felt so nice to be so brave,
My Mom and Dad were beaming.
But then the clock began to ring—
Oh shucks! I was just dreaming.

That was ten years ago. I had no idea then what Colette had gotten me into. Poetry has become the passion of my life and writing for children is what I enjoy most. I have now written many poems for children, and I have never forgotten Colette's instructions: "I want you to write a poem for me, Daddy. A good one that I can act out and make everybody laugh."

Elvis, Baseball, and Poetry

A wonderful thing about writing for children is the opportunity it gives me to speak to young audiences. What follows is a little story I use to convey to children the idea that poetry is a performance art. I ask them to imagine that I am a little kid whose favorite song is Elvis Presley's "Hound Dog." My mother comes home with a surprise:

"I have a surprise for you," she announces. "I went to the store today and bought your favorite song."

Excited, I open the bag, reach in, and pull out...a piece of paper?

"Maaaamaaaa!" I whine. "Where's the song?"

She smiles. "That *is* the song. It's sheet music. Look. These little black dots are the notes. They go up and down to show you when the tones rise and fall. And underneath you can read the words. 'You ain't nothing but a hound dog....' You see?"

"But Maaamaaa! I don't want to look at a piece of paper. I want to hear the music."

The words of a poem on paper are like the notes of a song on sheet music. The great poems of our language are written to be read out loud with expression. They are written to be performed. It's a simple idea and an important one.

Baseball is a game. When we teach little kids baseball we give them a glove, a ball, and a bat. We put them on a field, show them the bases, and let them play. Poetry is a performance art. When we teach children poetry by the performance method we give them poems to perform and put them in front of an audience of peers. It works for baseball, and I have come to learn that it works for poetry as well.

So we begin with the idea that an effective way to introduce children to poetry is to teach them to perform it. The first step in the process is to select poems that are easy to perform and that will entertain a young audience.

The Poetry Formula: Sound + Story + Character = Fun

A few months ago a neighborhood 12-year-old named Eric knocked on my door to get some help with a school assignment. The assignment was to select a poem and to identify it as being in the lyric, narrative, or dramatic style. He had chosen Edgar Allan Poe's "Annabel Lee," and he was stymied. Eric had correctly observed that the poem contained elements of all three categories. I agreed with him and suggested that he say so when he wrote his essay.

"Oh no, Mr. Brod. You don't know Ms. Smith. She wants it to be one or the other and that's the way it's gotta be."

I suspect that Ms. Smith was more tolerant than Eric described, but given the imperative of a forced decision, I suggested that he call it a lyric poem and he left happy. My interest was stimulated, so I did a little reading and learned that the authorities seem to agree that the division of poetry into lyric, narrative, and dramatic tends to be a little arbitrary and that poems often cross the lines. Indeed, when I applied the categories to the poems that chil-

dren like best, I found that their favorites *always* cross the lines. Children like poems with sounds that are fun to say (lyric); they like poems that tell a story (narrative); and they like poems in the voice of a character or characters with whom they can identify (dramatic).

So it would seem that we have arrived at a formula to help us choose poetry for children: Sound + Story + Character = Fun. Children love poems that fit the formula. Let's take a moment to examine each element to see how it works.

Sound

When I think about how children love the sound of poetry, I hear the voice of Bill Martin Jr describing the child's love for language. He tells us that a child's natural facility for language is driven by the joy of sound. I would add only that lyric poetry is the sound of language at full power. It comes as no surprise that children love it. Children love rhythm, rhyme, alliteration, assonance, and all the devices poets use to make the words feel good to say.

Story

Of all the ways we communicate ideas, telling stories is the most effective. Everyone likes a story. The great prophets of every civilization used stories. Professional speakers use stories to hold their audiences. And there is nothing that will draw the attention of a child more effectively than the words "Once upon a time...." To help a young performer capture the audience, use poems that tell stories.

"The Night I Caught the Burglars" is an example of a poem that tells a complete story. It has a hero, an antagonist, a conflict, a resolution, and a conclusion. It is difficult, however, to cram complete stories into relatively short poems, and it's really not necessary. The following poem has a hero, but the antagonist and conflict are only implied:

Always Be Polite When You Boss an Allosaurus

There was this giant skeleton,
Thirty feet from tail to head...
And I bet they couldn't make him brush
Before he went to bed.

His teeth were long and pointy
As sharp as they could be...
And I'd like to see them try to tell him
Not to watch TV.

*"Stop that you naughty dinosaur,
I've had about enough of you."*

Then crrr**runch**...
One less bossy grown-up
To tell us what to do.

Character

Poems are compelling when they have real characters who experience the feelings of real children. Children, like all of us, are often lonely and confused. They want to connect with others who feel like they feel, and they want to understand their feelings. In literature children meet characters whose circumstances and feelings are similar to their own. It is a hallowed moment. It is a moment of reassurance. It's a hug from Daddy to chase bad dreams away. "Someone else feels the way I feel. I am not alone."

Children feel less lonely when they discover an imaginary character with whom they can identify. They want to hear what he's going to say and see what he's going to do. The character becomes important because children see themselves in what he says and does. This is the heart and the essence and the purpose of literature. It's where children learn about themselves, where they struggle to understand their actions in the past and envision the possibilities for their future. When you select poems with real characters, you can be certain that in addition to giving children what they like, you will have given them what they hunger for, and often what they desperately need.

Now, this is important but it's a little hard to say. Characters inhabit poems in two different ways, and one is significantly more powerful than the other. There are poems in which the voice that recites the words talks about the character; then there are poems in which the voice that recites the words *is* the character.

Taking the allosaurus out for a walk.

The poem that follows is of the first kind. When you read it out loud you are an unidentified voice talking about a known character.

Skinny Minnie

She's not what she would seem
This sparkle frizzy Minnie,
Someday she'll be a young man's dream
But for now she's kind of skinny.

Minnie wonders about
what she will become.

This is a nice little poem. It permits a little girl to laugh at herself while it assures her that good things lie ahead. We do not, however, know anything about the person who says the words. The performer doesn't know who he's supposed to be; that makes the poem a bit difficult to perform. Now try this one. Read it out loud with expression. Become the character.

Dr. Womback's Needle

There'll be footsteps any second now
And through the door they'll burst,
Dr. Womback's needle
In the hands of Dr. Womback's nurse!

"Now this will pinch a little," she says
As I see the shiny steel
Of a fifteen-foot-long needle
She claims I'll hardly feel.

Someday I'll be big and strong
And she couldn't hurt me if she'd try,
But...now I'm just a little kid...
And I think I'm gonna cry.

Now that's a poem that almost performs itself. When you say the words you know exactly what you're supposed to be. You're a little kid at the doctor's office, you're about to get a shot, you're scared, and you're a little angry that this grown-up nurse person is about to hurt you. It's a poem with which a child can succeed in front of an audience.

During the spring of 1991, Bernice "Ms. Bee" Cullinan surveyed 2,500 children in kindergarten through grade 6 across the United States to find out which poems they preferred among the works of the nine National Council of Teachers of English award-winning poets. Teachers who read the poems aloud to students were surprised that their students' choices did not match their own.

Although the statistical analyses are not complete, Ms. Bee was able to draw some generalizations. She found that children like poems that make them laugh. They like poems that tell a story. They like poems they can understand. For example, "Mummy Slept Late and Daddy Fixed Breakfast" was a landslide winner from John Ciardi's poems. "I Left My Head" was the winner for Lilian Moore. "My Puppy" was the favorite from Aileen Fisher's work. "Kittens" by Myra Cohn Livingston,

"Flavors" by Arnold Adoff, and "Hughbert and the Glue" by Karla Kuskin were all chosen, too.

The data revealed that children do not like poems that are abstract or esoteric, and the primary feature they enjoy is humor. Teachers wrote, "I knew humor was important, but I didn't realize how important!" Ms. Bee draws the conclusion that if we are to turn children into poetry lovers, we must give them poems that are funny, understandable narratives.

How to Help Children Perform Poetry

So where are we? Poems are verbal art; encouraging children to perform poems is an effective way to introduce them to poetry; and the process begins with the selection of poems that are performable. Now comes the fun part—how to help children perform poems painlessly and well. Let me start by making a promise: this works, and you're going to love it. You may be in for a few surprises; many children surprise their teachers with their ability to perform. ("But she's so quiet, I never would have dreamed she had it in her.") So have faith in yourself and in your children, and let's do it.

Use the following method to make teaching poetry painless and fun. The steps should be spread out over time. You may, for example, do teacher performances for weeks or months before you proceed to group performance. When it feels right, go to the next step.

Teaching Idea

The Magic of Making Faces

Oral recitation has four basic elements: facial expression, voice inflection, body movement, and timing. The happiest thing I ever learned about helping children perform is that when a child makes the right face, everything else falls in place.

Try this exercise. Make a sad face. Droop your eyes, pout your bottom lip, tilt your head to the side, and say, "I am not very happy." You will find that voice, body, and timing tend to follow your expression.

Now try to defy nature. Make the same sad expression and try to say, "I am very happy" in a cheerful voice. You will find that it is very hard to sound happy when your face is sad.

Conduct the search for what a poem means and how to perform it by asking a single question: What face should I make when I say these words? Then make the face and say the words.

Imagine a nervous little girl who stands before an audience of 200. She makes a face, recites a line of poetry in character, the audience responds, and she feels the surge of her own potential. You can make it happen.

Teaching Idea

The Importance of a Good Audience

A performance is like a race car, guided by a steering wheel and driven by an engine: the performer is the steering wheel; the audience is the engine. Every good performer needs a good audience.

Recently I read for a large group of third and fourth graders. I told them how a good audience can make a good performance. Later I began to read poems. I started to pick up steam and soon I was really cooking. I then noticed a half dozen fourth-grade girls in the back row. They had been responding with their faces to my every word and now they were giggling with delight as the total effect became apparent. Their wonderful faces had taken charge and turned the day's performance into a moment of magic. They had made me an example of my own lesson.

Children in a poetry performance are no longer a "class"—they are an audience. They are an equal partner in the performance. They are alert and free to respond, and they always reward the performer's effort with applause. Shakespeare's *The Tempest* ends with a speech by Prospero. He drops the veil of theater, turns to the audience, and addresses it with a direct request for applause:

> But release me from my bands
> With the help of your good hands.
> Gentle breath of yours my sails
> Must fill, or else my project fails,
> Which was to please....

I love those lines. Prospero speaks for every performer and every artist and every work of art. We live to connect with an audience. Encourage children to be a good audience for you and for each other. When they become a good audience, you cannot help but produce good performances.

Avoid spending whole classes on poetry. Sessions should be short. Always leave them wanting more. Remember that poetry can be used as a break in classroom routine.

Step 1: Teacher Performance

Perform with full expression. Become the character. Be a little kid and hold nothing in reserve. Remember that you are the model; your performance will license your students to perform. You know you've gone far enough when you forget you're teaching. If you feel utterly ridiculous, you're almost there.

Note: Always evoke applause at the end of your performance. When you teach your class to be a good audience, you create a performance-friendly environment. A dramatic bow at the end of the reading will tell them to clap for you. If they do not respond, assume a pleading expression and clap for yourself. If they still do not respond, ask them to clap. By applauding for you they learn to applaud for each other.

Step 2: Group Performance

Recite single phrases with full expression and have the children as a group mimic your performance. This is lots of fun and will serve as a confidence builder. There's safety in numbers, and this is a painless way to help children discover the performer inside them. As they repeat the lines, watch their faces, react to them with smiles and laughter, and stimulate applause at the end.

Note: In the beginning, try to avoid choral reading of whole poems or long passages. Continuous choral reading forces children into expressionless sing-song recitation and defeats your purpose.

Step 3: Short Individual Performances

Ask for volunteers to perform a poem for the class. You will know who the "hams" are from the group performances. Encourage them, but be careful not to force a child prematurely into a pressure situation. Choose three or four children and have each perform a single line or short passage. Recite the line with full expression and have the child repeat after you. Reward each line with excitement and applause. Eventually you want each child in the class to have this experience, and enthusiastic acceptance will encourage participation.

Note: This is a big step. It takes courage for a child to let go in front of a class, especially for the first volunteers. I have found that it helps to kneel next to each performer. The more nervous the child is, the closer I get. The

physical closeness lends some much-needed support.

Step 4: Individual Performance

Take this very slowly and keep in mind that it may not be a good idea for every child in the class. Encourage the hams but do not force it. You may even develop a regular troupe and have one or two children perform a poem each day. The other children will not be left out—as members of the audience they are full participants in the process (and, of course, they should feel free to volunteer to be performers whenever they'd like).

Note: It is fine to memorize a poem, but a performer should always have the text of a poem in hand. Though I have performed each of my poems a thousand times and can say them in my sleep, I always feel better with the book in my hand. If nothing else, it's a good prop.

A Gift for the 21st Century

A child's first encounter with poetry happens only once. It is a moment of great promise, and the poems you choose are an important factor in determining how a child will respond to poetry. Give them poems that perform. Give them poems whose words feel good in your mouth when you make the sounds. Give them poems that tell stories in the voice of a character who feels their feelings and in whom they can discover themselves. Give them such poems and encourage them to perform. In performance the child and the poem become one. It's the start of a permanent relationship, and poetry will become a permanent part of their lives.

Here is the heart of it: Imagine humankind in the next century. Envision a people

Teaching Idea

Overcoming Stage Fright

A recent poll revealed that Americans fear public speaking more than death. A child who once faces an audience with a sense of "presence" is forever strengthened by the experience. This is what I say to help children muster the courage to perform.

The Light Bulb

When you're about to perform you're going to get nervous. Every performer gets nervous all the time. People who love you will say, "Don't be nervous," but that's like saying, "Jump in the lake but don't get wet." It's okay to be nervous. All performers get nervous. Just as a light bulb needs electricity to shine, a performer needs to be nervous.

The Ostrich

When you stand in front of an audience everyone is going to look at you and you're going to want to hide. All of us have something that we don't like about the way we look, so when everyone looks at us we try to cover up. We put our hands in our pockets or behind our backs, or we fold our arms. It's like the story about the ostrich who tries to hide by putting its head in the sand. There's a little ostrich in all of us and there isn't much we can do about it.

When I get in front of an audience I remember that I'm a little fat and I feel uncomfortable. It happens every time. There isn't anything I can do about it so I just laugh at myself. Here's a little secret and it helps to remember it. The audience doesn't care how you look. They want to see what you're going to do. So when you feel like the ostrich, laugh at yourself—and start doing what you're there to do. The audience will love you.

The Karate Ice Breaker

Just before you begin to speak, you may feel something in your way. It's like an invisible wall between you and the audience. You see all the faces and something inside you makes you want to hold back. This is a very important moment.

Have you seen the karate expert who breaks a block of ice with his bare hand? He cannot hold anything back. He hits the ice with all his might. That's what you can do. So when you stand before the audience and feel the invisible wall, remember the Karate Ice Breaker. Throw yourself to

continued next page

Bagert

the audience, don't hold anything back, and remember this secret about people: When you give yourself completely, the audience will love you completely, even if you make mistakes. You can lose your place and have to start over, you can mispronounce words, you can trip and fall on your face...none of it will hurt you. When you give yourself totally and hold nothing back, the audience is going to love you.

To perform, a child learns to accept nervousness, to laugh at self-consciousness, and to put the desire to give ahead of the fear of rejection. It's not everything a child needs to know, but it's a good start.

baptized in the sound of the great poems, men and women rich with insight and sensitive to the beat of their own hearts. Dream a generation at ease in the eternal struggle of beauty and the beast, a generation whose poems are clear crystal charms to light the darkness, a generation that will see itself as it is, laugh at its own foolishness, and maintain the courage to envision a better world.

Two hundred years ago, in *Prometheus Unbound*, Percy Shelley wrote these words:

To suffer woes which Hope thinks infinite;
To forgive wrongs darker than Death or Night;
To defy Power which seems Omnipotent;
To love, and bear; to hope till Hope creates
From its own wreck the thing it contemplates;...
This...is to be
Good, great, and joyous, beautiful and free;
This is alone Life, Joy...and Victory.

Ears that can hear such words and hearts that are open to receive their beauty is your gift to the 21st century. It is a gift you give today in the classrooms of 10,000 cities and towns.

Perform poems for your students. Give yourself with abandon and joy, and license performance by the children you hold in trust. Awaken inside them the power of their own presence, and breathe life into young spirits. The poet Homer was once a child; Virgil, Dante, Shakespeare, and Shelley were all once children. The great souls of our future are alive today; they sit in the small steel and plastic chairs of your classroom, and, for them, it is you who carry the fire. Envision their future and give wings to the poetry inside them.

In the second grade a little girl named Colette performed a poem for an audience of children and made them laugh. She is a young woman now, and the great adventure of life lies ahead of her. I am her Daddy and I'm a little scared. I am consoled by the fact that she carries inside her the resources she will need to flourish, and among those resources is a relationship with poetry. It is a spiritual chromosome activated in childhood. It will sustain her against the ravages of beasts and will awaken her soul to the quiet, powerful voice of beauty.

CHAPTER 3

Character Study
Responding to Literature: A Realistic Fiction Unit
Linking Literature to Life

Realistic Fiction
and the Real World

Dianne L. Monson

At the heart of good realistic fiction are characters who are interesting enough to capture a reader's imagination. If you ask children to tell you their favorite books, it is likely that you will hear the characters' names as often as you will hear the books' titles. A few years ago, the Book-of-the-Month Club asked its members to name their favorite children's books (Stein, 1989). Some responses were from children; others were from adults remembering books they loved in childhood. The choices included *Doctor DeSoto*, *Madeline*, *Heidi*, *Stuart Little*, *Charlotte's Web*, *A Bargain for Frances*, *Curious George*, *Paddington Helps Out*, *Harriet the Spy*, *Miss Rumphius*, and *The Great Gilly Hopkins*. There were other titles as well, but this sampling of books, all of which have strong title characters, shows clearly how important characters are to readers. Studies of children's reading interests have also highlighted a special interest in characters, showing that children prefer stories about characters who are attractive, clever, and successful (Monson & Sebesta, 1991). In short, children seem to like heroes.

A child's response to a story may show up initially as response to a character. When students identify Katherine Paterson's *The Great Gilly Hopkins* as a favorite book, for example, chances are they connect directly with Gilly. The most common response to literature made by children in the elementary grades is a personal one. A first step in helping students think about their favorite characters in ways that may lead to deeper literary understanding is therefore to create a link with people in their own lives.

The most important and basic response to a story is emotional. Rosenblatt (1969) describes literary experience as a transaction in which readers bring to their interpretation of text a whole set of understandings from their own lives—giving to the text as well as receiving from it, if you will—and in that way construct meaning from the story. A story that evokes laughter, wonder, sadness, curiosity, fear, or another emotion invites a reader to have a genuine interaction with the characters and the events in their lives.

In addition to emotional and personal responses and interpretations of a story's meaning, the common responses to literature are awareness of literary elements and critical judgment of the story's quality or of a character's behavior. When students are captivated by characters, they often have vivid memories of the story that can serve as a basis for judging other literature. For example, students often become emotionally involved with Julie in *Julie of the Wolves* by Jean George. When they later read another novel in which a protagonist faces difficult problems, they may draw comparisons, noting whether Julie seems more or less real or interesting than the character in the second book. When reflection on a book reaches this level, the reader has let an emotional response lead to a more intellectual judgment about the story's literary quality. At this point, if the reader also realizes that Jean George excels in describing characters and settings and uses them to advantage in her portrayal of Julie, he or she begins to understand some critical elements of literature.

Emotional responses may also lead readers to recognize that they share some of the fears and hopes of a character like Julie. Perhaps they will think about the way Julie tries to bridge two cultures. That may lead them to think about children who face similar kinds of conflicts. In that way, personal interpretation extends a story so readers recognize that some of its elements apply to situations close to their own lives.

In this chapter, I describe some activities that should help students in the intermediate and upper elementary grades come to a deeper understanding of the literature they read and gain a sense of the interaction among character, plot, and setting in realistic fiction.

Character Study

When students have had time to explore the personal qualities of story characters, encourage them to think about what the author did to develop those characters in such an interesting way. Reading aloud from a book with strong characterization provides a good opportunity to call attention to the author's use of description and dialogue to show what a character is like and how that person interacts with other characters in the story. Books with strong characters lend themselves to an investigation of the ways in which authors develop characters. Is description the major technique? Does the author make effective use of dialogue to reveal personal qualities of the characters? Are other subtle ways used to let readers know what sort of person a story character is? Does the person change over the course of the story? If so, what indicates the change?

Students may be brought together in response groups of four to six members to discuss questions they raise as they read or hear the story, or to talk over questions you ask them. The response time may begin with students sharing favorite parts of their books or talking about problems the characters are trying to deal with. Some teachers like to provide each group with a question of the day for their discussion. As students become able to function more effectively in response groups, they may draw their own questions from response journals or from problems that have come up as they read. Underlying this strategy is the desire to draw readers into the story, encouraging them to bring their own experiences to the reading.

To interest students in the techniques writers use to develop characters, you might begin a class collection of first lines or first paragraphs that introduce a character particularly well. Here are some examples:

"I was ten years old when my little brother Louis began driving my mother's car, and by the time I was eleven he had put over four hundred miles on it" (from *My Brother Louis Measures Worms* by Barbara Robinson).

"I am *not* a pest," Ramona Quimby told her big sister Beezus (from *Ramona the Pest* by Beverly Cleary).

Not every thirteen-year-old girl is accused of murder, brought to trial, and found guilty. But I was just such a girl... (from *The True Confessions of Charlotte Doyle* by Avi).

There in the doorway was a massive black head, the nose up and smelling, the tiny eyes bright with hungry anticipation. "Don't nobody yell," she said softly. "Just back up slow and quiet to the ladder and climb up to the loft" (from *Lyddie* by Katherine Paterson).

Each one of these brief excerpts suggests something about the person it describes. You want to know more and to decipher the technique the author is using to create such vivid impressions. Dialogue passages are revealing here; descriptive details are important, too. Introducing characters by using intriguing elements such as danger, humor, or an unusual situation is a common technique among writers. Children will enjoy adding to this list.

The role of voice in telling a story is also important. An author must decide whether to use the first or third person in writing. To give students some insight into the influence of

Response journals provide students with an opportunity to jot down their thoughts and questions about texts during or immediately after reading. These journal entries can then help to focus students' thinking about texts and can serve as a basis for later discussions or writing assignments. The following example from one student's response journal shows the sorts of comments and questions that are typically entered.

December 12: *Maniac Magee* by Jerry Spinelli

When Jeffrey jogged into Two Mills, he said "hi" to Amanda. She had a suitcase with her and he figured she was running away, too, so he tried to get into a conversation with her. I thought that was funny.

Amanda let him borrow a book but she told him not to come to her house. I'm not sure why.

Questions for Jeffrey/Maniac:

Why do you like books so much?

How did you manage to catch that football one-handed and not drop the book? Also, what did you like best—your perfect punt or the look on Hands Down's face when he caught it?

When did you stop feeling like Jeffrey and start feeling like Maniac? Was it after the frogball homer?

voice in revealing characterization, you might ask them to think about rewriting the first line of *My Side of the Mountain* in third person. Jean George's original reads, "I am on my mountain in a tree home that people have passed without ever knowing that I am here." A third person narrator might begin, "Sam was in a tree home on the mountain he thought of as his own." Or ask students to imagine the opening of *The Great Gilly Hopkins* in first person rather than third person. The original reads, "'Gilly,' said Miss Ellis with a shake of her long blonde hair toward the passenger in the back seat. 'I need to feel that you are willing to make some effort.' Galadriel Hopkins shifted her bubble gum to the front of her mouth and began to blow gently....'" If Gilly had to introduce herself, she might begin, "Galadriel Hopkins is my name and I am a foster child."

In both cases, the immediacy of the characterization is spoiled by the change in voice. The beginnings are absolutely right as they were written and published, and students can recognize that. Studying well-written books makes it clear that good authors choose the best means of presenting particular characters. In order to gain more awareness of the importance of voice, students may want to experiment in their own writing by trying out first lines in both first and third person.

With this background, students can be encouraged to keep reading response journals in which they record bits of description and dialogue that bring to life the personality of a character they enjoy in a book. Encourage responses by asking students to think about how characters are like themselves or people they know. What are the characters' most admirable qualities? Their bad qualities? At a particular point in the story, encourage students to jot down questions they would like to ask characters about their reasons for behaving as they do. When questions emerge naturally, that is an indication that the author has been successful in developing characters that children care about.

Responding to Literature: A Realistic Fiction Unit

This unit is constructed in three stages. The first is based on the observation that many upper elementary students have had little, if any, experience with formal response to literature. If that is true for your students, begin with a series of class sessions devoted to a book that all students read at the same time or that you read aloud. If your students are more advanced, you may want to begin with the second stage, in which students read independently from a choice of realistic fiction books, either contemporary or historical. The third stage is an enrichment section, building on study of characterization and other elements introduced with contemporary fiction but focusing on historical fiction.

Stage One

Lois Lowry's *Number the Stars* works well as an introduction to this unit because of its length and high quality. It could be read aloud in several sessions. The book, which appeals to students in the intermediate elementary grades, tells the story of a Danish family and its members attempts to help their Jewish friends flee German persecution during World War II. The story has many facets. Each of the characters is called on to bear some kind of burden. The emphasis on their personal qualities is what most appeals to students, though they will also find the descriptions of setting interesting.

In order to help students respond personally to the story, introduce the unit by setting up this situation for them: Suppose you are trying to write a description of someone you have just met but you need to know more about that person. What questions would you ask? Have children work together to create a list of questions. The list can then serve as a resource for noting characters' traits in *Number the Stars*. Ask children to try to identify what the author reveals about Annemarie, Ellen, and the other people in the story as you read aloud. Which of their questions can they answer after hearing the story?

In the opening scene of *Number the Stars*, two friends, Annemarie Johansen and Ellen Rosen, are racing home from school. When they are stopped by two German soldiers, they are terrified. The girls are all too aware of the soldiers' cold eyes and their shiny black boots. This sets the tone for the story that follows. The contrast between the bullying manner of the soldiers and the quiet but stubborn resistance of the Danes is apparent throughout.

The disappearance of the Hirsch family signals a change for Ellen Rosen and her family, and for Annemarie's family as well. The Rosens go into hiding and Ellen becomes part of Annemarie's family, taking the place of an older daughter who died some years earlier. When soldiers arrive to search the house, Annemarie helps save Ellen by quick thinking; she tears the Star of David necklace from Ellen's neck and conceals it in her own hand. As the story progresses, Ellen's bravery becomes important, too, especially when the Johansens organize a family visit to Uncle Henrik's fishing village—a trip that they hope will bring the Rosens to freedom in neutral Sweden.

The revelation of character traits in the book comes through a combination of dialogue, description, and action. Annemarie doesn't believe she is very brave, but as she talks with Uncle Henrik he convinces her that she is and must be. In the end, Annemarie does show extreme courage when she must pass a German patrol to bring a packet to a fishing boat that's ready to sail with Jewish refugees aboard. Determination and intelligence save her when she is stopped by the patrol. Only later does she learn that the packet contained a drug whose scent would keep the guard dogs from detecting the people hidden on board.

Through her experience of helping with the escape, Annemarie recognizes that the Rosens also have courage, as well as pride. Perhaps the bravest character, however, is one who is not central to the story. Peter Neilsen, a member of the resistance, engineers the Rosen's escape but is himself captured and executed by the Germans. His death underscores the terrible risks taken by—and the great courage of—all the Danes who tried to be the bodyguards of the Jews in Denmark.

Students can learn about understanding characters by retelling a story from one char-
acter's point of view. In *Number the Stars*, the story is told through Annemarie's eyes, but the other people involved have their own perceptions of events. Encourage students to retell the story as Mrs. Rosen or Mr. Johansen might tell it, or challenge them to try to see the uniforms of the soldiers and the faces of the Johansen family as Ellen Rosen might have observed them the night the soldiers came. Encourage students to write what Ellen might have written in her diary after that night.

By presenting a personal story, Lowry conveys the lessons of this global conflict in a way that children can relate to. The conflict in this book is essentially person against person—or, to be more accurate, person against political belief. As the story progresses, it becomes clear that everyone who opposes the Nazis as well as all the Jews living in Denmark are in danger from the Germans who occupy the country. Children will be struck by the qualities of the people who were brave enough to try to rescue those who had no hope. Lowry brings these qualities powerfully to life; students will find it easy to have a personal reaction to this book. As a follow-up, children might compare the setting and situation in *Number the Stars* with that in *The Upstairs Room* by Johanna Reiss.

Stage Two

After you've read and discussed *Number the Stars*, give students a choice of novels with contemporary settings that depict people facing conflicts or bearing burdens. Some that work well for character analysis are *The Eighteenth Emergency*, *The Summer of the Swans*, and *Good-bye, Chicken Little* (all by Betsy Byars), *Julie of the Wolves* (by Jean George), *One-Eyed Cat* (Paula Fox), and *Sea Glass* (Laurence Yep). The following brief response guides suggest some questions to ask to help

Jimmie sits by the icy
river on the cover of
Good-bye, Chicken Little.

students recognize how authors develop characters. Remind students that a character can be revealed through action, journals, letters, dialogue, descriptions, first-person statements, and comments made by the narrator.

The Eighteenth Emergency. When Benjie (called Mouse) is threatened by Marv Hammerman, the sixth grade bully, he falls back on an old game he and his friend Ezzie used to play—how to survive life's greatest emergencies. List as many of Mouse's "emergencies" as you can remember and tell how the boys planned to deal with them. How does Mouse plan to survive the emergency of his encounters with Marv? What happens instead? Do you agree that Mouse comes out a winner? Why or why not? What words or phrases would you use to describe Mouse's appearance, behavior, and feelings at the beginning of the story? At the end?

Good-bye, Chicken Little. What causes Jimmie to be so afraid that he begins to call himself Chicken Little? How does he react to his uncle's death? What finally helps him overcome his fears? Do you admire Jimmie or feel sorry for him? Do your feelings change as the story develops?

Julie of the Wolves. As you read or after you have finished, make a chart of the way Julie/Miyax behaves and thinks in each of her lives—as a girl living in the Eskimo culture and as a girl living in the white culture. You might organize it this way:

	Julie	Miyax
Dangers		
Behavior		
Dress		
Fears		
Happiness		
Other		

In addition, you may want to illustrate her home territory in Alaska and in San Francisco.

The author ends the story without letting us know what Miyax and Kapugen will say to one another. Write your own conversation.

If you are interested in the descriptions of wolf behavior in this book, do some research about wolves' habits and compare that information with what is given in the book.

One-Eyed Cat. As you read, think about these questions: Why does the one-eyed cat haunt Ned? When Ned thinks Mr. Scully has lost interest in the cat, why did Ned say he was afraid he'd have to carry the cat alone? Why does it seem to weigh 200 pounds? What do you think Ned's father would have told him if he had confessed his fears about blinding the cat? What adjectives or phrases would you use to describe each of the major characters?

Sea Glass. This story is told in the first person by the main character. Study the way Craig's character is revealed through his comments about himself, his relationship with his father, and his problems with other kids. Notice how Kenyon drops her façade and reveals her feelings when she talks with Craig alone, behind Uncle's place. Think about how the author lets you know that it is important to accept yourself as you are and not try to be someone you aren't. What words or phrases best describe Craig's looks, behavior, and feelings?

The Summer of the Swans. When you read the first description of Charlie, how did you picture him? Were you surprised when you learned his real age? Record some descriptions of Charlie that show his dependence on Sara and the loneliness he experiences when he is out of her sight. Consider Sara as a character. As you read, collect anecdotes that reveal her feelings about herself (a good

beginning is the episode where she describes herself). Jot down some evidence from the story that lets you know what her relationship is to Charlie. Take note of how Sara changes as the story progresses: What words or phrases would you use to describe her at the beginning of the story? At the end?

These sorts of questions can form the basis for response circle discussions and may be useful when students begin response journals. In all cases, the goal is to help students understand other people and their problems within the context of their own lives and to begin to understand the feelings we all share.

A number of activities can be used to encourage an affective response with these and other novels. Students can try role playing, for example. Ask students to write individual lists of five things they like to do and five things they don't like to do. Then have them respond to the same assignment as though they were a character in a book they have just read. It is best to let students keep these lists private, but do ask them to think about whether they are like or are different from the characters in the novels.

A related activity involves readers in the role of a best friend who is called upon to give advice to the story character. To introduce this activity, ask students whether they could be a best friend to the main character in the story they chose to read. Why or why not? Have they shared any of that character's experiences or had different experiences they could pass along that might help the person? To set this in motion, tell each student, "You are the best friend of a character in one of the books you have recently read. Identify an episode that caused that character unhappiness or concern. (Some likely ones are Ned's distress when he first sees the one-eyed cat or Sara's concern when she realizes that Charlie is missing.)

Teaching Idea

Character Profile

To encourage students to make personal connections with literary characters, ask them to fill out this fact sheet about a favorite character.

Think of your favorite book character and write the person's name in each blank below if the description fits him or her.

_____ is nice looking.

_____ is smart.

_____ gets good grades in school.

_____ is clever.

_____ is usually successful.

_____ has lots of friends.

_____ has an exciting life.

_____ is nice to other people.

Add other things you like about your character:

_____ is _____

_____

Now mark the place on each line that best describes your favorite character:

_____ is like me

a lot	some	not at all

_____ is like my best friend

a lot	some	not at all

_____ is like the most popular kid in class

a lot	some	not at all

Make up your own line:

_____ is like _____

_____

a lot	some	not at all

If your favorite character was more like you, how would she or he change?

If you could be more like your favorite character, how would you have to change?

What might you say to that person to help him or her deal with the situation?''

Bette Bao Lord's *In the Year of the Boar and Jackie Robinson* tells readers what it's like to experience a change in cultures through the eyes of a child moving from China to the United States. Katherine Paterson's *Park's Quest* presents the problem from a different point of view: Park learns that he has a Vietnamese half-sister. As readers interpret the events and compare the way they are depicted in the two books, they may recognize that some elements of the stories apply to situations close to their own lives.

Interpretation of fiction calls for drawing inferences about characters' feelings, the possible effects of an event on the lives of the people involved, or the way an event in a story relates to something similar to what the reader has experienced. To help readers draw inferences about the thoughts of characters, pose these questions: If a main character in the book you just finished were to write a letter to Annemarie of *Number the Stars* and, in the

Grandmother tells Bandit and Precious Coins that they will join their father in America in *In the Year of the Boar and Jackie Robinson*.

letter, point out some ways their lives are alike, what would the person say? What questions might he or she pose to Annemarie or Ellen? Then ask students to write the letter.

Another strategy for exploring characterization is to assign students to small groups, with each child representing a different book. Ask each one to introduce his or her main character, describe some of that person's physical characteristics, and give some information about the problems the person faced. Students might like to draw pictures of their characters. Next, have students tell what the character might say in response to these questions: If you were going to tell someone about yourself, what would you say? Do you think your problem is worse than the problems of the other people represented here? Why or why not?

To encourage students to evaluate some aspect of two books, ask them which character they like better, Annemarie Johansen or a main character from a novel with a contemporary setting. Why? Are the contemporary characters in that book like Annemarie in any way?

Stage Three

Reading and studying historical fiction is a natural extension of a unit on realistic fiction. Characters in both historical and more contemporary books share the same feelings—hope, love, hate, fear, joy, and so on. Both genres can describe personal, social, or political conflicts. Reading historical fiction, however, gives students a clearer picture of the importance of an author's treatment of time and place and the description of a story setting. Once students see these elements at work in historical novels, they will begin to recognize their role in fiction set in contemporary times.

The third stage of this unit allows students to choose one of several books with historical settings. If you want the whole group to read the same book, Esther Forbes's *Johnny Tremain* is a good choice. This well-written novel interests most students. Johnny's development and maturation from beginning to end is striking. The details of the Revolutionary War period in American history are accurate, as are references to the people who were influential in creating the new government.

If you prefer to offer students a choice of books to read, *My Brother Sam Is Dead* by Christopher and James Lincoln Collier is a good book to pair with *Johnny Tremain*. It presents a picture of Revolutionary War times through the eyes of a family torn by divided loyalties. The parents are loyal to King George, while the eldest son fights on the side of the revolutionaries. Whereas *Johnny Tremain* is set mainly in urban areas, *My Brother Sam Is Dead* has a rural setting. The two provide interesting material for comparison.

You might also offer students a choice of books that deal with problems encountered by people who settled in the United States at different times. *The Sign of the Beaver* (Elizabeth George Speare), *Dragonwings* (Laurence Yep), and *Journey to Topaz* (Yoshiko Uchida) are all effective and can be used in combination. The first book is set in the 1700s and portrays relationships between European settlers and Native Americans. The second explores the conditions faced by Chinese laborers living in San Francisco at the turn of the century, as described by a boy who comes from China to join his father in America. The third book portrays the prejudice against people of Japanese descent who were sent to internment camps during World War II.

In each book, a major character is in conflict with other people or with nature. The activities that follow are suggested as ways to help students recognize the qualities of major characters in the books they choose. They are appropriate for use with historical fiction selections as well as with the books suggested in Stage Two of the unit. Attention to literary elements of the books can highlight characterization, plot, and setting.

Characterization. One good activity for studying characterization that students particularly enjoy is staging a TV talk show. One student is the interviewer and two or three others play characters from books read during the unit. To make the characters seem more real, students should be encouraged to wear or carry some object that relates to the theme of the story. For example, in one classroom, two boys chose to be interviewed as Tim in *My Brother Sam Is Dead* and Sam in *The Sign of the Beaver*; both wore makeshift period costumes. The questions they answered included these: When did you begin to worry about what was happening? If you could have changed your life then, what would you have done? What do you think is your best quality? What do you think is your worst quality? If you could do anything you wanted, what would it be? Who would you most like to impress? Who means the most to you? This activity can be used with both historical and contemporary novels (Monson & McClenathan, 1979, pp. 100-104).

If your analysis of the literary elements of a book reveals strong characterization and successful use of dialogue, Readers Theatre is a logical extension activity. You may prepare the first scripts, but as students become more adept at Readers Theatre interpretations, they will want to select their own material and write their own dialogue. In all of this work, they should be reminded of the effectiveness of dialogue in character development. Readers

Theatre can be informal: no sets or costumes are used, and dramatic actions are limited to facial expressions and some gestures. Dramatic effect is achieved by interaction among readers. Participating students should stand in a semicircle so they can all make eye contact when they want to reinforce the relationships among characters. Since the narrator is important, a good reader should take that part.

Select a short, fairly self-contained episode that has several characters in addition to the narrator. The key is to choose selections from books with fine dialogue. Although the dialogue should be left untouched, it is sometimes necessary to shorten the narrative passages. Once the selection has been scripted, students can choose their parts. Students must have read the entire book, or at least enough of it to recognize the personal qualities of the characters they are representing, before they can make good choices. With that background, ask them to think about how they would describe the characters and then decide how the characters would speak.

Plot. Plot is, of course, central to readers' enjoyment of fiction. Ask students to think about these questions when you are guiding them to understand plot development: What is the source of conflict that influences the plot of this book? Does it stem from conflict between people? Between people and nature? People and society? Idea and idea? Is conflict within a person revealed by doubt and uncertainty or through a moral dilemma? How does the main character deal with the conflict?

To help students think about the way conflict is handled, have each one write a sentence on a strip of paper describing each kind of conflict the main character is involved in; on a separate strip, each student should write another sentence for the way the person tries to resolve the conflict. Put students into groups whose members have read several different books. Encourage them to look for cases where characters from different books are involved in similar kinds of conflicts and to consider which characters seem more successful in dealing with problems. As a follow-up, the sentence strips can be used to produce a display or a mobile showing common types of conflicts and resolutions in realistic fiction.

Setting. Books with strong descriptions of place and time, such as Avi's *The True Confessions of Charlotte Doyle*, can help students think about the setting of a story. Have students find evidence that the book does not have a contemporary setting (sailing ships crossing the ocean instead of modern ocean liners; lanterns instead of electric lamps being used for light; Charlotte's need to wear men's clothing because her skirts would be a hazard when she climbed the mast; and so forth). Then ask whether the story could take place now, encouraging students to present arguments either way. Next ask students to write information about the settings of novels depicting more modern times. What evidence can they find that allows them to identify the time the story takes place and its location? Is it rural, urban, or small town? Could they design a jacket for the book that would give a good sense of time and place?

Combining elements. A book that illustrates clearly the interdependence of characterization, plot, and setting is Katherine Paterson's *Lyddie*. The conflict here involves essentially person versus person as Lyddie seeks to earn enough money to save the family farm. Left alone on the farm with her younger brother, Lyddie struggles mightily to succeed. But against Lyddie's wishes, her mother lends the land out to creditors in payment of the family debts. In time, Lyddie finds her way to

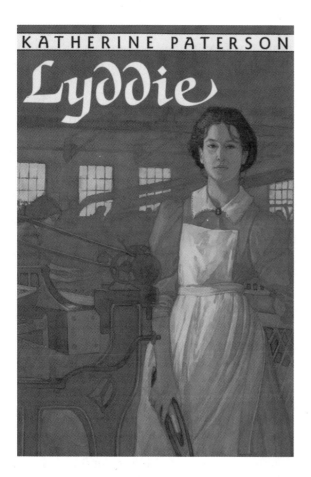

Lyddie in the factory, as depicted on the cover of Katherine Paterson's novel.

Lowell, Massachusetts, where she goes to work in a factory. Paterson shows Lyddie's maturation through the challenges she must meet to be successful in her work and, more important, in her intense effort to learn to read and write.

From beginning to end, Lyddie's courage shines through. In the opening scene, she saves the family by staring down a marauding bear. At the conclusion, Lyddie decides she will go to Ohio to a college that accepts women students. She will once again have to stare down a (figurative) bear, but she is determined to get an education.

The descriptions of a bleak farm existence and the punishing conditions in the factory are gripping portrayals of life in the mid-1800s. The relationships and mutual support among the factory girls is a positive side that lets us know how they survived difficult and health-threatening working conditions. The book offers a look at the workplaces, the homes, and the friendships that sustained poor people on the farms and in the cities of New England in the 19th century.

A sense of time and place also can be explored when students have read novels depicting different historical periods. Students can, for example, assume the identity of characters from the novels and discuss an issue as each character might see it (Cline & McBride, 1983). Some issues that provoke good discussion are whether children ought to take responsibility for helping out with work around the house or whether 12-year-olds should be given the freedom to stay out alone past 10:00 p.m. The contrast in answers from Lyddie, Gilly in *The Great Gilly Hopkins*, and Charlotte in *The True Confessions of Charlotte Doyle* makes an interesting discussion.

The ''Create a Town'' process (developed by Irene O'Neill, curriculum director of the Archdiocese of St. Paul in Minnesota) is a good activity for linking instruction on characterization, plot, and setting. It can be used particularly effectively to encourage creative reading, thinking, and writing about the land and people introduced in the many historical novels dealing with westward expansion. The first step involves reading and listening to a wide variety of books set in that period in U.S. history. Some choices include Carol Ryrie Brink's *Caddie Woodlawn*, Pam Conrad's *Prairie Songs*, Brett Harvey's *Cassie's Journey: Going West in the 1860's* and *My Prairie Year*, Patricia MacLachlan's *Sarah, Plain and Tall*, Ann Turner's *Dakota Dugout*, and Laura Ingalls Wilder's *Little House on the Prairie* and *Little Town on the Prairie*.

When students have been immersed in the problems faced by settlers, as well as descriptions of the territory they crossed and the areas they settled in, convene the group for a problem-solving activity. Their job is to create a town that might have existed sometime during the period of westward expansion. They are to decide where their town is located, what year it is, and what the town is called. As children brainstorm possible times and places, write their suggestions on the board. Then use a system of voting or discussion to let them decide which place and date they want to work with.

Let's say they decide to place their town in the prairies of North Dakota in 1876. The next task is to describe the setting as clearly and completely as possible. Encourage students to generate a list of words and phrases to describe the prairie. You may want to give them time to read for more information, or you may find it useful to read aloud from a book such as *One Day on the Prairie* by Jean Craighead George. The purpose here is to try to help students gain a sense of the sights, sounds, and smells the settlers encountered. Students might hunt for folk melodies that depict the pioneer times or make their own tapes of wind sighing through the prairie grass, meadow larks singing, and other prairie sounds.

The next step calls for brainstorming to identify the buildings that would likely make up the town. At this point, if time allows, you may want to initiate production of a mural. One group of students might be responsible for depicting the prairie itself, the country surrounding the town. Another group might draw or paint the town, showing a number of the buildings they have included in their town plan, or perhaps showing an aerial view of the whole locale. Several other groups might be responsible for more detailed paintings of houses and important buildings in town. With this format, the mural would proceed from left to right, showing the approach to the town, the town in general, and a focused look at a few buildings.

The most interesting job comes next—deciding who the important people in the town will be. This leads easily from brainstorming to writing. After students have generated a list of people they think would make their town come alive (and who would be necessary to make the community prosper), offer them the challenge of becoming one of the characters. They will need some prewriting time to get ready. Some may want to read or reread books with prairie settings. Some will want to discuss their favorite characters; others will be more interested in simply creating the person they would like to have been if they had lived in 1876.

Students may begin by drawing a picture of their character or by finding a photo or magazine picture of a person of that era. They should develop a written description of the person, including physical characteristics and a personality sketch. You might ask them to describe the town as seen through the eyes of their characters. In this extension, they can develop friendships among characters, create stories about the town and its people, and chronicle some of the history of the place.

If students enjoy the Create a Town activity, they will expand on it, creating dialogue between characters and even producing their own Readers Theatre scripts and productions. This activity can be adapted to virtually any unit in the social studies curriculum, from study of the community in the primary grades to study of world history in middle school. The essential component is access to a collection of well-written books set in the appropriate time period.

Linking Literature to Life

The activities described here can help you achieve several goals in teaching a literature unit. First, and perhaps most important, they help students become emotionally involved with major characters. Some of the activities build on an emotional engagement to involve students intellectually as well, inviting them to notice techniques good authors use to create believable, well-rounded characters. As students consider the kinds of conflicts faced by people in contemporary and historical fiction, they become aware of times they have had to deal with similar problems. Recognizing concerns that unite people is one step toward recognizing universal themes that permeate all good literature. These activities aim at encouraging students to respond to texts and to one another. I hope that striving to teach literature with this goal in mind will help us engage the hearts as well as the minds of students.

References

Cline, R., & McBride, W. (1983). *A guide to literature for young adults*. Chicago, IL: Scott, Foresman.

Monson, D., & McClenathan, D. (Eds.). (1979). *Developing active readers: Ideas for parents, teachers, and librarians*. Newark, DE: International Reading Association.

Monson, D., & Sebesta, S. (1991). Children's reading interests. In J. Flood, J. Jensen, D. Lapp, & J.R. Squire (Eds.), *Handbook of research in the teaching of English language arts*. New York: Macmillan.

Rosenblatt, L.M. (1969). *Literature as exploration* (rev. ed.). New York: Noble.

Stein, S. (Ed.). (1989). *Calling all kids! The books our readers loved best*. Camp Hill, PA: Book-of-the-Month Club.

Children's Books

Avi. (1990). *The true confessions of Charlotte Doyle*. New York: Orchard.

Brink, C.R. (1935). *Caddie Woodlawn*. New York: Macmillan.

Byars, B. (1970). *The summer of the swans*. New York: Viking.

Byars, B. (1973). *The eighteenth emergency*. New York: Viking.

Byars, B. (1979). *Good-bye, Chicken Little*. New York: HarperCollins.

Cleary, B. (1968). *Ramona the pest*. New York: Morrow.

Collier, J.L., & Collier, C. (1974). *My brother Sam is dead*. New York: Four Winds.

Conrad, P. (1985). *Prairie songs*. New York: HarperCollins.

Forbes, E. (1943). *Johnny Tremain*. Boston, MA: Houghton Mifflin.

Fox, P. (1984). *One-eyed cat*. New York: Bradbury.

George, J. (1959). *My side of the mountain*. New York: Dutton.

George, J. (1972). *Julie of the wolves*. New York: HarperCollins.

George, J. (1986). *One day on the prairie*. New York: Crowell.

Harvey, B. (1986). *My prairie year*. New York: Holiday House.

Harvey, B. (1988). *Cassie's journey: Going west in the 1860's*. New York: Holiday House.

Lord, B.B. (1986). *In the year of the boar and Jackie Robinson*. New York: HarperCollins.

Lowry, L. (1989). *Number the stars*. Boston, MA: Houghton Mifflin.

MacLachlan, P. (1985). *Sarah, plain and tall*. New York: HarperCollins.

Paterson, K. (1978). *The great Gilly Hopkins*. New York: Crowell.

Paterson, K. (1988). *Park's quest*. New York: Lodestar/Dutton.

Paterson, K. (1991). *Lyddie*. New York: Dutton.

Reiss, J. (1972). *The upstairs room*. New York: Crowell.

Robinson, B. (1988). *My brother Louis measures worms*. New York: HarperCollins.

Speare, E.G. (1983). *The sign of the beaver*. Boston, MA: Houghton Mifflin.

Spinelli, J. (1990). *Maniac Magee*. Boston, MA: Little, Brown.

Turner, A. (1985). *Dakota dugout*. (Ill. by R. Himler.) New York: Macmillan.

Uchida, Y. (1971). *Journey to Topaz*. New York: McElderry.

Wilder, L.I. (1935). *Little house on the prairie*. New York: HarperCollins.

Wilder, L.I. (1941). *Little town on the prairie*. New York: HarperCollins.

Yep, L. (1975). *Dragonwings*. New York: HarperCollins.

Yep, L. (1979). *Sea glass*. New York: HarperCollins.

CHAPTER 4

Current Events
Favorite Topics
Historical Events
Books to Read Aloud

Interacting with Informational Books

M. Jean Greenlaw

If you haven't been to the "numbered" section of the library's children's collection in some time, you are in for a welcome surprise. We have come a long way from the days when the only nonfiction books in that section of the library marched across the shelves in a dreary procession of similar colors, formats, and titles, often written by the same group of authors to a standard formula and used exclusively for researching class reports or projects. Now we have a bold profusion of titles, books written by authors who care about their subjects and produced by publishers who treat each book as a unique addition to the body of literature.

These books are gaining some much-deserved attention in the classroom as more professionals are focusing on their value and the ways they can be used to enhance the curriculum and, of course, students' knowledge. The National Council of Teachers of English, for example, established the annual Orbis Pictus Award in 1991 to honor a work of nonfiction, and a committee of NCTE has written a book on using nonfiction entitled *Using Nonfiction Trade Books in the Elementary Language Arts* (edited by Evelyn Freeman and Diane Person).

A greater volume of informational books for children is being published each year, and the range of subjects these books discuss is becoming increasingly broad. This means that teachers have a vast number of books to choose from and a wide range of possibilities for incorporating them into a literature-based reading program. In what follows, I suggest ways some specific books can be used to teach particular topics. I hope this discussion will serve as a springboard to incorporating many more books on many different subjects into both reading instruction and content area teaching.

Current Events

School curricula should not exist in a vacuum, determined exclusively by district, state, or provincial guidelines or by rigid adherence to textbooks. Students live in a world that is changing daily, and education must have a connection to that real world. Teachers and students who watch news programs and read materials about current events will find much to discuss and to learn from.

The eruption of Mount Pinatubo in the Philippines, for example, could provide the impetus for a science unit on volcanoes (Seymour Simon's *Volcanoes* would be a good resource) or for an examination of other devastating eruptions. Ron and Nancy Goor explore the ruins of a famous Roman town in *Pompeii*, and Patricia Lauber looks at a more contemporary site in *Volcano: The Eruption and Healing of Mount St. Helens*.

Many children are very interested in animals. Recently I saw two television newscasts that showed segments highlighting endangered animals: one presented the plight of the Kodiak bear, which is being encroached on dangerously by humans; the other concerned a California program aimed at saving the condor from extinction. Either of these topics could spur extensive reading and research on endangered animals; a study of a similar case nearer to the students' home is one possibility. Numerous fine books on animal conservation are available to use as resources.

Ecology and environmental concerns are, of course, much in the news. This topic can provide many teaching opportunities, and in many cases excellent informational books are available for use in the classroom. For example, numerous accounts of the Exxon Valdez oil spill and its aftereffects have been published. Students could read several, determine

Teaching Idea

Endangered Animals

Discuss the idea of endangered animals and extinct species with students, perhaps reading aloud from Margery Facklam's *And Then There Was One*. Ask students to conduct research to identify species that are endangered or near extinction. Students can form groups to learn more about specific species and to discuss the volatile subject of the rights of animals versus the rights of humans.

Several books on specific animals have been published and might be useful for this type of study. Among them are George Ancona's *Turtle Watch*, Dorothy Hinshaw Patent's *Where the Wild Horses Roam*, Adele Vernon's *The Hoiho*, and Aubrey Lang's *Eagles*.

Teaching Idea

New Zoos

Zoos used to contain little more than animals in cages. Today, many zoos have completely changed the way animals are cared for and displayed; some are even involved in attempts to save endangered species. Read about some of these new zoos. Have students compile a list of attributes of a humane zoo. If there is a zoo nearby, students can invite a staff member to come and speak to them about the zoo's policies.

Resources on this topic include Peggy Thompson's *Keepers and Creatures at the National Zoo*, Jake Page's *Smithsonian's New Zoo*, Patricia Curtis's *Animals and the New Zoos*, Georgeanne Irvine's *Protecting Endangered Species at the San Diego Zoo*, and Nat Segaloff and Paul Erickson's *A Reef Comes to Life*.

who the author is in each case, and decide whether the tone of the account is colored by bias. Be sure to draw attention to emotional words used to influence the reader. A closer comparison of tone and factual information can be made between two books, possibly Terry Carr's *Spill! The Story of the Exxon Valdez* and Roland Smith's *Sea Otter Rescue: The Aftermath of an Oil Spill*. These books offer a number of contrasts for study. For instance, Carr's book contains only three pages on the efforts to rescue oil-covered sea otters, but in that short section he reveals the cost of saving each otter (quoted at US$80,000). Smith's 48-page book, specifically on sea otter rescue, makes no mention of the cost. Students can speculate about why this information is missing.

Favorite Topics

Students at different ages often develop consuming interests in certain topics. It is wise to take advantage of such interests and promote investigation of these topics in class projects. The same subject might captivate different students in different ways and lead to quite different undertakings. The exploration of space, for example, has fascinated many people for decades. Younger students might set out to construct a timeline of space exploration; middle grade students might be interested in all of the spin-offs from space research that are now part of our daily lives; high school students might get enmeshed in

Teaching Idea

Digging for Dinosaurs

Some people spend their workdays at dinosaur digs; others visit sites where digs are in progress. What happens on a dig? Where are there sites that can be visited? Discover the answers to these questions and see whether there are any sites in your area. Use references such as Aliki's *Digging Up Dinosaurs*, Kathryn Lasky's *Dinosaur Dig*, and Caroline Arnold's *Dinosaur Mountain: Graveyard of the Past*.

Working at a dinosaur dig in Aliki's *Digging Up Dinosaurs*.

Teaching Idea

The Particulars
of Dinosaurs

Encourage your students to select one aspect of the world of dinosaurs that particularly intrigues them—maybe it's how dinosaurs provided for their young or what might have happened to make them extinct. Have the students conduct individual or small group research and then report back to the class. Among books on specific aspects of dinosaurs are Miriam Schlein's *Discovering Dinosaur Babies*, Patricia Lauber's *Living with Dinosaurs* and *Dinosaurs Walked Here and Other Stories Fossils Tell*, and Caroline Arnold's *Dinosaurs Down Under: And Other Fossils from Australia*.

learning specifics about the controversy surrounding whether the United States should participate in building a space station.

Local or regional issues can also be a rich source for study. Some students may want to learn about the history of an annual event or holiday. Topics like these can lead to a variety of reading and writing activities. Older students may even write articles for the local newspaper. A study of the lore and legends of cowboys might intrigue another group of students. Allow the students to tell you what they want to learn about at least once during the year. If the whole class doesn't agree on a common topic for study, several topics can be studied in small groups.

Dinosaurs have been a source of fascination for countless students. Dinosaur remains are discovered fairly frequently, and new information about dinosaurs is still being uncovered. These new findings are discussed in several recently published books; students might be interested in comparing these books with earlier ones to see how far the study of dinosaurs has come. Select several informational books about dinosaurs published over a considerable range of years. Have students compare information on specific dinosaurs and create a chart of the differences in each

book. For example, they can compare information presented in Helen Roney Sattler's *The Illustrated Dinosaur Dictionary*, published in 1983, with her *The New Illustrated Dinosaur Dictionary*, published in 1991. As well as including updated information on the dinosaurs discussed in the first edition, 50 new dinosaurs have been added in the later work. Another good source of information is Patricia Lauber's *The News about Dinosaurs*. In this book the author juxtaposes what was once believed to be true about dinosaurs with the latest information.

Historical Events

Anniversaries of major historical events usually generate news coverage as well as books for children and adolescents. The alert teacher anticipates upcoming events and works with the librarian to see that materials are available to enable a class to get as much knowledge about those events as possible.

The bicentennial of the French Revolution, for example, might have raised students' interest in *The Rights of Man, the Reign of Terror*, Susan Banfield's fine book on that piece of history. In the United States, the linked bicentennials of the Constitution and the Bill of

Travel, as today's students think of it, is relatively easy. But what were the conditions on Columbus's voyages? Create a dramatization of one voyage by using information found in such sources as Peter and Connie Roop's *I, Columbus: My Journal 1492-3*, Olga Litowinsky's *The High Voyage: The Final Crossing of Christopher Columbus*, and Nancy Levinson's *Christopher Columbus: Voyager to the Unknown*.

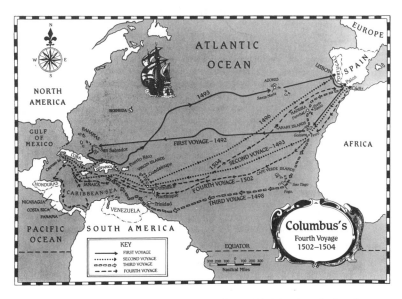

Columbus's voyages depicted in a map from *Christopher Columbus: Voyager to the Unknown.*

Teaching Idea

Traveling with Columbus

Whatever personal beliefs one holds about the impact of Columbus's voyages, it is obvious that vast changes occurred because of them. The Smithsonian Institution in Washington, D.C., has mounted a major exhibition about these events called "Seeds of Change" and has published a companion book (edited by Herman Viola and Carolyn Margolis). Using this and other resources, have students research the short- and long-term effects of the voyages. Then have them create a class or school exhibit, making use of local historians and museums. Remember to explore the possibilities of how the world might have been different if it had not been for Columbus.

Teaching Idea

The Impact of Columbus

Rights in the late 1980s captured the attention of the media and the public. Milton Meltzer's *The Bill of Rights* traces that document's history and clarifies the bill's importance. The Statue of Liberty in New York's harbor, which recently turned 100, is the subject of Jonathan Harris's *A Statue for America*. On a related note, New York's old immigration station on Ellis Island is now a museum; the history of that emotional place is told in several books, including *Ellis Island: Gateway to the New World* by Leonard Fisher.

One anniversary that is of historical interest to much of the world is the 1992 quincentenary of Columbus's first voyage to the Americas. This event, which has spawned numerous books, should be examined far beyond 1992. There are so many ramifications of Columbus's voyage and so many viewpoints about it that discussions on this topic will extend far past the quincentenary year. What was the world like in 1492? What social, political, and cultural events were taking place in Europe? And what was happening in the Americas? What impact did Columbus's arrival have on the Native Americans and on the world as a whole? Resources such as Norman Finkelstein's *The Other 1492: Jewish Settlement in the New World* and Milton Meltzer's *Columbus and the World Around Him* help highlight this period and provide new insights.

Books to Read Aloud

When you reach for a book to read aloud to your students, do you ever choose an informational book? When we think of read-alouds, we generally think of stories. But if you delve into the world of informational books, you'll find a large number of well-written and fascinating works that would be ideal for reading aloud. Younger children will sit entranced by *It's an Armadillo!* by Bianca Lavies or *Is This a House for Hermit Crab?* by Megan McDonald. Upper-elementary students will be moved to tears by Ann Turner's *Nettie's Trip South* or Fay Stanley's *The Last Princess: The Story of Princess Ka'iulani of Hawai'i*. Middle and high school students will be fascinated by the information in books such as James Giblin's *The Riddle of the Rosetta Stone* and Russell Freedman's *Franklin Delano Roosevelt*. Don't miss these and other wonderful informational books that will expand students' horizons while providing excellent models of writing style.

Conclusion

The jury is in. It is impossible to ignore this vast wealth of informational books waiting to be read. The days of boring book reports are over and a new era of interaction is upon us. Enjoy!

Reference

Freeman, E., & Person, D. (1992). *Using nonfiction trade books in the elementary language arts.* Urbana, IL: National Council of Teachers of English.

Children's Books

Aliki. (1988). *Digging up dinosaurs.* New York: Crowell.

Ancona, G. (1987). *Turtle watch.* New York: Macmillan.

Arnold, C. (1988). *Dinosaur mountain: Graveyard of the past.* (Photos by R. Hewitt.) New York: Clarion.

Arnold, C. (1990). *Dinosaurs down under: And other fossils from Australia.* (Photos by R. Hewitt.) New York: Clarion.

Banfield, S. (1989). *The rights of man, the reign of terror.* New York: Lippincott.

Carr, T. (1991). *Spill! The story of the Exxon Valdez*. New York: Watts.

Curtis, P. (1991). *Animals and the new zoos*. New York: Lodestar.

Facklam, M. (1990). *And then there was one*. (Ill. by P. Johnson.) Boston, MA: Little, Brown.

Finkelstein, N.H. (1989). *The other 1492: Jewish settlement in the New World*. New York: Scribners.

Fisher, L.E. (1986). *Ellis Island: Gateway to the New World*. New York: Holiday House.

Freedman, R. (1990). *Franklin Delano Roosevelt*. New York: Clarion.

Giblin, J.C. (1990). *The riddle of the Rosetta Stone*. New York: Crowell.

Goor, R., & Goor, N. (1986). *Pompeii*. New York: Crowell.

Harris, J. (1985). *A statue for America*. New York: Four Winds.

Irvine, G. (1991). *Protecting endangered species at the San Diego Zoo*. New York: Simon & Schuster.

Lang, A. (1990). *Eagles*. (Photos by W. Lynch.) Boston, MA: Little, Brown.

Lasky, K. (1990). *Dinosaur dig*. (Photos by C. Knight.) New York: Morrow.

Lauber, P. (1986). *Volcano: The eruption and healing of Mount St. Helens*. New York: Bradbury.

Lauber, P. (1987). *Dinosaurs walked here and other stories fossils tell*. New York: Bradbury.

Lauber, P. (1989). *The news about dinosaurs*. New York: Bradbury.

Lauber, P. (1991). *Living with dinosaurs*. (Ill. by D. Henderson.) New York: Bradbury.

Lavies, B. (1989). *It's an armadillo!* New York: Dutton.

Levinson, N.S. (1990). *Christopher Columbus: Voyager to the unknown*. New York: Lodestar.

Litowinsky, O. (1991). *The high voyage: The final crossing of Christopher Columbus*. New York: Delacorte.

McDonald, M. (1990). *Is this a house for hermit crab?* (Ill. by S.D. Schindler.) New York: Orchard.

Meltzer, M. (1990). *The Bill of Rights*. New York: Crowell.

Meltzer, M. (1990). *Columbus and the world around him*. New York: Watts.

Page, J. (1990). *Smithsonian's new zoo*. Washington, DC: Smithsonian.

Patent, D.H. (1989). *Where the wild horses roam*. (Photos by W. Munoz.) New York: Clarion.

Roop, P., & Roop, C. (Eds.). (1990). *I, Columbus: My journal 1492-3*. New York: Walker.

Sattler, H.R. (1983). *The illustrated dinosaur dictionary*. New York: Lothrop, Lee & Shepard.

Sattler, H.R. (1991). *The new illustrated dinosaur dictionary*. New York: Lothrop, Lee & Shepard.

Schlein, M. (1991). *Discovering dinosaur babies*. (Ill. by M. Colbert.) New York: Four Winds.

Segaloff, N., & Erickson, P. (1991). *A reef comes to life*. New York: Watts.

Simon, S. (1988). *Volcanoes*. New York: Morrow.

Smith, R. (1990). *Sea otter rescue: The aftermath of an oil spill*. New York: Cobblehill.

Stanley, F. (1991). *The last princess: The story of Princess Ka'iulani of Hawai'i*. New York: Four Winds.

Thompson, P. (1988). *Keepers and creatures at the National Zoo*. (Photos by P.S. Conklin.) New York: Crowell.

Turner, A. (1987). *Nettie's trip south*. (Ill. by R. Himler.) New York: Macmillan.

Vernon, A. (1991). *The hoiho*. (Photos by D. Schneider.) New York: Putnam.

Viola, H.J., & Margolis, C. (1991). *Seeds of change*. Washington, DC: Smithsonian.

SECTION TWO

Trade books can serve either as the focus of or as resources for a range of study units. Sometimes they are best used to enhance an area of instruction targeted for special attention; at other times they can be a springboard for intensive cross-disciplinary study.

This section outlines ways literature can be used to teach certain themes, whether in the content areas or as part of a detailed literature study within the language arts program. Chapter 5 describes how trade books can be used to enhance studies of visual art, drama, and music and to encourage children to view reading as an aesthetic experience. Chapter 6 describes a year-long study of popular children's author Tomie dePaola undertaken by a third grade class. This activity not only boosted the children's reading ability but also became the impetus for explorations in other content areas and the creation of class writing and publishing projects. Bill Martin Jr is the focus of chapter 7, which outlines a number of activities based on this author's many well-loved books. In the classrooms described here, children's enthusiasm for Martin's writing led to improved literacy skills and increased interest in learning.

Compelling books whose characters and plots reflect life among a wide variety of cultures are the subject of chapter 8. Using these works in the classroom will help students better understand and appreciate the different cultures and peoples with whom they live. Chapter 9 continues the discussion of different cultures and countries with its exploration of award-winning books from Australia, Canada, Great Britain, New Zealand, and the United States. The chapter concludes with a listing of award winners from 1980-1991.

Thematic Units

CHAPTER 5

Enriching the Arts and Humanities

Sam Leaton Sebesta

The literature base in reading instruction is more firmly established now than it was when this book's predecessor, *Children's Literature in the Reading Program* (Cullinan, 1987), was published. Now we can refine the concept without fear that it will lose its footing and fall into the Gulf of Discarded Methods.

Literature-based programs emphasize trade books and activities centered on them—that much is agreed. However, there appears to be tacit disagreement over the purpose of the literature beyond its utility in teaching the fundamentals of how to read. The *efferent* stance is that literature is used for acquiring skills or information: "The reader's attention is centered on what should be retained *after* the actual reading-event" (Rosenblatt, 1985, p. 37). For instance, if a pupil is directed to read a selection in order to answer a set of comprehension questions, to locate and define a list of vocabulary items, or to identify examples of figurative language, the literary experience may be entirely efferent. The opposite view is *aesthetic*. Rosenblatt calls it an aesthetic transaction: "The reader's attention is focused on *what he is living through during the reading-event*" (p. 38). Pupils read to experience the work. They respond to that experience, which Rosenblatt calls an "evocation." An aesthetic response session for a novel such as Paula Fox's *The Village by the Sea* would not begin with comprehension questions or an examination of character traits or style. It might begin with open, student-generated discussion; with role-playing to explore Emma's encounter with her mysterious uncle and aunt; or with filling a page of a free-writing response journal.

Why is the distinction between efferent and aesthetic important? Why does it come at the beginning of a chapter about literature and the humanities? First, because literature-based programs need a balance between efferent and aesthetic types of response. The efferent stance emphasizes utility and cognitive growth; the aesthetic stance emphasizes enjoyment, emotion, and personal involvement. There is evidence that some literature-based programs lean almost exclusively toward one stance or the other (Cox & Zarrillo, 1990). To be aware of the distinction is the first step in finding a healthy balance. Second, because books about the arts and humanities offer special opportunities to develop the aesthetic stance. They are doorways to visual arts, drama, and music—to the "continuously renewed delight" offered by the humanities (Dewey, 1929, p. 7).

Literature and the Visual Arts

One way to foster an aesthetic response is to encourage intermediate students to try on the role of the artist, first by considering what it might have been like to be one of the past masters. Piero Ventura's *Michelangelo's World* introduces the great sculptor and painter in first person. We learn of Michelangelo's first venture to Rome—to sell a fake antique sculpture—as if in his own words. We experience the brawls, the rivalry between Michelangelo and Leonardo da Vinci, and the triumphs: the sculpting of David from a 15-foot too-narrow block of marble and the acrobatics involved in painting frescoes on the ceiling of the Sistine Chapel. Cartoon figures and diagrams enliven the account. How pleased I think Michelangelo would be with this reincarnation! It places an artist's life nearer to the reader's own, bringing aesthetic response through engagement and involvement.

Teaching Idea

Sliding into Art

Three enchanting picture books show children visiting art museums and entering, literally, the paintings they view. *Katie's Picture Show* by James Mayhew is a pleasant adventure in London's National Gallery until Katie goes sliding into a bottomless pit of modern art. A similar fate awaits Lulu in Posy Simmonds's *Lulu and the Flying Babies*, drawn in cartoons but respectful of museum art. Most surprising is *Rembrandt's Beret, or the Painter's Crown* by the Brothers Alcorn, who know a secret passage from the Uffizi gallery to the Pitti Palace—it contains portraits of famous painters who step out to meet you.

Use all three or just one. Then use the technique. Seat children in front of one painting or let them choose their own in an art gallery. If those options aren't available, use books of reproductions such as Philip Yenawine's *Colors* and *Stories*, both from the Museum of Modern Art in New York. Then say this: "Look at the picture until you think you've memorized it. Then look at it some more. Then, like Katie or Lulu or Tiberius in the books we've read, tell or write or draw what happens to *you* as you slide into the painting."

Lulu is chastized by a flying baby in *Lulu and the Flying Babies.*

Meet Edgar Degas by Anne Newlands, also written in the first person, begins with a reproduction of a self-portrait and these words: "If I seem to be staring at you, I'm not. I'm staring at myself, in a mirror." The quips that follow are actually astute directives to make us examine closely the 13 paintings reproduced in full page in this remarkable book. From there, it is just an arm's reach to the more comprehensive *Picture This: A First Introduction to Paintings* by Felicity Woolf, with its detailed commentary and reproductions of paintings created between 1400 and 1950. People who stand in front of a painting and say, "Isn't that pretty?" or "What's that supposed to be?" should read this book. Its author, a former secondary school teacher, comments on the time and setting of each painting. She tells us enough about the content of a painting to make us study it closely and long to see the original, close up. She excites our interest in the artist's process by telling a little about how each painting was done.

If all of this seems a bit heavy, you can lighten up with *Visiting the Art Museum* by Laurene Krasny Brown and Marc Brown, in which a family of five puzzles through ten art galleries, describing the Discus Thrower (sculpted in 450 BC) as a "nude frisbee player" and discovering when they leave that they see the world outside the museum afresh. Or turn to *Cartoons and Cartooning* by Harvey Weiss, which suggests that the 230-foot-long Bayeux tapestry is "the longest and most unusual cartoon strip ever made," and urges you to "jump in and get started" on your own.

Of course, you don't have to have the books cited here to build a visual arts component to a reading program emphasizing aesthetic response. These are just examples; there are many other good books, old and new, to choose from. Surround children with art-

works and books about them. Avoid the abstract ("This picture makes us feel gentle and calm") when you talk about visual art—and avoid rushed judgments ("I don't like this picture because I don't like sunflowers"). Instead, have students try some activities such as these:

- You are the artist. Why did you do this picture or sculpture? How did you do it? What did you use? What do you want us to get from it?

- Walk into this picture. Where do you stand? What do you see? Where else might you go, as you walk into the background or out of the border? What will you do next?

- Select and pose as one of the characters in a painting. What might the character be saying? Thinking?

- Report on an artist; write or tell your report in the first person, as if you were the artist.

These direct point-of-view activities are not as unusual as they may appear. Fantasy writers including E. Nesbit, Philippa Pearce, and P.L. Travers have used them (see, for example, chapter 2 in *Mary Poppins*). The second act of the musical *Sunday in the Park with George* by Stephen Sondheim and James Lapine begins with 16 characters in a Seurat painting coming to life, singing their way through the years on a gallery wall.

As every good teacher of reading and writing knows, reception and production in language arts go together. Responding to art includes creating art, and books can almost literally guide the hand and eye. Two dependable standbys are *23 Varieties of Ethnic Art and How to Make Each One* by Jean and Cle Kinney and *How to Make Whirligigs and Whimmy Diddles and Other American Folk-*

Teaching Idea

Learn the Process; Appreciate the Product

Visual art production enhances reception. Start with an art lesson in which students experience an art process used in picture books, *before* you show them the picture book. Here are two examples.

A Plasticine Experience

In *Playing with Plasticine* Barbara Reid tells how to "paint a picture" with this clay-like material. It's simple. You mold a flat setting out of one set of colors and then you mold three-dimensional characters out of a contrasting set of colors. Place characters on the setting and photograph the scene. It's a unique type of illustration, and usually a pleasant surprise.

Then, after practicing the art process, bring out picture books that use it. *Effie*, written by Beverley Allinson and illustrated by Barbara Reid, now brings gasps of recognition and appreciation. *A Man and His Hat*, a rhyme tale by Letitia Parr, is illustrated with photographed "clay animations" by Paul Terrett. Children appreciate and interpret these picture books more thoroughly as a result of their own art experience.

Ukiyo-e ("Floating World")

Ukiyo-e is a 300-year-old Japanese art process in which wood block prints are used to imitate brush strokes, which allows the prints to be reproduced. Give children the experience, using potatoes, plastic knives, and dark tempera paint. Cut the potato to get a design (bamboo, flowers, trees), dip it into the paint, and print on coarse paper. Try smearing with fist and fingers if this helps bring out the sense of "floating."

Then bring out a masterpiece: The illustrations of Leo and Diane Dillon for *The Tale of the Mandarin Ducks* (by Katherine Paterson) are inspired by *Ukiyo-e* techniques. Note the aesthetic response of children, who now perceive the art with a sense of the process that created it.

craft Objects by Florence Pettit. Although these crafts books first appeared in the 1970s, they are still to be found, well-worn but serviceable, in many libraries. Or place S. Adams Sullivan's *Bats, Butterflies, and Bugs: A Book of Action Toys* and Robin West's *Far Out: How to Create Your Own Star World* in a "following directions" learning center. These two easy-to-follow and exciting crafts books both call for readily found materials. The art objects that can result from these four how-to books are terrific; children need no coaxing to create them. All of these books, by the way, have been used effectively in cross-age cooperative learning groups, with primary and intermediate pupils working together.

Books that help children explore the possibilities of an art medium are popular. Henry Pluckrose's *Crayons* received many affirmative votes on its way to being selected as a "Children's Choice" book. Why? Because it seems to sit down beside children, with their ubiquitous crayon collections, to offer suggestions that range farther and farther from the old instruction to "draw a picture and color in the spaces." A hot iron, a swash of ink, scissors, glue—put these common materials together with crayons and the result can be a creation that seems to have been visited by a fairy godmother. In the same series is Jeannie Hull's *Clay*, with ideas on how to experience the process of creating art with this most satisfying material.

Now have students look again at picture books. Their involvement with great artwork and artists and with their own creations will lead them to fresh insights about a genre that is sometimes mistakenly confined to preschool and primary levels. Here are four examples of picture books that can be used with intermediate-grade students to encourage aesthetic response to visual art, in different ways.

Claude and Frédéric Clément's *The Painter and the Wild Swans*, adorned with Japanese calligraphy, is *about* art—a painter's search for a place of beauty "impossible to capture" and his transformation into a swan are shown in a remarkable series of paintings. If you wished to find a place of such beauty, where would you look? How would you try to portray it?

The picture books of Deborah Nourse Lattimore, with their links between art, archaeology, and ancient history, are extraordinary. *The Prince and the Golden Ax: A Minoan Tale* ends with a miracle: The famed blue monkeys of Thera are transformed into frescoes on the temple wall and thereby escape their pursuer. The monkeys also somehow escaped the real-life volcanic eruption that destroyed most of the island. Pupils introduced to these dancing figures can find out all about their survival through the centuries from guidebooks and reference sources—as good as any treasure hunt!

Chris Van Allsburg takes you where photographer and scientist fear to go in *Two Bad Ants*, which depicts the motivations and tribulations of the two ants, whose journey plummets them into "a boiling brown lake" that is actually a coffee cup. Subsequent episodes, too scary to detail here, include trips into the garbage disposal and an electric socket. It's the enlarged, solidly precise drawings done from an ant's beleaguered perspective that communicate the odyssey and that can inspire child artists to experiment with other unusual perspectives.

Don't overlook Maurice Sendak's compositions for Wilhelm Grimm's *Dear Mili* for intermediate students. What do you see first as you examine a picture, and how does Sendak direct your eye from the focus of the picture to the details that make the scene powerful?

Cover of Jean Fritz's biography of the fourth president of the United States.

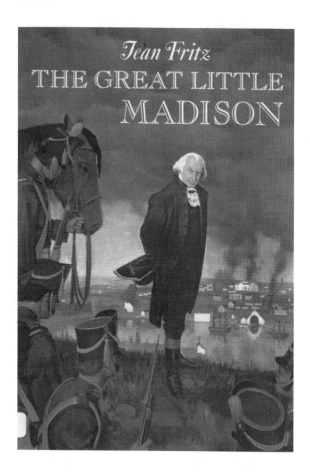

Jean Fritz
THE GREAT LITTLE
MADISON

Finally, help children notice that the visual arts play a part in the lives of characters they read about. In Betsy Byars's *The Blossoms and the Green Phantom*, Junior will show "the whole world" his never-before-imagined flying pyramid made out of air mattresses and garbage bags. Junior has the artist's desire to astonish and please. In the previously mentioned *The Village by the Sea*, two lonely girls find solace in constructing a miniature town out of "found" materials on the beach. It's a place wherein they can imagine a happier world than theirs seems to be. Or hark back to the Ireland of a thousand years ago, to the story of Cormac, whose art of illuminating manuscripts helps him face the Viking raid in Mary Stolz's *Pangur Ban*.

Literature and Drama

Drama is a show-and-tell way of responding to literature. When question answering and literary analysis threaten to overbalance the efferent stance, drama and oral interpretation can intervene to assert the aesthetic approach. Here are some ideas to help accomplish this task.

Creative Drama

Creative drama is improvisational; that is, it is done without a script. It can be done in segments large or small; children can play a crucial scene rather than a whole story, or one episode in a biography such as Jean Fritz's *The Great Little Madison*.

A creative drama session begins with identifying what is to be played. If the technique is new to children, encourage them to select literature with concentrated action and a strong theme. A good topic for beginning creative drama is "Folk Tales from Around the

World.'' If you choose this topic, these books are excellent candidates for dramatic interpretation: *The Golden Goose* from Germany (by the Brothers Grimm), *Rama and Sita* from India (Govinder Ram), *The Magic Horse* from Persia (Sally Scott), *Iktomi and the Boulder* from the Plains Indians (Paul Goble), and *Anansi and the Moss-Covered Rock* from West Africa (Eric Kimmel).

You can discuss the story and plan the action, or you can jump right in. Some teachers start with pantomime: children mime what the characters do, while others tell or read the scene. Then the enactment is evaluated—how can we make it better?—and replayed. Gradually, the characters construct dialogue to go with the mime, discovering that speech is easier when action is clear. During this time, the teacher provides leadership by focusing discussion, coaching the enactment, and drawing an imaginary curtain to keep scenes brief and to the point. Pace, in fact, can be the most important feature of creative drama sessions.

In sum, here are the steps for a creative drama session:

1. Select a scene with plenty of action.

2. Choose actors to mime the scene.

3. Evaluate: What was convincing in the mime? How can we make it better?

4. Play it again. Evaluate. Begin adding dialogue created on the spot by the players.

5. Add other scenes to make a full creative drama.

Teachers who are reluctant to try creative drama sometimes say, ''But aren't children self-conscious in front of an audience?'' The answer is that creative drama is not performed in front of an audience. Everyone participates, whether a whole class or a subgroup. True, some students participate as scenery or extras, but they will become major players during re-enactments. In short, creative drama is a cooperative venture. Everyone gets into the act.

As students become familiar with the process, encourage them to select episodes with rounded, dynamic characters and settings that are integral to the story (Lukens, 1990). Try, for instance, the scene in which Mary Lennox discovers Colin in *The Secret Garden* (chapter 13 of Frances Hodgson Burnett's classic) or a modern counterpart, such as Maggie's first meeting with the dolls in Sylvia Cassedy's *Behind the Attic Wall* (chapter 18) or Annemarie's encounter with the Nazi soldiers in Lois Lowry's *Number the Stars* (chapter 15). (A useful guide for these sessions is McCaslin's [1990] *Creative Drama in the Classroom.*)

Formal Drama

In contrast to creative drama, formal drama uses a script and may be played in front of an audience, shifting the emphasis from process to product. It requires memorization, rehearsal, and a director to help players envision the effect their presentation will have on an audience. Props, costumes, and scenery may be used but should be minimal. It's the performance that counts.

Is formal drama worth the time and effort it takes? Much depends on the quality of the script and direction. A good director helps players focus on character interaction and intent. A good script may be an original literary work or an adaptation. It should have emotional appeal, a distinct style, and a worthwhile theme. Experts seem to agree that in recent times more and more suitable scripts have become available for formal drama for and with children. Nancy Willard's drama version of *East of the Sun and West of the Moon* is a literary accomplishment, whether read in an armchair or played on a stage. *Escape to Freedom: A Play about Young Frederick Douglass* by Ossie Davis can be played in full or done as a "serial," its five scenes performed at the rate of one per week. The second volume of *Plays Children Love* (edited by Coleman Jennings and Aurand Harris) is a fine resource for the intermediate grades, with scripts of classic and modern plays, including Paul Sills's famed Story Theatre version of "The Golden Goose." A good source to guide production of these formal dramas is Judy and Judy's (1982) *Putting on a Play*.

Readers Theatre

Readers Theatre gives students access to the whole field of oral interpretation. Readers Theatre is like playing the piccolo: It sounds easier than it really is. It harkens back to radio drama days, when well-spoken dialogue built the scenery and the character descriptions in listeners' minds. It's a high art, at the heart of reading to elicit aesthetic response. Here are a few suggestions, drawn from many teachers' experiences.

Start with engaging literature that's heavy on dialogue, such as children's favorite scenes from the time-tested Freddy series (e.g., *Freddy and the Men from Mars* by Walter Brooks, chapter 1) or the enormously popular Babysitters Club series. Leaving out the "he saids" and "she exclaimeds," assign only description that's absolutely necessary to one or more narrators. Type a script or, if feasible, simply have pupils bracket off their speeches in pencil in the paperback.

Allow for lots of practice. First, have students read the whole script silently and then try out various roles. There's no memorization of parts, but impress on students the need to read fluently. Have them look for contrasts, perhaps two characters who are opposites. Have them look for high points—places where the mood is strong and where there's an important turning point.

At intermediate levels, you can teach some of the techniques used by radio performers. With *overlap*, the first word of a character's line is spoken at the same time as the last word of the speech that precedes it; this technique helps pick up the pace. *Topping* means that each speech is given greater intensity than the one that precedes it, so that there is a dramatic or comic build-up. *Pause*, to be effective, is preplanned and marked in the script; it's a chance for the audience to respond.

Throughout the rehearsal and performance, emphasize voice, not action. Voice plus a few sound effects should communicate the entire experience. One teacher has her students stand behind a large mock-up of a radio as they rehearse to emphasize that all must be done with voice.

Readers Theatre is a good introduction to the broader field of oral interpretation, which includes choral speaking and dramatic reading. These are old arts renewed by literature that demands to be read aloud. Some contemporary examples include Paul Fleischman's books of poetry for two voices, *Joyful Noise* and *I Am Phoenix*. (The Caedmon Company markets a professional reading of these two books on audiotape.) Excellent excerpts for reading aloud abound in *The Random House Book of Humor for Children* (selected by Pamela Pollack). Every child is aesthetically enriched for having heard, watched, or performed the great opening page of Russell Freedman's *Lincoln: A Photobiography* or for experiencing the style of Rosemary Sutcliff in the White Hart episode of *The Shining Company* (pp. 29-39). It's more than "getting the words right"—it is bringing sound and imagery to listeners through the art of oral interpretation.

Literature and Music

Children need more variety in music than they're likely to hear on TV and in the shopping mall. In certain situations, it pays to visit a used-record store, select a variety of compositions, and play records or tapes as background during part of each school day. Without comment, give pupils an hour of Grieg every day for a week. During the *next* week, someone is likely to request a little Grieg during journal time. Try a composer-of-the-week theme, and notice how quickly intermediate-grade students pick up on the names and different styles of Grieg,

Teaching Idea

Be-an-Expert Kit

"You can be an expert. You can know more about _____ than anyone else in this room, this school, this block, and maybe this town. Here's what you do. Unpack this kit. Listen to the tapes. Study the maps. Read the books. When you're ready, ask for the EXPERT QUIZ. You can do this by yourself or with a partner."

My first Be-an-Expert Kit was on Mozart, celebrating the 200th anniversary of his death. I taped the best-known, most sprightly airs from my Mozart records. I also taped the brief but rather difficult text of Lisl Weil's *Wolferl: The First Six Years in the Life of Wolfgang Amadeus Mozart*. I added two fairly easy, well-focused biographies: *Mozart Tonight* by Julie Downing and *Mozart: Scenes from Childhoods of the Great Composers* by Catherine Brighton. As an option, I added *The Mozart Season* by Virginia Euwer Wolff, a novel about a 12-year-old violinist getting ready to play a Mozart concerto in competition.

Students can check out the kit for three weeks. When they finish, they request the EXPERT QUIZ, which I prepare and seal in an envelope. The quiz isn't picky, but it does require information that a person ought to have if she or he claims to be an expert on, say, Mozart: *Which opera has a statue that moves? If you play a clavichord, do you sit down at it, blow into it, or tuck it under your chin?*

Put the Be-an-Expert materials in uniform-size boxes bought at the hardware store. Start the year with six of them on a range of arts-related topics. Invite contributions. I'm waiting for a family to come back from Salzburg with more Mozart materials!

Tchaikovsky, Wagner, Gershwin, Ellington, and the Beatles.

All of these musicians and a year's worth more are introduced in thumbnail sketches in Piero Ventura's *Great Composers*, which also contains brief descriptions of Asian music-making. Lisl Weil's 32-page *The Magic of Music* presents history, music fundamentals, and an array of instruments in a manner so appealing that students will likely pass the book around for reading and enjoying all through the school year. If that doesn't do it, try *Orchestranimals* (Vlasta Van Kampen and Irene Eugen), a sophisticated picture book starring a penguin conductor badgering (Do penguins badger? This one does!) his tardy menagerie of players into performing "Crash Concerto." Who's missing? Crash, of course. Part of the musical score appears on each frantic page, so have a piano handy if it isn't too heavy.

Enthusiasm for dance—both movement that tells a story to a musical background and movement that simply responds to music—has, I think, increased over the past 50 years. *Black Dance in America: A History Through Its People* (James Haskins) is a thoughtful account that culminates with descriptions of the work of Alvin Ailey and Judith Jamison, disco dancing, break dancing, and other trends in the modern dance scene. Ballet, once available to only a few adults (and fewer children), has expanded its audience enormously, both live and on TV. As a result, more and more children now have the interest and background to view Margot Fonteyn's perfect rendition of *Swan Lake* in book form, with illustrations by Trina Schart Hyman, right down to its bittersweet ending and the great dancer's afternote: "*Swan Lake* is the only ballet I never felt strong enough to perform twice in the same day." For the fourth-grade balletomane, there is also a highly detailed pop-up book called *Ballet in Motion* (Craig Dodd and Shirley Soar) with the most amazing flying scene (from *The Sleeping Beauty*) this side of aeronautics.

How long will it be before a teacher can easily gain access to videos of musical performances to show in the classroom, accompanied by books such as the ones I've described here? Perhaps it can be done now, or surely it will be possible by the turn of the century. Dance, at any rate, is accessible to almost everyone, even without professional companies or electronics. The simplest mime of a folktale or myth or narrative poem becomes dance when it is practiced and set to a drum beat.

Books invite singers. Raffi's songbooks are brightly designed and decked out with piano or guitar accompaniment to which can be added all sorts of rhythm instruments. (Of course, you can obtain Raffi's recordings of the songs if you need a back-up.) Try *The Raffi Everything Grows Songbook* or Raffi's little volume devoted to a Calypso song, *Tingalayo*. A popular blending of pictures, prose narrative, and story-ballad-with-music is Jimmy and Savannah Jane Buffett's version of *The Jolly Mon*. Researchers who point out the virtues of fluency and repeated reading will be pleased with the daily use of songbooks, song charts, and lyric sheets in your classroom!

In the modern world, background music is taken for granted. We hum along in the car, bus, or shopping mall without notice. Books can bridge the distance between music as a subliminal experience and music as a consciously sought avenue to peace of mind and re-creation. Well, perhaps peace of mind isn't quite the appropriate phrase for Mariah in Mildred Pitts Walter's *Mariah Loves Rock*. She's near hysteria in her wish to attend the concert of her hero, rock star Sheik Bashara.

But at least Mariah's story makes sense to those who love and seek music. The spontaneous plot-connected chants that head the chapters of Walter Dean Myers's *The Mouse Rap* are another instance of modern students seeking music.

Discuss the role that music plays—or can play—in our lives. Invite students on a yearlong quest as they read to discover book characters for whom music is a significant part of life. Can they find, for instance, the books and characters with musical motifs in the works of Katherine Paterson, Margaret Mahy, Patricia MacLachlan, and Madeleine L'Engle?

The Aesthetic Experience

Books about the arts and humanities are available in every genre, hence appealing to a wide range of readers. Their appeal is primarily aesthetic, a domain often neglected in reading instruction. They fill a great need to bind reading and other arts to aesthetic experience.

Aesthetic experience is not composed of a cluster of skills. It is holistic. Students grow in their response repertoire through holistic activity. They dance, paint, mime, chant, and dramatize their responses. They read interpretively, to find and sometimes to share the imagery, mood, and wonder.

Response journals, or a place in a journal to write about one's responses to the arts, can be fostered in the intermediate grades. So, too, can response groups, who meet to discuss in "grand conversations" (Eeds & Wells, 1989) their reactions to visual arts, drama, and music—and the books that help make the arts and humanities accessible to a new generation.

References

Cox, C., & Zarrillo, J. (1990). *Teaching with literature in the elementary school: A qualitative study applying Rosenblatt's transactional theory*. Paper delivered at the annual convention of the American Educational Research Association, Chicago, IL.

Cullinan, B.E. (Ed.). (1987). *Children's literature in the reading program*. Newark, DE: International Reading Association.

Dewey, J. (1929). Experience, nature, and art. In *Art and education* (pp. 3-12). New York: Barnes.

Eeds, M., & Wells, D. (1989). Grand conversations: An exploration of meaning construction in literature study groups. *Research in the Teaching of English, 23*(1), 4-29.

Judy, S., & Judy, S. (1982). *Putting on a play*. New York: Scribner's.

Lukens, R.J. (1990). *A critical handbook of children's literature* (4th ed.). Glenview, IL & Boston, MA: Scott, Foresman/Little, Brown.

McCaslin, N. (1990). *Creative drama in the classroom* (5th ed.). White Plains, NY: Longman.

Rosenblatt, L.M. (1985). The transactional theory of the literary work: Implications for research. In C.R. Cooper (Ed.), *Researching response to literature and the teaching of literature* (pp. 33-53). Norwood, NJ: Ablex.

Children's Books

Alcorn, J. (1991). *Rembrandt's beret, or the painter's crown*. (Ill. by S. Alcorn.) New York: Tambourine.

Allinson, B. (1991). *Effie*. (Ill. by B. Reid.) New York: Scholastic.

Brighton, C. (1990). *Mozart: Scenes from childhoods of the great composers*. New York: Doubleday.

Brooks, W.R. (1954/1986). *Freddy and the men from Mars*. (Ill. by K. Wiese.) New York: Knopf.

Brown, L.K., & Brown, M. (1986). *Visiting the art museum*. New York: Dutton.

Buffett, J., & Buffett, S.J. (1988). *The jolly mon*. (Ill. by L. Davis.) San Diego, CA: Harcourt Brace Jovanovich.

Burnett, F.H. (1962). *The secret garden*. (Ill. by T. Tudor.) New York: Lippincott.

Byars, B. (1987). *The blossoms and the green phantom*. (Ill. by J. Rogers.) New York: Delacorte.

Cassedy, S. (1983). *Behind the attic wall*. New York: Crowell.

Clément, C. (1986). *The painter and the wild swans*. (Ill. by F. Clément.) New York: Dial.

Davis, O. (1978). *Escape to freedom: A play about young Frederick Douglass*. New York: Viking.

Dodd, C., & Soar, S. (1988). *Ballet in motion: A three-dimensional guide to ballet for young people*. New York: Lippincott.

Downing, J. (1991). *Mozart tonight*. New York: Bradbury.

Fleischman, P. (1985). *I am Phoenix: Poems for two voices*. (Ill. by K. Nutt.) New York: HarperCollins.

Fleischman, P. (1988). *Joyful noise: Poems for two voices*. (Ill. by E. Beddows.) New York: HarperCollins.

Fonteyn, M. (Reteller). (1989). *Swan Lake*. (Ill. by T.S. Hyman.) San Diego, CA: Gulliver.

Fox, P. (1988). *The village by the sea*. New York: Orchard.

Freedman, R. (1987). *Lincoln: A photobiography*. New York: Clarion.

Fritz, J. (1989). *The great little Madison*. New York: Putnam.

Goble, P. (1988). *Iktomi and the boulder*. New York: Orchard.

Grimm, J., & Grimm, W. (1987). *The golden goose*. (Trans. by S. Saunders; ill. by I. Seltzer.) New York: Scholastic.

Grimm, W. (1988). *Dear Mili*. (Trans. by R. Manheim; ill. by M. Sendak.) New York: Farrar, Straus & Giroux.

Haskins, J. (1990). *Black dance in America: A history through its people*. New York: Crowell.

Hull, J. (1989). *Clay*. (Photos by C. Fairclough.) New York: Watts.

Jennings, C.A., & Harris, A. (Eds.). (1988). *Plays children love: Volume II*. New York: St. Martin's.

Kimmel, E.A. (1988). *Anansi and the moss-covered rock*. (Ill. by J. Stevens.) New York: Holiday House.

Kinney, J., & Kinney, C. (1976). *23 varieties of ethnic art and how to make each one*. New York: Atheneum.

Lattimore, D.N. (1988). *The prince and the golden ax: A Minoan tale*. New York: HarperCollins.

Lowry, L. (1989). *Number the stars*. Boston, MA: Houghton Mifflin.

Mayhew, J. (1989). *Katie's picture show*. New York: Bantam.

Myers, W.D. (1990). *The mouse rap*. New York: HarperCollins.

Newlands, A. (1989). *Meet Edgar Degas*. New York: Lippincott. (Originally published in Toronto, Ont., by Kids Can Press, 1988.)

Parr, L. (1991). *A man and his hat*. (Ill. by P. Terrett.) New York: Philomel. (Originally published in Sydney by Collins Ltd., 1989.)

Paterson, K. (1990). *The tale of the Mandarin ducks*. (Ill. by L. Dillon & D. Dillon.) New York: Lodestar.

Pettit, F.H. (1972). *How to make whirligigs and whimmy diddles and other American folkcraft objects*. New York: Crowell.

Pluckrose, H. (1987). *Crayons*. (Photos by C. Fairclough.) New York: Watts.

Pollack, P. (Selector). (1988). *The Random House book of humor for children*. (Ill. by P.O. Zelinsky.) New York: Random House.

Raffi. (1989). *The Raffi everything grows songbook*. (Ill. by children from New York and Toronto.) New York: Crown.

Raffi. (1989). *Tingalayo* (Raffi Songs to Read series). (Ill. by K. Duke.) New York: Crown.

Ram, G. (1987). *Rama and Sita* (Folk Tales of the World series). New York: Bedrick/Blackie.

Reid, B. (1988). *Playing with Plasticine*. New York: Morrow. (Originally published in Toronto, Ont., by Kids Can Press, 1988.)

Scott, S. (Reteller & Illustrator). (1985). *The magic horse* (originally "The Ebony Horse" from the "Arabian Nights," trans. by R.F. Burton). New York: Greenwillow.

Simmonds, P. (1988). *Lulu and the flying babies*. New York: Knopf.

Stolz, M. (1988). *Pangur Ban*. New York: HarperCollins.

Sullivan, S.A. (1990). *Bats, butterflies, and bugs: A book of action toys*. Boston, MA: Little, Brown.

Sutcliff, R. (1990). *The shining company*. New York: Farrar, Straus & Giroux.

Van Allsburg, C. (1988). *Two bad ants*. Boston, MA: Houghton Mifflin.

Van Kampen, V., & Eugen, I.C. (1989). *Orchestranimals*. New York: Scholastic.

Ventura, P. (1989). *Great composers*. (Trans. by M. Casey.) New York: Putnam. (Originally published in Milan by Arnoldo Mondadori, 1988.)

Ventura, P. (1989). *Michelangelo's world*. New York: Putnam. (Originally published in Milan by Arnoldo Mondadori, 1988.)

Walter, M.P. (1988). *Mariah loves rock*. New York: Bradbury.

Weil, L. (1989). *The magic of music*. New York: Holiday House.

Weil, L. (1991). *Wolferl: The first six years in the life of Wolfgang Amadeus Mozart*. New York: Holiday House.

Weiss, H. (1990). *Cartoons and cartooning*. Boston, MA: Houghton Mifflin.

West, R. (1987). *Far out: How to create your own star world*. (Photos by B. Wolfe & D. Wolfe; drawings by R. Kiedrowski.) Minneapolis, MN: Carolrhoda.

Willard, N. (1989). *East of the sun and west of the moon: A play*. (Ill. by B. Moser.) San Diego, CA: Harcourt Brace Jovanovich.

Wolff, V.E. (1991). *The Mozart season*. New York: Henry Holt.

Woolf, F. (1990). *Picture this: A first introduction to paintings*. New York: Doubleday. (Originally published in London by Hodder & Stoughton, 1989.)

Yenawine, P. (1991). *Colors*. New York: Museum of Modern Art/Delacorte.

Yenawine, P. (1991). *Stories*. New York: Museum of Modern Art/Delacorte.

CHAPTER 6

An Author Study: Tomie dePaola

Joanne Lionetti

What began in my whole language classroom as a typical author study grew into a project of such magnitude that it lasted a whole year. I had no way of knowing in September when I first shared Tomie dePaola's *The Art Lesson* with my third grade class that his work would be invaluable in helping to change a "low-ability" (according to their scores on standardized tests), easily frustrated group of children into a highly motivated community of readers. One student wrote in his response log: "Befor I started reading Tomie's books, I hated to read but Tomie turned my life arownd now I *LOVE* to read." This is the chronicle of his and the other children's transformation.

The Beginning

The Art Lesson was so popular with my students that I decided to build an author study unit around Tomie dePaola. In order to familiarize the children with dePaola's style, I first needed to acquire many of his books. Our school librarian gladly sent all her copies down to my room and set about ordering more. She also provided some background information about the author. Our reading specialist and I searched our local libraries and some book club catalogs. With the 16 books I gathered, the encouragement of my principal, and my own enthusiasm, I launched the author study. I didn't know where our study would take us, but I was anxious to find out.

Each day I shared a new book with the children in our readers/writers workshop. We read the dedications, studied the illustrations, and discussed the story. We always read the information about the author and noted the book's copyright date. The book would then quickly become an old favorite as the children shared it in school and at home. I created "task cards" which the children worked on in small groups: They selected books, counted

Tommy hides a box of 64 crayons under his sweater in this illustration from *The Art Lesson.*

Figure 1
Examples of Task Cards

♥ ♥ Counting Hearts ♥ ♥

Tomie dePaola likes to draw ♥s

1. Choose 2 of Tomie's books.

2. Write the names of the books in your response log.

3. Count the number of hearts in each book.

4. Record the number in your response logs.

5. Fill in the graph (Make a graph)

6. Glue the graph into your response log.

♥ ♥ ♥ ♥ ♥ ♥ ♥

Wondering About Words

1. Read your favorite book.

2. When you are finished, find a word you are wondering about.

3. Write the word in your response log.

4. Write what you think it means (use the pictures and other words to help you).

Take the challenge of champions Look up the word and write its meaning.

Comparing Characters

Sometimes different characters in different books share the same experiences.

1. Read Nana Upstairs and Nana Downstairs and Now One Foot, Now the Other

2. In your response log answer these questions

1. How are Bobby and Tommy alike?
2. How are they different?
3. How are Nana Upstairs and Bob the same?
4. How are they different?

How About That

Tomie has some very good ideas. He had a super idea for the last page of The Art Lesson.

1. Look at the last page
2. The pictures in front of Tomie are from other books.
3. Make a list in your response log of which books the pictures are from.

the number of hearts drawn (Tomie's trademark!), and made graphs of their findings; they arranged book titles in order of their copyright dates; through modeling, they learned to do character analyses and comparisons; they distinguished reality from fantasy, and related stories to events in their own lives. (A few examples of these task cards appear in Figure 1.) The children wrote about the books in response logs and then shared the logs with one another. Through these activities the children became increasingly familiar with dePaola's style and learned more about the author himself since many of his books are autobiographical.

Enthusiasm Rises

Our stockpile of books started to grow as the children became more engaged. They began going to their own community libraries and bringing in "Tomie books" to share. Books were renewed time and time again; I don't doubt that for quite a few months all the Tomie dePaola books in the Nassau County library system could be found in Room 27! The children were hooked, and before long they were bringing in their own copies, purchased for them by their parents. I knew then that the enthusiasm was spilling out of the classroom and into the children's homes. Our community of readers was broadening as parents and siblings willingly became involved. We began to keep a running list of books as we read them, and the children delighted in watching the list grow.

While the children became immersed in the study, I had many opportunities to observe them and assess their growth. Working in pairs as "book buddies," they read books aloud into a tape recorder; the tapes were then used by younger children in the school. I used the tapes as a means of evaluating my students' oral reading. I also spent time each day sharing books with individual children and recording pertinent information. The children's response logs reflected their writing skills, and our book talks enabled me to see how well they understood various literary concepts. As they worked in groups or alone, moving from one activity to another, they became more eager to take risks and less frustrated in their reading. One of their favorite activities was to sit in the "author chair" and read their favorite Tomie book to the class. The other children gathered around the reader and listened intently, accepting all approximations of difficult words in the text and applauding at the story's end.

The task cards gave children the opportunity to work at their own pace, but I felt it was important to work together as a whole community as well. After our shared reading we began using Tomie's books for group activities. We honed our baking skills by making bread dolls after we read *Watch Out for the Chicken Feet in Your Soup*; we made popcorn and grew plants from unpopped kernels when we read *The Popcorn Book*; we located new places on the map after reading various folktales and enjoyed some special Italian bread that was sent in by a parent after one child shared *Tony's Bread* at home. We had great fun making our own quicksand based on *The Quicksand Book* and learned to identify the clouds outside the classroom windows after reading *The Cloud Book*. I used Tomie's books to teach quotations, title selection, sequencing, notetaking, and matching text to illustration. Our work became integrated across disciplines. The children were clearly learning to see the value of books as they read for a variety of purposes.

A blizzard of popcorn in
The Popcorn Book.

An Author Biography

After a while the children had gleaned so much information about the author that I thought it would be appropriate for them to learn about biographies. They regarded themselves as authors; they loved to write their own books and stories and were quite proud that they knew so much about Tomie. The conditions seemed right, so I suggested we try

to write a biography of him. My suggestion met with great enthusiasm.

By the time we were ready to begin the biography, three months had gone by and the children had read 26 of his books. Our first task was to work together to list all the facts we'd learned. The children had retained a great deal of information from their reading. They knew about Tomie's family background, his likes and dislikes as a child, where he grew up, his schooling, and a few details of his present life. They were able to give a physical description: "He has curly gray hair. He wears glasses. He has a nice smile and a wrinkly face and a fat chin."

After we compiled our list, I played an interview Tomie had taped for a book club. The children asked to hear the tape again and again. "He sure has a great laugh," one child exclaimed; the others agreed. Hearing the author's voice brought to life an image they held lovingly in their minds. We used the tape to add information to our list. Then we were ready to begin the rough draft of our biography.

I divided the author's life into three parts: Little Tomie, Medium Tomie, and Big Tomie. I cut the points from our list into individual strips and the children placed the facts under the correct category in this "biography map" (Figure 2). Using that information, the children worked in groups to compose pieces about each part of Tomie's life. Decisions had to be made all along the way about what information to use, where to put it, and what each member of the group should do. The children took charge of each task—it was cooperative learning all the way.

Every day we met and discussed progress and set a goal for the day. Then the children

Figure 2
A Biography Map

Little Tomie
- liked his grandma's chicken soup
- had an Italian and Irish grandma
- liked to make up and listen to stories

Medium Tomie
- drew on every thing
- was a good tap dancer
- grew up in Connecticut

Big Tomie
- lives in a barn
- was a teacher
- puts himself in his books
- finished art school in 1956

went to their groups and set about writing, revising, and discussing their work. After about 40 minutes, we met again to share our progress and problems. The children read and reread, wrote and rewrote, deleted and added until the story met everyone's approval. They learned new skills as they needed them. They were determined to share their knowledge about the author by writing a book that did justice to the man they had grown to love. When the text was done, decisions had to be made about the illustrations. The children worked diligently, matching their illustrations with the text. They even adopted Tomie's style by making borders and using many hearts.

After the biography was written and illustrated, we agreed on a title (*The Art of the Heart Man*), and a dedication ("To Tomie dePaola—a wonderful author and illustrator who has a great laugh"). Then we composed our "About the Authors" page:

> The authors go to Marion Street School. They read *26* Tomie dePaola books. They fell in love with Tomie's illustrations and stories. They wrote this book to share what they know about the wonderful Heart Man.

The finished product was truly a labor of love, and the process did much to add to the children's growth. The book was then published—multiple copies were made, bound, and laminated—and the proud authors each took a book home to share. The reviews were all so positive that when one of the children suggested sending a copy to Tomie, we decided to do so. We wrote letters to him and passed them and a copy of the book to the school's reading specialist, who had worked with me on the project. She sent our book to Tomie's publishing company in New York, where it began quite a journey.

An editor at the publisher's office sent *The Art of the Heart Man* to Tomie, who read it and sent it along to Bernice Cullinan, who saw the beauty of the book and understood the work behind it. After a few weeks we received letters from the editor, Tomie, his assistant, and Bee, all full of praise for the book. The day the mail came the children swelled with pride and celebrated the fact that they had been invited into the community of published authors. I could see the children's confidence growing, and knew I was a witness to all that Frank Smith (1988), who introduced me to the concept of membership in communities, describes in *Insult to Intelligence*.

Our study did not end with the biography, but rather continued to grow as a result of it. Through Tomie's assistant and with the continued support of my principal, we were able to arrange a telephone conversation with the author. We used the days before the conference to prepare a list of questions to ask Tomie: How do you choose which books to illustrate? How long does it usually take to write a book? Did you ever get a book rejected? Why do you put hearts in your books? We practiced on the speaker phone and prepared our comments.

Finally the big day arrived. The air was filled with excitement and anticipation as the children gathered around the speaker phone and watched me dial. When Tomie came to the phone, the children were beside themselves with delight. One girl was so filled with emotion that when she stepped up to the phone she gave a big sigh and said, "Tomie dePaola, your books are great!" Tomie answered all our questions and the children hung on his every word. His enthusiasm for and appreciation of their work did much to encourage them to do more reading and more writing.

During the telephone conference Tomie told about going off to kindergarten with dreams of learning to read. The children loved to listen to this story on the tape we made of the conference. It became apparent to me that we had the elements at hand to write another book, so we began to explore the genre of realistic fiction. Using the taped story, we worked together on weaving fiction with fact to develop a story line. The children proved adept at this task, and it was clear that they based their work on the many books they had read. One has only to read their second published book, *When Do I Learn to Read? A Retold Story*, to see the influence of their favorite author. The illustrations could be called "primitive dePaolas"; they indicate the children's awareness of the importance of pictures in telling a story. The book is well sequenced, is laced with quotations, and uses a rich vocabulary.

The Joy of Reading

By the time this book was finished, the school year was drawing to a close. The list of books we'd read went from ceiling to floor; the final count of Tomie books in the class library was 88. We had come a long way since September and our meager inventory of 16 books.

It was quite apparent to me that the experience the children had that year changed them as readers and writers. They had grown to view reading as something enjoyable, something they could do with success. What happened in this class is testimony to the fact that children learn to become good readers by reading a lot and that a talented author can lead children to discover the joy of reading. In doing so, that author gives a gift that will last forever.

My third grade students said it best in their "About the Authors" section of their final book: "When the authors get old, they will still remember Tomie because he helped them LOVE reading."

Reference

Smith, F. (1988). *Insult to intelligence: The bureaucratic invasion of our classrooms* (rev. ed.). Portsmouth, NH: Heinemann.

Children's Books

dePaola, T. (1973). *Nana upstairs and Nana downstairs*. New York: Putnam.

dePaola, T. (1974). *Watch out for the chicken feet in your soup*. Englewood Cliffs, NJ: Prentice Hall.

dePaola, T. (1975). *The cloud book*. New York: Holiday House.

dePaola, T. (1977). *The quicksand book*. New York: Holiday House.

dePaola, T. (1978). *The popcorn book*. New York: Holiday House.

dePaola, T. (1981). *Now one foot, now the other*. New York: Putnam.

dePaola, T. (1989). *The art lesson*. New York: Putnam.

dePaola, T. (1989). *Tony's bread*. New York: Putnam.

CHAPTER 7

Chicka Chicka Boom Boom Zooms with Pre-K Kids
Chicka Chicka Boom Boom Clicks with Fourth Graders
A Class Vote
Making Connections

The Magic of Martin

Deborah A. Wooten

As a staff developer, teacher, and mother, I have shared Bill Martin Jr's books for years with audiences of many ages and backgrounds. His books are imaginatively crafted with rhythm, rhyme, and a host of other literary elements that give them extremely wide appeal. They also have the ability to touch each reader in a special way. Some of his books, such as the perennial favorite *Brown Bear, Brown Bear, What Do You See?*, make brilliant use of the repetition that so engages prereaders. Others, such as *Knots on a Counting Rope* (written with frequent collaborator John Archambault), are geared for an older audience—although I have read *Knots* to kindergartners with great success. Because Martin is such a prolific writer, he is an excellent choice for a class author study, and no matter what subject I find myself teaching, I can always find a Bill Martin Jr book to complement the thematic or interdisciplinary unit.

I do not know Bill Martin Jr personally, but his name pops up frequently in my conversation and my teaching. I have savored and shared his books for years. I could relate countless experiences concerning the special touch of Bill Martin Jr's books; the following vignettes are only a few that illustrate the magic of Martin.

Chicka Chicka Boom Boom Zooms with Pre-K Kids

Not long ago I gave a copy of Martin and Archambault's colorfully illustrated alphabet book *Chicka Chicka Boom Boom* to a prekindergarten teacher I know. The book became the nucleus of a huge project when she noticed that her students repeatedly asked her to read it aloud, listen to them read it, or listen while they told their own version. Her students responded enthusiastically to other books, too, but in a classroom vote, *Chicka Chicka Boom Boom* was chosen as the absolute favorite.

Because this book was so popular, the teacher and one of her colleagues decided to structure a unit around it. They opted to let the children themselves decide what kind of project they would like to do; the teachers would be available to help the children develop and implement their ideas. A noisy discussion ensued with the children suggesting a variety of activities, but a consensus was reached when one loud voice said, ''Let's make a coconut tree!''

''Okay. What do you want it to look like?'' the teachers prompted.

The children chimed in with suggestions: ''Bending....'' ''With fat letters....'' ''With real coconuts!'' ''Let's paint it!'' That last idea was met with unanimous approval. Before long, after much painting, cutting, measuring, discussion, laughter, and anticipation, a six-foot coconut tree was created.

Some of the children's comments and responses to teachers' questions posed during the creation process were written down on charts that were later hung in various places for the children to refer to. The tree itself was hung in the hallway for the whole school to enjoy. Coconuts were brought in, and the children predicted what was inside. The class shook them, felt them, and weighed them, and talked about their findings. Again, the responses were recorded on a chart. One girl commented that it sounded like the ocean inside the coconut. Later they drank the coconut milk and ate its meat. They shredded coconut to make macaroons one week and co-

The cover of *Chicka Chicka Boom Boom,* a book that proved popular with a wide variety of readers.

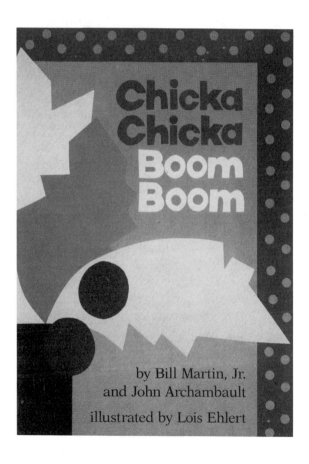

Chicka Chicka Boom Boom

by Bill Martin, Jr. and John Archambault

illustrated by Lois Ehlert

conut cupcakes the next. Then they crushed the coconut hulls and attached them to their tree to add a touch of realism.

A week later, some of the students wanted to write about what could happen to the letters in the alphabet. They questioned why Martin and Archambault had made some of the letters have accidents, and this led to a discussion about real accidents. Then they wanted to know if they could use their imaginations to come up with other kinds of accidents for the letters. One of the students invented an accident for J: "J fell in a raisin, because it's fun!" The children's ideas were written down and hung all around the classroom.

Imagination plays a role in helping children remember a story. *Chicka Chicka Boom Boom* served as a learning "treasure map," helping the children explore by taking risks in their thinking and using language as a tool to discover new knowledge. By hearing stories read aloud, children learn the rules of narrative patterns before they learn to read or write themselves, and this knowledge in turn improves verbal communication skills (Fox, 1985; Meyer & Rice, 1984; Weaver, 1988). Steffensen, Joag-Dev, & Anderson (1979) report that reading (and, by extension, being read to) is also a major source of vocabulary growth. Children have a natural propensity to manufacture language (Thomas, 1990). The interesting language opportunities sparked by a Bill Martin Jr book nurture this developmental process.

I was amazed at all the activities and ideas that were inspired by just this one book. The children were actively involved and invested much attention and effort in this unit of study. They were clearly interested in *Chicka Chicka Boom Boom,* and we know that interest is crucial in developing a positive attitude in reading and learning (Asher, 1979). This is one reason why *Chicka Chicka Boom Boom* successfully added to the children's linguistic data pool and preexisting schema (Harste, Woodward, & Burke, 1984), and that, in turn, stimulated them to make sense of and use language that was new to them.

Chicka Chicka Boom Boom Clicks with Fourth Graders

Wondering if it would appeal to older children, I read *Chicka Chicka Boom Boom* with a class of fourth grade students. The teacher and I were anxious to share the book with these children because we enjoyed it so much ourselves. One morning, we settled all the kids around us and I began to read the rhythmical text. Something magical happened. The students started snapping their fingers and clapping their hands to the rhythm of the book. I glanced up from my reading to see them moving from side to side in unison. When I finished, they begged me to read the book again and again. Each time I read, more kids chimed in until all 29 voices were chanting at once. I left knowing that we had all gained enormous pleasure from sharing *Chicka Chicka Boom Boom*.

At lunch that day I was in the schoolyard and a small group of girls jumping rope caught my eye. As I moved toward them, I realized that they were using the language of *Chicka Chicka Boom Boom* for their jump-rope chant. A group of first graders joined in; they had heard *Chicka Chicka Boom Boom* read aloud in their classroom earlier in the week.

It seems that the appeal of this book knows no bounds. In spite of differences in these children's ages and backgrounds, they were unanimous in their enthusiasm for the book—and their teachers shared their feelings. The students were experiencing the positive impact of literature on language development. The fact that these children used language from a book even while at play shows that *Chicka Chicka Boom Boom* had become important to them outside the walls of the school.

Each time I share *Chicka Chicka Boom Boom* with children, we all learn something new. Even my own three-year-old daughter taught me something one day when I was looking for the book's dust jacket, which she had removed. I said, "Katie, you have to keep the jacket on the book to protect it." Her reply was, "It doesn't work, Mommy, because of the ABCs." What she meant was that because the endpapers have the alphabet written on them, the jacket's flaps cover a portion of the letters that she now holds very dear.

A Class Vote

A kindergarten teacher and I decided to work together to launch a Bill Martin Jr author study in her classroom. Because classroom experience and research indicate that students learn more when they are involved in the learning process as much as possible, we decided to consult with the children from the outset. We gathered the 18 kindergartners around us, and I explained that they were going to select the order in which we would all read the books. I would introduce each of the eight books, and then every student would vote for the book he or she wanted read first.

I could feel the children's anticipation growing as I described each book. Then we voted. The teacher prepared to write the titles

Teaching Idea

Layers of Learning

Chicka Chicka Boom Boom provides many opportunities to learn about books and stories as well as about subjects in other content areas. The deeper the teacher and students probe into the book, the more layers of learning they can uncover. Below are a few potential subjects for study.

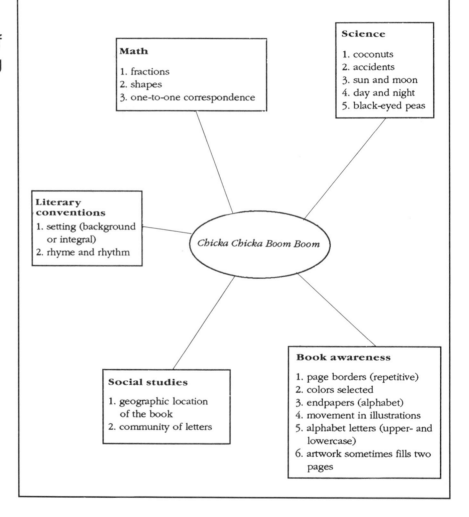

Math

1. fractions
2. shapes
3. one-to-one correspondence

Science

1. coconuts
2. accidents
3. sun and moon
4. day and night
5. black-eyed peas

Literary conventions

1. setting (background or integral)
2. rhyme and rhythm

Chicka Chicka Boom Boom

Social studies

1. geographic location of the book
2. community of letters

Book awareness

1. page borders (repetitive)
2. colors selected
3. endpapers (alphabet)
4. movement in illustrations
5. alphabet letters (upper- and lowercase)
6. artwork sometimes fills two pages

in the order we would read them on a chart to be displayed in the Bill Martin Jr corner. We winked at each other when we realized that this would be a math lesson as well as a reading lesson.

The vote resulted in a tie between *The Ghost-Eye Tree* and *Brown Bear, Brown Bear, What Do You See?* for the first read-aloud choice. The kindergartners knew without discussion what this meant: negotiations began immediately as each one went to bat for his or her choice. After some of the students successfully marketed their choice to their peers, *The Ghost-Eye Tree* was overwhelmingly picked as the first choice. The teacher announced that *Brown Bear, Brown Bear* would be read second.

Then, without any instruction, all 18 kindergartners raced to the read-aloud section of the room. They all said the book's title with me as if they were upper graders. They listened quietly to the story until I elicited their verbal participation. As I read, I looked to the students to complete certain predictable words and passages. The rhythm and rhyme in *The Ghost-Eye Tree* made it easy for the students to be a part of this story. Listening to this book also acquainted the children with the special uses of language in storybooks: this isn't language to get something done, but language to represent experience and to encourage the contemplation and evaluation of that experience (Britton, 1970). Even though we each had our private response to the experience of hearing the story, however, we were united in our enjoyment of it.

When I had finished reading, the teacher wrote down the students' responses to the story on sentence strips to be added to a chart in the Bill Martin Jr corner. One of the kindergartners said, "I like the imagination and when the tree said eeeeoooowowowowowowoooowowowo, you know, on that page." And flipping through the book, she was able to find the pages where the tree is shown making this eerie sound. Many of the students said they liked the scary parts best of all. Another student said, "I like when he pulled down his hat.... That boy's the toughest."

The most lively discussion was centered around one of the illustrations of the tree. Some students thought that bats were flying around it; a couple of others argued that because the story was set in autumn, they must be leaves. These students managed to win the others over to their point of view. Not only had they comprehended the story, but they were drawing conclusions that reached beyond the literal meaning of the book.

Making Connections

The most special moments for me in teaching are when the right book connects with a student to meet a specific need. For example, one day I had a conference with a sixth grader. A colleague sat in on the conference, as did the girl's teacher. I was visiting this classroom for the first time and had not met this student prior to the conference. The interview centered around her composition notebook. As I read it, I was struck by the imagery in her writing. I commented on this quality only to discover that the student's father was blind and that she spent a great deal of time describing things to him. I immediately asked the teacher to lend me her copy of *Knots on a Counting Rope*. I explained to the student that this book is written in two voices and asked her to help me read: she read the part of the blind grandson and I took the part of the grandfather. Even though we only had time to

Teaching Idea

Springboards for Discussion

Bill Martin Jr's books embrace a number of themes that can be used as springboards for discussion with children. Teachers can guide these discussions to help children connect the events and ideas in the stories with their own lives. Here are some suggestions to use with two of Bill Martin Jr's books, both of which were written with John Archambault.

Knots on a Counting Rope

1. Blindness and other disabilities
2. Multicultural interaction
3. Grandparent/ grandchild relationships
4. Dialogue
5. Folklore
6. Descriptive imagery
7. Value of and love for story

The Ghost-Eye Tree

1. Sibling interaction
2. Fear
3. Country life
4. Imagination
5. Seasons (autumn)
6. Patterns, recurring lines in the story

read a few pages, the child asked to continue on her own. The memory of this connection between student and story is something I will always cherish.

Part of the magic of Bill Martin Jr is that the simplicity of his themes provides a framework that readers of all ages and developmental levels can latch onto. When these simple tales and charming characters are revealed in the author's rhyming, rhythmic language, they are nearly impossible to resist. With books such as these, children are given the resources for building a lifelong love of reading and a solid foundation for the learning that will enhance and enrich their lives.

References

Asher, S.R. (1979). Referential communication. In G. Whitehurst & B.J. Zimmerman (Eds.), *Function of language cognition*. San Diego, CA: Academic.

Britton, J. (1970). *Language and learning*. London: Penguin.

Fox, C. (1985). Opening moves. In M. Meek (Ed.), *Bedford Way paper* (#17). London: Institute of Education, University of London.

Harste, J.C., Woodward, J., & Burke, C. (1984). *Language stories and literacy lessons*. Portsmouth, NH: Heinemann.

Meyer, B.J., & Rice, G.E. (1984). The structure of text. In P.D. Pearson (Ed.), *Handbook of reading research* (pp. 319-351). White Plains, NY: Longman.

Steffensen, M.S., Joag-Dev, C., & Anderson, R.C. (1979). A cross-cultural perspective on reading comprehension. *Reading Research Quarterly, 15*(1), 10-29.

Thomas, L. (1990). *Et cetera, et cetera: Notes of a word-watcher*. Boston, MA: Little, Brown.

Weaver, C. (1988). *Reading process and practice from socio-psycholinguistics to whole language*. Portsmouth, NH: Heinemann.

Children's Books

Martin, B., Jr. (1967/1983). *Brown bear, brown bear, what do you see?* (Ill. by E. Carle.) New York: Henry Holt.

Martin, B., Jr, & Archambault, J. (1985). *The ghost-eye tree*. (Ill. by T. Rand.) New York: Henry Holt.

Martin, B., Jr, & Archambault, J. (1987). *Knots on a counting rope*. (Ill. by T. Rand.) New York: Henry Holt.

Martin, B., Jr, & Archambault, J. (1989). *Chicka chicka boom boom*. (Ill. by L. Ehlert.) New York: Simon & Schuster.

Note: The author would like to thank Annie Molinari, Tara Ellington, Marilyn Copeland, and Judy Davis, teachers in the New York City Public School system, for their contributions to this chapter.

CHAPTER 8

Extending Multicultural Understanding

Rudine Sims Bishop

"E pluribus unum"—from many, one. It is the motto on the Great Seal of the United States, and until 1956 it was the official motto of the nation. For many years, it was the fashion to emphasize the last word of this motto—to stress the homogeneity of the American people, the metaphor of the melting pot. In this last decade of the 20th century, however, it is important to recognize and come to grips with the pluralistic nature of the society in which we all live.

In the age of shifting populations, increased immigration and emigration, and the "global village," societies everywhere are changing. In the United States, demographic data indicate that the fastest-growing segments of the population are those groups that have been known traditionally as minorities. In California, no one sociocultural group constitutes a majority. The East Coast is experiencing a similar phenomenon: by the end of the decade, one in three residents of New York City will be a member of a "minority" group. Projections are that by the middle of the next century the "minorities" taken together will constitute the majority of the country's population. The United States has become a multicultural society.

Given that the so-called minorities are becoming the new majority, it would be useful to seek a new term, one that does not carry the connotation of "less important" that has come to be associated with *minority*. Virginia Hamilton (1989), in her acceptance speech for the 1988 Boston Globe-Horn Book Award for *Anthony Burns: The Defeat and Triumph of a Fugitive Slave*, used the term *parallel culture*: "If this were the life of any ordinary individual not of a parallel culture who became enormously famous..." (p. 83). Because of its connotation of similarity and equality, I think "parallel culture" is an acceptable alternative

to "minority" and so will borrow Hamilton's term for this chapter.

World events demonstrate that maintaining a harmonious multicultural society is not always easy. Solutions to complex and stubborn social and economic problems are often not readily apparent. If people are to solve these social problems, it will be necessary to develop greater empathy and understanding for each other. One possible place to begin is by sharing with children and young adults good literature that illuminates the human experience in all its diversity.

This chapter offers a rationale for including such literature in the curriculum and recommends some specific books that might serve as exemplars. The chapter concludes with an appendix of additional titles that could enrich a classroom.

Good literature can develop and extend understandings and attitudes important to living in our multicultural society. Through reading, young people can begin to understand the effects of social and economic problems on the lives of ordinary individuals. In the United States, for instance, racism and poverty are two of the worst problems, and they disproportionately victimize people who are members of parallel cultures. Inevitably, some of the books that center on characters from those groups and their experiences address such social issues. For example, Mildred Taylor's saga of the Logan family, including *Roll of Thunder, Hear My Cry*, *Let the Circle Be Unbroken*, and *The Road to Memphis*, vividly evokes the spirit of an African-American family that refuses to be defeated by racism, greed, and oppression. By sharing, however briefly, the lives of that family, young people can come to understand the potentially devastating effects of such negative forces on the everyday lives of real people.

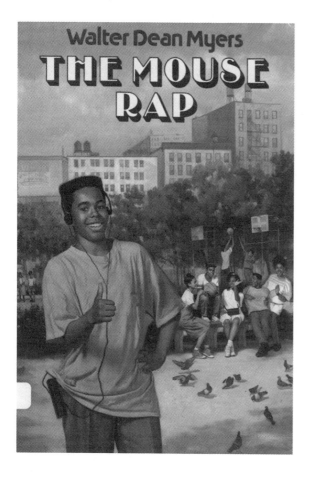

The Mouse Rap tells the story of Mouse and his friends' adventures in Harlem during one summer vacation.

Literature can also show how we are connected to one another through emotions, needs, and desires—experiences that are common to all. One of the reasons Katherine Paterson's *Bridge to Terabithia* has such wide appeal is that it speaks to just those kinds of experiences—the importance of friendship, the need to belong, the inevitability of death. Understanding our common humanity is a powerful weapon against forces that would divide and alienate us from one another.

At the same time, books can help us understand, appreciate, and celebrate the differences among us—those things that make each cultural group unique. Walter Dean Myers's urban novels, such as *The Mouse Rap*, for instance, reflect very clearly the linguistic and cultural traditions that are an important part of growing up in many African-American communities. Such books help young people understand how each group enriches the society as a whole.

Children's literature is also one of the ways we transmit values to our young people. It lets them know what adults in their society consider appropriate ways of behaving, believing, and assessing who and what are important. Children who find their own experiences mirrored in books receive a kind of affirmation of themselves and their culture. Children who find that people like themselves and experiences similar to their own are excluded, misrepresented, or belittled receive another message altogether. They learn that they are not valued members of their society, and that reading can be a negative or hurtful experience.

As recently as 25 years ago, the world of children's literature, with a few exceptions, treated parallel cultures in the United States in one of two ways: they were either ignored or stereotyped and cast in the role of comic re-

Bishop

lief. As a result of the Civil Rights movement, and partly because of the Elementary and Secondary Education Act, that situation changed during the middle and late 1970s. Greater numbers of books about African Americans appeared, and many more positive and authentic images were presented. Although books about African Americans represented the largest number, books about other groups, such as Hispanics, Native Americans, and Asian Americans, also became somewhat more plentiful during that time, as did books set in other countries.

The first half of the 1980s saw a diminishing of the number of books about people of color published in the United States. At mid-decade, only about 1 percent of children's books published each year were about African Americans, and the picture was even more dismal for other groups. For example, between 1972 and 1982 only 56 children's books about Puerto Ricans were published; in 1980 not one such book appeared (Nieto, 1983). At the moment, "multiculturalism" is a buzzword in educational circles, and publishers seem eager to offer books that fit under the rubric "multicultural literature." This promising trend has resulted in an increase in the number of books featuring people from parallel cultures. However, because more children's books are being published annually, the percentage of children's books focusing on people of color is still much smaller than the percentage of such people in the population.

In any case, a number of high-quality children's books about people from parallel cultures within the United States, as well as from other countries, are available. The remainder of this chapter will discuss some of the ways such books can be used in classrooms, particularly in the intermediate and upper-elementary grades.

Start with Information

Understanding requires knowledge, and it would be logical to begin developing multicultural understanding through knowledge gained by reading nonfiction. Most nonfiction for young readers that focuses on parallel cultures is either biography or history. A few books—typically photo essays or photo documentaries—examine the lives of individuals or groups; others examine special topics, such as the music, dance, or art of a particular group.

Some of the most highly regarded books about parallel cultures in the United States come from the pen of Milton Meltzer, the historian and biographer. Meltzer has written about several groups, including Hispanic Americans, Chinese Americans, and Jewish Americans. The first of his History in Their Own Words series, *The Black Americans*, is a compilation of primary-source materials—diaries, journals, speeches, newspaper accounts, letters—that tell the history of black Americans from 1619 to 1983. Another book that presents African-American history through primary-source materials is Julius Lester's Newbery honor book *To Be a Slave*, which gives excerpts from the narratives of former slaves. It covers the period from 1619 through the Reconstruction.

Brent Ashabranner and Russell Freedman have contributed books that provide information about and foster understanding of both historical and contemporary experiences of North America's indigenous peoples—the Native Americans—and immigrants of today and yesterday. Books like Ashabranner's *Into a Strange Land*, *To Live in Two Worlds*, and *The New Americans* and Freedman's *Immigrant Kids* and *Indian Chiefs* can provide much-needed factual accounts for pupils studying American life and history. Together with his-

Teaching Idea

Using Nonfiction

Nonfiction should be both informative and artistic. Good nonfiction lends itself to being read aloud.

Biographies often read like novels and are a good first step into nonfiction. Several biographies are available in picture book format and are particularly suitable for reading aloud. Two examples are Allen Say's *El Chino*, the story of a Chinese American who became a matador, and *The Last Princess*, Fay Stanley's longer story of Princess Ka'iulani of Hawaii.

History need not be dull. Try reading aloud Walter Dean Myers's dramatic historical account *Now Is Your Time: The African American Struggle for Freedom*. Myers weaves into this chronicle the history of individuals and families, including his own family and the Dandridge family, of which Martha Washington was a member.

Pueblo Storyteller by Diane Hoyt-Goldsmith and *Family Pictures/Cuadros de Familia* by Carmen Lomas Garza offer glimpses into the lives of families from parallel cultures. *Pueblo Storyteller*, a photo essay, describes the customs and traditions of the Cochiti people. *Family Pictures*, a bilingual (Spanish/English) book illustrated with paintings, has a more personal focus. Both first-person accounts, however, offer models for classroom writing and reporting, perhaps on the families and communities of the students. Students can be encouraged to create their own pictures or, when appropriate, take photographs to illustrate their own documentaries or essays.

Sheila Hamanaka's *The Journey: Japanese Americans, Racism and Renewal* makes a useful companion piece to Yoshiko Uchida's *Journey to Topaz*. *The Journey*, based on Hamanaka's dramatic five-panel mural, provides a context into which readers can place Uchida's fictional account. *The Journey* might also inspire students to create their own murals to synthesize and display their understandings of the topic.

torical fiction, they can provide richer, more detailed information about some of the groups that make up the United States.

Well-written biographies can also help students understand the lives of individual members of different cultural groups and their contributions to society. The subjects of biographies have expanded in recent years beyond athletes, entertainers, and other traditional choices and now include writers, artists, civil and human rights activists, and others who are heroes to their own people. *Portraits: Biography and Autobiography in the Secondary School* (Fleming & McGinnis, 1985) presents several different ways of approaching biography in the classroom. It offers both discussion questions and classroom activities.

As is true of all literature from and about parallel cultures, nonfiction works are best read and discussed as part of a broader study of history and peoples, rather than being confined to certain holidays or commemorations. Of course, such literature should never be restricted to classrooms in which the groups being studied are represented in the student body. Nonfiction about parallel cultures can serve the same classroom purposes as other nonfiction: it provides informational content for curricular studies, models of ways students can demonstrate their own knowledge about a topic, and extensions of or companion pieces for fiction.

Folklore

Every culture has developed a folklore. The folktales of any group can give insight into its traditional dreams, wishes, values, humor, and other characteristics. Folktales of the "root cultures" from which modern Americans are descended can help students feel con-

nected to their history and ancestry. For example, in *The Rainbow People*, Laurence Yep retells some of the stories collected in Oakland, California's Chinatown during the 1930s. The stories are set in China, but they were told in the Californian immigrant community and brought comfort and hope to the Chinese men who had come to work in America but had been unable to bring their families. In his introduction, Yep states that "the stories also expressed the loneliness, anger, fear, and love that were part of the Chinese-American experience" (p. x).

Folktales survive because they are usually good stories, suitable for all ages. Any teacher who is concerned about multicultural understanding should have an abundance of folktales in the classroom. Many collections are available in the folklore sections of libraries. In addition, single tales in picture book format abound. These tales can often be used with older students as well as younger ones, particularly when the tale is unfamiliar.

Because folktales come from an oral tradition, they lend themselves to being read aloud. Sometimes, in an attempt to retain the flavor of the language of the original storytellers, the compiler of a collection uses nonstandard language to tell the stories or parts of them. For example, Virginia Hamilton, in the introduction to her collection of black folktales, *The People Could Fly: American Black Folktales*, states: "I use a reasonably colloquial language or dialect, depending on the folktale. Moderate colloquialisms are understandable and readable. They reflect the expressiveness of the original slave teller, and later the free black storyteller" (p. xii). Sometimes teachers have been concerned that they cannot adequately reproduce the dialect as written or that their attempts to read a story in dialect will be seen as insulting or even racist. In the case of *The People Could Fly*, a bit of practice with a tape recorder and a conscious effort not to compound the colloquialisms presented in the stories with an affected southern accent might demonstrate that the stories are indeed readable as written. It is also useful to remember that the tales come from an oral tradition in which each teller adds his or her own touch to the stories. They can be changed in the telling or in the reading.

Whether simply enjoying the folktales or searching out the similarities and differences in stories from different cultures, students who become acquainted with a variety of folk stories are well on their way to understanding what it means to live in a multicultural world. Comparing and contrasting stories has the added benefit of fostering critical thinking and discussion among students.

Realistic Fiction

Realistic fiction describes life as it is today (or, in the case of historical fiction, as it was yesterday), and provides readers with insights

Teaching Idea

Comparing Folktales

Older children can study and contrast folktales from a number of cultures to note the ways in which different cultures treat the same story elements.

Since various motifs appear in tales from many cultures, students can examine folktales to discern similarities and differences in the ways those motifs are used. For example, tricksters appear in the stories of many groups. The Bruh Rabbit character in African-American folklore, brought from Africa and later replaced by the slave character John, is a trickster (see "He Lion, Bruh Bear and Bruh Rabbit" from *The People Could Fly*). Students can look for tricksters in stories from other cultures (e.g., the African Anansi the Spider, the Native American Coyote) and compare their exploits.

Students can also compare variants of the same story. *The Seven Chinese Brothers* as retold by Margaret Mahy, for example, is a recently published version of the familiar *The Five Chinese Brothers* (told in a 1938 version by Claire Hutchet Bishop). In addition to charting and discussing the differences in the illustrations and story lines, older students can discuss how the setting of Mahy's version—during the building of the Great Wall—affects the story. The book can then be a companion piece to Leonard Everett Fisher's *The Great Wall of China*.

Bishop

about human nature and people's roles in society. (For further exploration of ways to use realistic fiction in the classroom, see chapter 3.) In the case of realistic fiction about parallel cultures, the best attempts to mirror and illuminate the experiences of growing up in such a culture are likely to come from authors who are very close to that experience—and usually from authors who are themselves members of the group. Other authors may have different perspectives and different purposes, and although the books they produce may capture "universal" aspects of living and may be of high quality, these authors are still writing from an "outsider's" view. Teachers trying to extend multicultural understanding may want to seek out literature written from the inside.

In the past two decades a number of African-American writers and artists have created a substantial body of African-American literature for children and young adults. Two of these writers—Virginia Hamilton and Mildred Taylor—have been awarded the prestigious Newbery Medal. Others (for example, Lucille Clifton, Eloise Greenfield, Walter Dean Myers, Sharon Bell Mathis, Rosa Guy, Brenda Wilkinson, Alice Childress, Julius Lester, and Mildred Pitts Walter) have produced a variety of quality literature for intermediate and young adult readers. A number of writers and artists have been newly published in the past several years—Angela Johnson, Elizabeth Fitzgerald Howard, Patricia McKissack, and Pat Cummings, to name a few.

Far fewer writers from other parallel cultures in the United States are represented in children's book publishing. Among Asian-American writers, probably the best known is Laurence Yep, a Chinese American. He has produced a number of novels, some of which—*Sea Glass* and *Child of the Owl*, for example—focus on growing up as a Chinese American in contemporary times. He has also explored Chinese immigrant experiences in *Dragonwings*, which is set in San Francisco at the time of the great earthquake, in his collections of folktales, and in *The Star Fisher*, the fictionalized account of his grandparents' and mother's sojourn in West Virginia. Yep also has written science fiction and fantasy, and recently an autobiography entitled *The Lost Garden*. Also well known is Yoshiko Uchida, whose books tell of the experiences of Japanese Americans in the Depression years (*A Jar of Dreams* and *The Best Bad Thing*) and in the World War II relocation camps (*Journey to Topaz* and *Journey Home*).

The major children's book publishers are publishing few Native American writers. Although some nonfiction and some historical fiction are available, there is very little contemporary fiction featuring Native Americans. Most of the current books relating to Native Americans are retellings of folktales and are written by non-Native authors.

The same is true for Hispanic Americans. One noteworthy collection of short stories does focus on growing up in a contemporary Hispanic family and community in California. Gary Soto's *Baseball in April* is full of warmth, humor, and evocations of the experiences and emotions shared by young people everywhere in the United States.

Realistic fiction provides both a mirror in which students can see themselves and a window through which they can view the lives and experiences of others. At times the window is also reflective, allowing readers to see the connections between themselves and the characters in the book, as well as with all humans.

In the classroom, the most important activity to do with realistic fiction is simply to share it with the students, inviting them to become an interpretive community of readers who make and share meaning with each other and with the teacher. Beware of overanalyzing literature, however. The teacher's purpose in literature discussions is to guide students to a deeper understanding of and appreciation for the literature. Not every book shared in the classroom needs to be the object of extended, formal study. Sometimes just reading it and inviting response is enough.

Poetry

Although the amount of children's poetry from parallel cultures is limited, teachers should be able to locate and select a few poems appropriate for choral reading, as accompaniments to fiction selections, or to be appreciated for their own sake. A reading of *Bridge to Terabithia*, for example, can be enriched by hearing "Poem" from *Don't You Turn Back: Poems by Langston Hughes*, edited by Lee Bennet Hopkins and illustrated with striking woodcuts by Ann Grifalconi.

Teaching Idea

Discussing Realistic Fiction

After students have read or listened to a book, invite them to talk about their reactions to it. To stimulate thinking, you might ask open-ended questions such as these:

- Why did the main character respond the way he or she did to the conflict in the book? What could he or she have done instead?
- Might the main character's experience have been different if he or she had not been from a parallel culture? In what way?
- Does this book remind you of any other books? In what way?
- What does the title mean to you?

To focus attention on literary elements or the author's craft, you might ask the following kinds of questions:

- How important is the setting to the book? What difference would it have made if this book had been set in another time or place?
- In what ways is the main character the same at the end as he or she was at the beginning of the book? How is he or she different?
- How has the author helped you get to know the characters? Or helped you envision the setting?
- Who is telling the story? What effect does that perspective have on the way the story unfolds?

Eloise Greenfield's collection *Nathaniel Talking* includes "Nathaniel's Rap," which seems to invite students to participate by providing rhythmical accompaniment. Virginia Driving Hawk Sneve's *Dancing Teepees: Poems of American Indian Youth* contains diverse voices and offers an opportunity for readers to think about what it might mean to grow up as a Native American.

A Vehicle for Change

Reading is not a passive activity. Each time we read a good piece of literature, we are changed by the experience. Books can help us see the world in a new way. It is this capacity to change us and to change our perspective on the world that makes literature an ideal vehicle for understanding cultures and experiences different from our own. Teachers who make the effort to incorporate literature from various cultures into the curriculum can contribute to making tomorrow's world a more humane and considerate one.

The cover of *Dragonwings*, a 1976 Newbery Honor book.

References

Fleming, M., & McGinnis, J. (Eds.). (1985). *Portraits: Biography and autobiography in the secondary school*. Urbana, IL: National Council of Teachers of English.

Hamilton, V. (1989). Author's acceptance speech for the Boston Globe-Horn Book Award for nonfiction. *The Horn Book Magazine, 65*(2), 183-185.

Nieto, S. (Ed.). (1983). Puerto Ricans in children's literature and history texts: A ten-year update. *Interracial Books for Children Bulletin, 14*(1 & 2).

Children's Books

Ashabranner, B. (1983). *The new Americans: Changing patterns in U.S. immigration*. New York: Dodd Mead.

Ashabranner, B. (1984). *To live in two worlds: American Indian youth today*. New York: Dodd Mead.

Ashabranner, B. (1987). *Into a strange land: Unaccompanied refugee youth in America*. New York: Dodd Mead.

Bishop, C.H. (1938). *The five Chinese brothers*. (Ill. by K. Wiese.) New York: Coward, McCann.

Fisher, L.E. (1986). *The Great Wall of China*. New York: Holiday House.

Freedman, R. (1980). *Immigrant kids*. New York: Dutton.

Freedman, R. (1987). *Indian chiefs*. New York: Holiday House.

Greenfield, E. (1989). *Nathaniel talking*. (Ill. by J.S. Gilchrist.) Village Station, NY: Black Butterfly Press.

Hamanaka, S. (1990). *The journey: Japanese Americans, racism and renewal*. New York: Orchard.

Hamilton, V. (1985). *The people could fly: American black folktales*. New York: Knopf.

Hamilton, V. (1988). *Anthony Burns: The defeat and triumph of a fugitive slave*. New York: Knopf.

Hopkins, L.B. (Ed.). (1969). *Don't you turn back: Poems by Langston Hughes*. (Ill. by A. Grifalconi.) New York: Knopf.

Hoyt-Goldsmith, D. (1991). *Pueblo storyteller*. (Photos by L. Migdale.) New York: Holiday House.

Lester, J. (1968). *To be a slave*. New York: Dial.

Lomas Garza, C. (1990). *Family pictures/Cuadros de familia*. San Francisco, CA: Children's Book Press.

Mahy, M. (Reteller). (1990). *The seven Chinese brothers*. (Ill. by J. Tseng & M. Tseng.) New York: Scholastic.

Meltzer, M. (1984). *The black Americans: A history in their own words*. New York: Crowell.

Myers, W.D. (1990). *The mouse rap*. New York: HarperCollins.

Myers, W.D. (1991). *Now is your time: The African American struggle for freedom*. New York: HarperCollins.

Paterson, K. (1977). *Bridge to Terabithia*. New York: Crowell.

Say, A. (1990). *El Chino*. Boston, MA: Houghton Mifflin.

Sneve, V.D.H. (1989). *Dancing teepees: Poems of American Indian youth*. (Ill. by S. Gammell.) New York: Holiday House.

Soto, G. (1990). *Baseball in April*. San Diego, CA: Harcourt Brace Jovanovich.

Stanley, F. (1991). *The last princess: The story of Princess Ka'iulani of Hawai'i*. (Ill. by D. Stanley.) New York: Four Winds.

Taylor, M. (1976). *Roll of thunder, hear my cry*. New York: Dial.

Taylor, M. (1981). *Let the circle be unbroken*. New York: Dial.

Taylor, M. (1990). *The road to Memphis*. New York: Dial.

Uchida, Y. (1971). *Journey to Topaz*. New York: Scribners.

Uchida, Y. (1979). *Journey home*. New York: Atheneum.

Uchida, Y. (1981). *A jar of dreams*. New York: Atheneum.

Uchida, Y. (1983). *The best bad thing*. New York: Macmillan.

Yep, L. (1975). *Dragonwings*. New York: HarperCollins.

Yep, L. (1977). *Child of the owl*. New York: HarperCollins.

Yep, L. (1979). *Sea glass*. New York: HarperCollins.

Yep, L. (1989). *The rainbow people*. New York: HarperCollins.

Yep, L. (1991). *The lost garden*. Englewood Cliffs, NJ: Julian Messner.

Yep, L. (1991). *The star fisher*. New York: Morrow.

Appendix:
Books about People from Parallel Cultures (for use in grades 4-6)

Contemporary Fiction

Ada, A.F. (1991). *The gold coin*. (Ill. by N. Waldman; trans. by B. Randall.) New York: Atheneum.

Boyd, C.D. (1985). *Breadsticks and blessing places*. New York: Macmillan.

Boyd, C.D. (1987). *Charlie Pippin*. New York: Macmillan.

Guy, R. (1989). *The ups and downs of Carl Davis III*. New York: Delacorte.

Hamilton, V. (1987). *The mystery of Drear House*. New York: Greenwillow.

Hamilton, V. (1990). *Cousins*. New York: Philomel.

Mohr, N. (1986). *Going home*. New York: Dial.

Myers, W.D. (1988). *Me, Mop, and the Moondance Kid*. New York: Delacorte.

Myers, W.D. (1988). *Scorpions*. New York: HarperCollins.

Paulsen, G. (1985). *Dog song*. New York: Bradbury.

Tate, E. (1987). *The secret of Gumbo Grove*. New York: Watts.

Taylor, M. (1987). *The friendship*. New York: Dial.

Taylor, M. (1987). *The gold Cadillac*. New York: Dial.

Taylor, M. (1990). *Mississippi bridge*. New York: Dial.

Thomas, J.C. (1986). *The golden pasture*. New York: Scholastic.

Walter, M.P. (1986). *Justin and the best biscuits in the world*. New York: Lothrop, Lee & Shepard.

Walter, M.P. (1988). *Mariah loves rock*. New York: Bradbury.

Walter, M.P. (1990). *Mariah keeps cool*. New York: Bradbury.

Yarbrough, C. (1989). *The shimmershine queens*. New York: Putnam.

Yee, P. (1990). *Tales from Gold Mountain: Stories of the Chinese in the New World*. (Ill. by S. Ng.) New York: Macmillan.

Historical Fiction

Goble, P. (1987). *Death of the iron horse*. New York: Bradbury.

Gregory, K. (1989). *Jenny of the Tetons*. San Diego, CA: Harcourt Brace Jovanovich.

Hamilton, V. (1989). *The bells of Christmas*. San Diego, CA: Harcourt Brace Jovanovich.

Hansen, J. (1986). *Which way freedom*. New York: Walker.

Hansen, J. (1988). *Out from this place*. New York: Walker.

Folktales and Traditional Literature

Hamilton, V. (1988). *In the beginning: Creation stories from around the world*. (Ill. by B. Moser.) San Diego, CA: Harcourt Brace Jovanovich.

Hamilton, V. (1990). *The dark way: Stories from the spirit world*. (Ill. by L. Davis.) San Diego, CA: Harcourt Brace Jovanovich.

Joseph, L. (1991). *A wave in her pocket: Stories from Trinidad*. (Ill. by B. Pinkney.) New York: Clarion.

Lester, J. (1987). *The tales of Uncle Remus: The adventures of Brer Rabbit*. New York: Dial.

Lester, J. (1988). *More tales of Uncle Remus*. New York: Dial.

Lester, J. (1990). *Further tales of Uncle Remus*. New York: Dial.

Lewis, R. (1988). *In the night, still dark*. (Ill. by E. Young.) New York: Atheneum.

Lewis, R. (1991). *All of you was singing*. (Ill. by E. Young.) New York: Atheneum.

Rohmer, H., Chow, O., & Viadure, M. (1987). *The invisible hunters/Los cazadores invisibles*. San Francisco, CA: Children's Book Press.

Rohmer, H., & Wilson, D. (1987). *Mother scorpion country/La tierra de la madre escorpion*. San Francisco, CA: Children's Book Press.

Nonfiction and Biographies

Ekoomiak, N. (1990). *Arctic memories*. New York: Henry Holt.

Hoyt-Goldsmith, D. (1990). *Totem pole*. (Photos by L. Migdale.) New York: Holiday House.

Lyons, M.E. (1990). *Sorrow's kitchen: The life and folklore of Zora Neale Hurston*. New York: Scribners.

McKissack, P. (1989). *Jesse Jackson: A biography*. New York: Scholastic.

Meltzer, M. (1976). *Taking root: Jewish immigrants in America*. New York: Farrar, Straus & Giroux.

Meltzer, M. (1980). *The Chinese Americans*. New York: Crowell.

Meltzer, M. (1982). *The Hispanic Americans*. New York: Crowell.

Meltzer, M. (1982). *The Jewish Americans: A history in their own words*. New York: Crowell.

Poetry and the Arts

Delacre, L. (1990). *Las Navidades: Popular songs from Latin America*. New York: Scholastic.

Greenfield, E. (1988). *Under the Sunday tree*. (Paintings by A. Ferguson.) New York: HarperCollins.

Mattox, C.W. (Adaptor). (1989). *Shake it to the one that you love the best: Play songs and lullabies from black musical traditions*. El Sobrante, CA: Warren-Mattox Productions.

Price, L. (Reteller). (1990). *Aida*. (Ill. by L. Dillon & D. Dillon.) San Diego, CA: Harcourt Brace Jovanovich.

CHAPTER 9

Award Winners from Five English-Speaking Countries

Sylvia M. Hutchinson
Ira E. Aaron

Children's literature awards exist in many countries around the world and are administered by a variety of organizations. Each awarding agency chooses the best writing or best illustrations according to its own criteria. However, the availability of an award-winning book is by no means limited to the country in which that book was originally published or given an award. One of the most interesting of the many recent changes in the publishing industry is the rapid growth in the availability of juvenile books across national borders. Over the past few years, for example, U.S.-based publishers have published noticeably more books by writers and illustrators from other countries. Numerous mergers and takeovers in the industry have created more multinational publishing companies, which frequently publish juvenile titles in more than one country. Also frequent is the publication of the same book by different publishers in different countries, either because of separate agreements negotiated by an author or agent or because of sublicense arrangements between publishers.

Members of the International Reading Association, through their attendance at annual conventions and world congresses, have learned a great deal about children's books from several English-speaking countries. Conventions and congresses in Great Britain, Australia, and Canada have introduced members to some of the top writers and illustrators of children's books in those host countries. Children's books published outside the United States have also been the focus of various pieces published in the Association's journals over the years.

This chapter focuses on award-winning children's books from five English-speaking countries: Australia, Canada, Great Britain, New Zealand, and the United States. For each country, one award for illustration and one for writing is discussed; an additional in-between category appears in the discussion of Australia's award winners, since in that country the writing award is offered in two age categories. The national library associations administer the awards in all countries except Australia, where the Children's Book Council of Australia—a coalition of groups concerned with children's books—handles the awards. Other awards for outstanding children's books exist, but we selected these particular awards as the focus for our chapter because we considered them to be the most prestigious. We were also impressed by the library associations' involvement in the selections.

With the exception of the U.S. awards, the Caldecott and Newbery medal books, our comments here discuss only award winners from 1980 through 1991. For each of the 11 prize categories, two books are reviewed in detail (the particular books selected for review reflect our personal preferences). All the winners since 1980 are listed separately, at the end of the chapter.

The vast majority of these books are still in print in the countries in which they were originally published; many of them are also available in other countries. The current availability of *all* the Caldecott and Newbery winners (these U.S.-based prizes were established in 1938 and 1922 respectively) is discussed in a separate section.

Our concluding section makes some general observations about similarities and differences in the five countries' winners.

Australia's Books of the Year

Picture Book of the Year

Almost half of the winners of the Australian picture book award are classified as realistic fiction. Death and grieving have not traditionally been topics for children's books, even if these books were realistic fiction. Increasingly, however, children's literature (including picture books) is addressing such serious topics. *The Very Best of Friends*, written by Margaret Wild and illustrated by Julie Vivas, tells the story of a marriage rooted in a loving friendship, the death of a husband, and a difficult period of grief. In this 1990 award winner, James and Jessie, a farm couple, are devoted to one another. James is very fond of William, the cat, but Jessie only tolerates William because of James. One Sunday morning, James dies suddenly. Acceptance of his death comes hard for both Jessie and William. In her grief, Jessie neglects William; she puts him outside and bolts the cat flap. William runs wild. Eventually, Jessie begins to recover; she starts to heal by making peace with the cat, and the reader knows that soon Jessie and William will become "the very best of friends." Despite the sadness in the story, the text and illustrations add an occasional touch of humor.

The 1989 Picture Book of the Year is quite different from the 1990 winner. Hidden animals and coded messages in the illustrations and a mystery about who stole Elephant's birthday meal make Graeme Base's *The Eleventh Hour: A Curious Mystery* fascinating for inquisitive readers. The number 11 plays a key role in the story: eleventh birthday, eleventh month, eleventh day, eleventh hour, and so on. The colorful, detailed, comical illustrations combine with the rhyming text to lure the reader into attempting to solve the puzzle. Interestingly, the edition of this book available in the United States has a six-page explanation on how to solve the puzzle sealed in the back of the book. This section is not included in the original Australian edition.

Book of the Year: Younger Readers

Overnight, a mysterious carousel appears in town in Emily Rodda's *The Best-Kept Secret*. The carousel's magic is that it takes riders seven years into the future. Not everyone can get aboard, but ten-year-old Joanne can. She, along with a few other townspeople, makes the journey and spends one hour in the future. The lost six-year-old whom Joanne meets and helps is her yet-to-be-born brother—now she knows why her mother wants a larger house! The reason the secret of the carousel is so well kept is that once the journey is over the riders cannot quite remember anything about the trip. This book, Rodda's third to be selected for the award, won the 1990 prize. (Her *Pigs Might Fly* and *Something Special*, both illustrated by Noela Young, won in 1987 and 1985 respectively.) In 1991 Rodda became a four-time winner of the same award with *Finders Keepers*.

Australia celebrated its 200th birthday in 1988, the year *My Place*, written by Nadia Wheatley and illustrated by Donna Rawlins, won this award. This fictionalized history of Australia describes a particular place where children live as it was in 1988, 1978, 1968, and on back through the decades to 1788 when only Aborigines lived in Australia. Each spread covers a year in text and illustration, with a map of "my place" as a child would draw it. Descriptions touch on almost all important aspects of Australian history. The 21 two-page stories are written from the perspective of children as young as "nearly 7" and as old as 12, who tell of their communities and their families. This book will appeal to a wide age range and may prompt readers to wonder what their "place" was like in the past.

Book of the Year: Older Readers

John Marsden's *So Much to Tell You* is the sad story of a 14-year-old girl trying to recover from the trauma of having had her face disfigured by acid thrown by her father (her mother was the intended victim). Marina's emotional scars exceed her physical problem; one of the scars is an inability to speak following the incident. Through Marina's diaries, the reader follows her ups and downs in hospitals and in a boarding school. She slowly begins to recover physically, but her inability to speak remains. She arranges to go to a country hospital near where her father is imprisoned when she learns that he needs treatment for a minor hand injury. When she sees her father she says "Hello, Dad," and then, "I've got so much to tell you." This book won the award in 1988.

The 1984 award winner was Patricia Wrightson's *A Little Fear*, a serious story with a few comical episodes. Tired of her daughter's overprotection, Mrs. Tucker "escapes" from a senior-citizen home to an isolated cottage she has inherited. There she adopts a dog she names Hector. A spirit called a Njimbin, who has ruled the area for centuries, resents the intrusion of the old woman and her dog. The Njimbin mobilizes the insects and the rats, but Mrs. Tucker and Hector fight back. Readers will especially enjoy learning how Mrs. Tucker plans her revenge when she decides to go back to a home near her daughter.

Canadian Kudos

Amelia Frances Howard-Gibbon Medal

Pupils and even teachers have sometimes resisted reading poetry because of its figurative language and its frequently romantic themes. Happily, though, much of contemporary children's poetry deals with everyday topics in straightforward language. The 1990 winner of this award for illustration is *Til All the Stars Have Fallen*, a book of Canadian-authored poems selected by David Booth and illustrated by Kady MacDonald Denton. Poems in the collection range from the serious to the humorous to the whimsical. The illustrations make use of watercolors, collage, and occasionally the layout of the text itself. One poem, in which "tomato" is the only word, is printed in red ink in the shape of a tomato; in a poem about jumping from steps, the letters are printed to look like steps. Booth's introduction, in poetry-like prose, is an outstanding explanation of what poetry is and how poems should be read.

The illustrations and text in Ian Wallace's *Chin Chiang and the Dragon's Dance*, the 1985 winner, tell the story of a young Chinese boy's fear of dancing the dragon's dance, even though he has dreamed of it for as long as he can remember. Colorful and detailed illustrations appear on the lefthand pages, with the text on the right. Wallace's watercolors give the story a Chinese flavor.

Book of the Year for Children

The 1990 award book in this category takes the reader back to the summer of 1940, when England feared invasion by German forces. Kit Pearson's *The Sky Is Falling* relates the experiences of ten-year-old Norah and her five-year-old brother, Gavin, who are evacuated with other British children to the safety of Canada. After arriving in Toronto, the children are taken into the home of a wealthy widow and her grown daughter. Norah learns early that the widow really wanted only Gavin but had to take both children. Pearson relates the touching story of the children's insecurities and difficulties in trying to accept and be accepted by their adoptive family. As the author states in an afterword, almost 8,000 children from Britain were evacuated to Canada during World War II. This story is fiction, but it is modeled on the experiences of real evacuees. Pearson's time-warp novel, *A Handful of Time*, won this award in 1988.

The 1985 award winner, Jean Little's *Mama's Going to Buy You a Mockingbird*, presents the emotion-packed story of children's reactions to their father's illness and ultimate death. Because of their father's illness, Jeremy, almost 12, and his 8-year-old sister, Sarah, spend a miserable summer with Aunt Margery. When they learn that their father has cancer, they become even more miserable. After their father dies, the children, along with their mother, face a number of problems, including the necessity of moving into a smaller and more affordable home. Coming to terms with his father's death begins for Jeremy when he hears his mother singing the line "Mama's going to buy you a mockingbird" from the traditional song, instead of "Papa's going to buy you a mockingbird." The understanding of loss becomes even clearer when early on Christmas morning Jeremy sees his mother's small, half-filled Christmas stocking, which she has prepared for herself. For the first time, he realizes that his parents had been filling each other's stockings. Before other family members get out of bed, Jeremy replaces his

mother's stocking with a larger one and then fills it to the brim. He tops it off with Hoot, a polished stone owl given to him by his father a few months before his death. Jeremy knows his mother has a special feeling for Hoot.

Great Books from Great Britain

Kate Greenaway Medal

This award is given for illustration. In the 1989 medal winner, Michael Foreman's autobiographical *War Boy: A Country Childhood*, a young boy shares his experiences and views about World War II and its impact on the Suffolk coast. The writer/illustrator presents these everyday experiences as he remembers them years later. The book opens with a fire-bomb crashing through then three-year-old Foreman's bedroom roof. In a nostalgic recollection of the soldiers and sailors who were based near his home and whom the little boy came to know and care about, he sketches the war as he saw it. The book closes with a letter from one of the former servicemen who had known Foreman's family in those days; it is an expression of sadness at the death of Foreman's mother. Illustrations include photographs, diagrams, sketches, pastels, and reproductions of posters. They are simple and occasionally reflect the illustrator's sense of humor. Two Greenaway medals were awarded in 1982, and both winning books were illustrated by Foreman: *Sleeping Beauty and Other Fairy Tales* by Angelo Carter and *Long Neck and Thunder Foot* by Helen Piers.

The 1986 winner of this award is an interestingly illustrated and humorous modernization of the Snow White story. *Snow White in*

Young Michael Foreman and friends play in the ruins of a bombed building where flowers had begun to bloom, in *War Boy: A Country Childhood*.

New York, written and illustrated by Fiona French, places Snow White in New York in the 1920s. The wicked stepmother is Queen of the Underworld; Snow White's "woods" are the dark streets between New York's tall buildings; her seven dwarfs are seven members of a jazz band she joins as lead singer. She is "poisoned" by a cocktail cherry but is later awakened by a stumbling pallbearer; her handsome prince, a reporter, is among the mourners who turn out expecting to attend her funeral. The pictures range from brilliant and happy to dark and somber as the story unfolds. Snow White's funeral procession is presented mostly in black and gray; when she awakens, the colors become brighter. For children to enjoy this book, they first should be familiar with a traditional story of Snow White.

Carnegie Medal

A wise teacher, recognizing that two of her young students have similar problems, arranges for one to help the other in Anne Fine's *Goggle-Eyes* (published in the United States as *My War with Goggle-Eyes*), the 1989 award winner. Kitty has had a lot of experience handling her mother's boyfriend, but for Helly the situation is new. Kitty tells Helly all about Old Goggle-Eyes, her mother's boyfriend. His razor-sharp tongue made him easy to hate but, despite herself, Kitty grew to like him. Though Old Goggle-Eyes didn't believe it a worthwhile effort, he went along with Kitty and her mother to a sit-in near a nuclear submarine base, and he looked after Kitty and her younger sister when their mother was arrested for demonstrating. Old Goggle-Eyes wasn't so bad after all.

A mysterious young man called MCC takes over when he becomes a volunteer salesman at the antique shop owned by Alisa and her mother in Geraldine McCaughrean's *A Pack of Lies*. This 1988 winner consists of 12 stories "manufactured" by MCC Berkshire to personalize the antiques he wants to sell to unsuspecting customers; the stories together are the "pack of lies." An epilogue helps to clear up, at least partially, unanswered questions about MCC. McCaughrean has a good sense of humor and is masterful in her use of language.

New Zealand's Best

Russell Clark Award

Pamela Allen has won two Australian Picture Book of the Year awards (for *Bertie and the Bear* in 1984 and *Who Sank the Boat?* in 1983). In 1986 she received New Zealand's Russell Clark Award for *A Lion in the Night*. Her text and cartoon-like pictures tell a rollicking tale about a lion entering a castle and stealing a baby girl. Pictures disclose the glee of both the baby and the lion as they are chased across the kingdom by the Queen, the King, the Admiral, the Captain, the Sergeant, and a little dog. The lion tricks their pursuers and gets the baby safely home, and the story has a happy ending. Was the baby dreaming? Maybe....

Gwenda Turner's *The Tree Witches*, the winner in 1984, is about the antics of two girls and a boy who pretend to be witches. They go about in disguises and play tricks on others. A tree house serves as their convenient hideout. When they encounter a new boy in the neighborhood, they recruit him to join the group. The color pictures look almost like photographs.

Esther Glen Award

The 1988 winner of this award was Tessa Duder's *Alex* (published in the United States as *In Lane Three, Alex Archer*). Fifteen-year-old Alex is one of her country's best swimmers, and she wants to win a place on the team representing New Zealand at the 1960 Rome Olympics. To do this, she must beat out her top rival, Maggie. Because of the cost in energy and time of her six years of training, Alex has very few friends. She falls in love with Andy, an athletic and intelligent boy who understands and encourages her in her swimming. In an emotional scene, Duder tells of how Alex learns that Andy has been run over and killed by a drunken driver. A short section printed in italics at the beginning of each chapter relates Alex's feelings and thoughts about swimming. The author has been a champion swimmer herself, and her knowledge about and love for the sport shine through the story. The 1989 Esther Glen Award went to Duder's *Alex in Winter*, a continuation of Alex's story and her attempt to cope with the loss of Andy.

The Changeover: A Supernatural Romance, written by Margaret Mahy, was awarded both the 1985 Esther Glen Award and the 1984 Carnegie Medal (the latter in Great Britain). Laura has the "gift," and she recognizes that 16-year-old Sorry Carlisle also has it. A spell is put on Laura's 3-year-old brother, Jacko, and he almost dies. Laura, with the help of Sorry's family, has to use her own supernatural powers (the "changeover") in order to rescue Jacko. The plot branches out when Kate, Laura's mother, becomes friendly with Chris Holly, and Laura's father and his new wife come to visit Jacko in the hospital. The story is a mixture of realistic fiction and fantasy. Mahy makes superb use of figurative language, often with a humorous twist (she mentions, for example, "punishing the grass edges with some instrument of gardening torture"). Mahy's *The Haunting*, another mixture of realism and the supernatural, won both New Zealand's 1983 Esther Glen Award and Great Britain's 1982 Carnegie Medal.

Medalists from the United States

Randolph Caldecott Medal

The 1990 Caldecott Medal winner was Ed Young's *Lon Po Po: A Red-Riding Hood Story from China*. Children who know the traditional English version of Red Riding Hood will enjoy this quite different Chinese version with its beautiful illustrations. When a mother leaves her three children at home alone while she goes to visit their grandmother, a wolf dressed as an old woman gains entry into the house by pretending to be their grandmother, or Po Po. The three sisters soon learn that the wolf is an imposter and outwit him by climbing a tall tree to gather nuts which the wolf is led to believe are delicious and magical. The children tell the wolf that the nuts must be "plucked directly from the tree." But alas, the wolf cannot climb! Justice prevails when the children happen to let go of the rope as they

are pulling the wolf up in a basket.

Chris Van Allsburg's *The Polar Express*, winner of this award in 1986, is one of America's top selling children's books, with more than 800,000 copies in print. The story and illustrations appeal to nearly all children—and to those who are children at heart. It is Christmas Eve, and the young narrator, hearing "hissing steam and squeaking metal," goes out to find the Polar Express. He gets aboard and joins others on the way to visit Santa. The narrator, chosen to receive the first gift of Christmas, asks for one of the sleigh bells. Back aboard the train, he realizes that he has lost the bell through a hole in his pocket, but the next morning he finds the bell under the Christmas tree, along with a note from Santa suggesting that he sew up the hole. The sleigh bell is special: his parents cannot hear it; his sister can for a time and then cannot; but he can hear it always. Only those who believe can hear the bell!

John Newbery Medal

The 1991 Newbery award winner was Jerry Spinelli's *Maniac Magee*. Orphaned at the age of 3 and homeless by choice at 11, Jeffery (later known as Maniac) leads an unbelievable life. An uncle and aunt with whom he lives never speak to each other; in fact, they have nothing to do with each other, although they live in the same house. To escape this setting, Maniac leaves—and a legend begins. Maniac is outstanding at everything. He solves racial problems, he is a tremendous athlete, and almost overnight he teaches an old man—a former baseball player—to read by using a baseball analogy. Children will recognize the tall tale element in the story, but most still will cheer for homeless Maniac, who can make a home anywhere.

Lois Lowry's *Number the Stars*, the 1990 Newbery winner, is a chilling yet heartwarming story. In 1943 Denmark, a Jewish girl is taken into a Gentile home and disguised as a family member to hide her from Nazi soldiers. Several narrow escapes occur, including a tense scene in which the soldiers want to know why Ellen has black hair when the other children in the family have light hair. As Lowry explains in an afterword, the story is modeled on real events that occurred in Denmark during World War II. The Danish resistance helped large numbers of Jews cross the border into neutral Sweden. On the last page of the book, Lowry reproduces part of a real letter from a young Danish man to his mother, written on the night before he was executed for his role in the resistance.

Availability of Caldecott and Newbery Books

As of this writing, all 54 Caldecott Medal books (1938-1991) are in print in the United States; of the 70 Newbery winners (1922-1991), all but 2—James Daugherty's *Daniel Boone*, the 1940 winner, and Monica Shannon's *Dobry*, the 1935 winner—are in print. Thirty-seven of the Caldecott winners are available in both paperback and hardcover; 4 in paperback only; and 8 in hardcover only. Fifty-six of the Newbery winners are available in paperback and hardcover; 4 in paperback only; and 8 in hardcover only. (Twenty-three Newbery Medal winners are also available in large-print format.)

Common Threads

We discussed in detail only a small number of titles in this chapter, but we did read and study carefully *all* the award-winning

Maniac Magee always seems to be on the move.

J E R R Y   S P I N E L L I

Maniac Magee

books listed in the bibliography. In the course of the study we noted a number of similarities about the award winners. Some of these, along with a few general statements, follow.

• The books in this study more frequently fell into the fantasy genre than any other literary category. Approximately two-thirds of the picture books were either modern or traditional fantasy stories. Approximately half of the award winners in the writing categories were fantasy. This includes the supernatural (stories of ghosts, witches, time travel, and magic), an interesting finding given that books dealing with the supernatural often face censorship challenges in schools for promoting the "occult."

• Family relations, nontraditional or dysfunctional families, substance abuse, war, and death are facts of modern life that children may have to deal with. They are also the subjects of a number of these award-winning books.

• Good writers and illustrators are being published in all countries, but the quality of even these award-winning books varied.

• The setting for most books did not play a major role in the stories, although most of the award-winners were set in the country in which the books were published. Characterization was usually far more important than setting.

• World War II is the setting of award-winning books from Canada, Great Britain, New Zealand, and the United States. Clearly, the issues and themes that came out of that war have continuing relevance to a new generation of readers.

• Award-winning books from other countries add to children's knowledge and appreciation of people and events from other cultures, places, and times. Perhaps most important, though, these books help children realize that some problems are universal and that children from other countries have the same basic emotions that they do.

Children's Books

Allen, P. (1982). *Who sank the boat?* South Melbourne, Victoria: Nelson Australia.

Allen, P. (1983). *Bertie and the bear*. South Melbourne, Victoria: Nelson Australia.

Allen, P. (1985). *A lion in the night*. Auckland: Hodder & Stoughton.

Base, G. (1988). *The eleventh hour: A curious mystery*. Ringwood, Victoria: Viking O'Neil.

Booth, D. (Selector). (1989). *Til all the stars have fallen: Canadian poems for children*. (Ill. by K.M. Denton.) Toronto, Ont.: Kids Can Press.

Carter, A. (1982). *Sleeping Beauty and other fairy tales*. (Ill. by M. Foreman.) London: Victor Gollancz.

Duder, T. (1987). *Alex*. Auckland: Oxford University Press.

Duder, T. (1989). *Alex in winter*. Auckland: Oxford University Press.

Fine, A. (1989). *Goggle Eyes*. London: Hamish Hamilton.

Foreman, M. (1989). *War boy: A country childhood*. London: Pavilion.

French, F. (1986). *Snow White in New York*. Oxford, UK: Oxford University Press.

Little, J. (1984). *Mama's going to buy you a mockingbird*. Markham, Ont.: Penguin Books Canada.

Lowry, L. (1989). *Number the stars*. Boston, MA: Houghton Mifflin.

Mahy, M. (1982). *The haunting*. London: J.M. Dent.

Mahy, M. (1984). *The changeover: A supernatural romance*. London: J.M. Dent.

Marsden, J. (1987). *So much to tell you*. Glebe, NSW: Walter McVitty.

McCaughrean, G. (1988). *A pack of lies*. Oxford, UK: Oxford University Press.

Pearson, K. (1987). *A handful of time*. Markham, Ont.: Puffin.

Pearson, K. (1989). *The sky is falling*. Markham, Ont.: Penguin Books Canada.

Piers, H. (1982). *Long Neck and Thunder Foot*. (Ill. by M. Foreman.) London: Viking Kestrel.

Rodda, E. (1984). *Something special*. (Ill. by N. Young.) North Ryde, NSW: Collins/Angus & Robertson.

Rodda, E. (1986). *Pigs might fly*. (Ill. by N. Young.) North Ryde, NSW: Collins/Angus & Robertson.

Rodda, E. (1988). *The best-kept secret*. North Ryde, NSW: Collins/Angus & Robertson.

Rodda, E. (1990). *Finders keepers*. Norwood, SA: Omnibus.

Spinelli, J. (1990). *Maniac Magee*. Boston, MA: Little, Brown.

Turner, G. (1983). *The tree witches*. Auckland: Penguin Books (NZ).

Van Allsburg, C. (1985). *The polar express*. Boston, MA: Houghton Mifflin.

Wallace, I. (1984). *Chin Chiang and the dragon's dance*. Toronto, Ont.: Groundwood.

Wheatley, N. (1987). *My place*. (Ill. by D. Rawlins.) Blackburn, Victoria: Collins Dove.

Wild, M. (1989). *The very best of friends*. (Ill. by J. Vivas.) Ringwood, Victoria: Hamish Hamilton.

Wrightson, P. (1983). *A little fear*. Surry Hills, NSW: Century Hutchinson.

Young, E. (1989). *Lon Po Po: A red-riding hood story from China*. New York: Philomel.

Appendix: Bibliography of Award Winners, 1981–1991

The bibliography lists all the award winners in the 11 categories since 1980, organized by country. The publisher given for each book is that of the original edition. The letters at the end of each entry indicate the countries in which the book has subsequently been published ("A" for Australia, "C" for Canada, "G" for Great Britain, "N" for New Zealand, and "U" for the United States). When books are also published in another country, the publisher quite often is different from that of the original publication. Note also that even if the books have not been published separately in numerous countries, they still may be easily available through local distributors or sales agents. Information on the availability of any of the following titles in your home country can be obtained through bookstore personnel or library staff.

Australia

Picture Book of the Year. This award was first presented in 1956; two awards were made in 1989.

1991—Graham, Bob. (1990). *Greetings from Sandy Beach*. Port Melbourne, Victoria: Lothian Publishing.

1990—Wild, Margaret (1989). *The very best of friends*. (Ill. by Julie Vivas.) Ringwood, Victoria: Hamish Hamilton (an imprint of Penguin Books Australia). G, U.

1989—Baillie, Allen. (1988). *Drac and the gremlin*. (Ill. by Jane Tanner.) Ringwood, Victoria: Viking O'Neil (an imprint of Penguin Books Australia). U; Base, Graeme. (1988). *The eleventh hour: A curious mystery*. Ringwood, Victoria: Viking O'Neil (an imprint of Penguin Books Australia). G, U.

1988—Graham, Bob. (1987). *Crusher is coming*. North Ryde, NSW: Collins (a division of HarperCollins Australia). G, U.

1987—Morimoto, Junko. (1986). *Kojuro and the bears*. North Ryde, NSW: Collins (a division of HarperCollins Australia).

1986—Denton, Terry. (1985). *Felix and Alexander*. Melbourne: Oxford University Press. G, U.

1985—no award.

1984—Allen, Pamela. (1983). *Bertie and the Bear*. South Melbourne, Victoria: Thomas Nelson Australia. G, U.

1983—Allen, Pamela. (1982). *Who sank the boat?* South Melbourne, Victoria: Thomas Nelson Australia. G, U.

1982—Omerod, Jan. (1981). *Sunshine*. Ringwood, Victoria: Viking Kestrel (an imprint of Penguin Books Australia). G, U.

1981—no award.

Book of the Year: Younger Readers. This award was first presented in 1982.

1991—Rodda, Emily. (1990). *Finders keepers*. Norwood, SA: Omnibus Books. U.

1990—Adams, Jeanie. (1989). *Pigs and honey*. Norwood, SA: Omnibus Books.

1989—Rodda, Emily. (1988). *The best-kept secret*. North Ryde, NSW: Angus & Robertson (now Collins/Angus & Robertson, a division of HarperCollins Australia). G, U.

1988—Wheatley, Nadia. (1987). *My place*. (Ill. by Donna Rawlins.) Blackburn, Victoria: Collins Dove (a division of HarperCollins Australia). U.

1987—Rodda, Emily. (1986). *Pigs might fly*. (Ill. by Noela Young.) North Ryde, NSW: Angus & Robertson (now Collins/Angus & Robertson, a division of HarperCollins Australia). U.

1986—Steele, Mary. (1985). *Arkwright*. South Yarra, Victoria: Hyland House.

1985—Rodda, Emily. (1984). *Something special*. (Ill. by Noela Young.) North Ryde, NSW: Angus & Robertson (now Collins/Angus & Robertson, a division of HarperCollins Australia). U.

1984—Dunn, Max. (1983). *Bernice knows best*. (Ill. by Ann James.) Melbourne: Oxford University Press.

1983—Klein, Robin. (1982). *Thing*. (Ill. by Alison Lester.) Melbourne: Oxford University Press. G, U.

1982—French, Simon. (1981). *Cannily, cannily*. North Ryde, NSW: Angus & Robertson (now Collins/Angus & Robertson, a division of HarperCollins Australia). G.

Book of the Year: Older Readers. The first award was presented in 1946.

1991—Crew, Gary. (1990). *Strange objects*. Port Melbourne, Victoria: Heinemann (an imprint of Octopus Publishing Group Australia).

1990—Klein, Robin. (1989). *Came back to show you I can fly*. Ringwood, Victoria: Viking Kestrel (an imprint of Penguin Books Australia). U.

1989—Rubinstein, Gillian. (1988). *Beyond the labyrinth*. South Yarra, Victoria: Hyland House. U.

1988—Marsden, John. (1987). *So much to tell you*. Glebe, NSW: Walter McVitty Books. G, U.

1987—French, Simon. (1986). *All we know*. North Ryde, NSW: Angus & Robertson (now Collins/Angus & Robertson, a division of HarperCollins Australia). G.

1986—Fowler, Thurley. (1985). *The green wind*. Chatswood: Rigby Publishers (an imprint of Lansdowne Press).

1985—Aldridge, James. (1984). *The true story of Lilli Stubeck*. South Yarra, Victoria: Hyland House. G, U.

1984—Wrightson, Patricia. (1983). *A little fear*. Surry Hills, NSW: Hutchinson (now Century Hutchinson Australia). U.

1983—Kelleher, Victor. (1982). *Master of the grove*. Ringwood, Victoria: Penguin. U.

1982—Thiele, Colin. (1981). *The valley between*. Chatswood: Rigby Publishers (an imprint of Lansdowne Press).

1981—Park, Ruth. (1980). *Playing beatie bow*. South Melbourne, Victoria: Thomas Nelson Australia. G, U.

Canada

Amelia Frances Howard-Gibbon Medal. This award for illustration was established in 1971.

1991—Molley, Tolowa. (1990). *The orphan boy*. (Ill. by Paul Morin.) Don Mills, Ont.: Oxford University Press. U.

1990—Booth, David. (Selector). (1989). *Til all the stars have fallen: Canadian poems for children*. (Ill. by Kady M. Denton.) Toronto, Ont.: Kids Can Press. U.

1989—Lunn, Janet. (1988). *Amos's sweater*. (Ill. by Kim LaFave.) Toronto, Ont.: Groundwood Books (a division of Douglas & McIntyre).

1988—Gay, Marie-Louise. (1987). *Rainy day magic*. Don Mills, Ont.: Stoddart (a division of General Publishing Co.). G, U.

1987—Gay, Marie-Louise. (1986). *Moonbeam on a cat's ear*. Don Mills, Ont.: Stoddart (a division of General Publishing Co.). G.

1986—Wynne-Jones, Tim. (1985). *Zoom away*. (Ill. by Ken Nutt.) Toronto, Ont.: Groundwood Books (a division of Douglas & McIntyre). U.

1985—Wallace, Ian. (1984). *Chin Chiang and the dragon's dance*. Toronto, Ont.: Groundwood Books (a division of Douglas & McIntyre). G, U.

1984—Wynne-Jones, Tim. (1983). *Zoom at sea*. (Ill. by Ken Nutt.) Toronto, Ont.: Groundwood Books (a division of Douglas & McIntyre). U.

1983—Climo, Lindee. (1982). *Chester's barn*. Montreal, P.Q.: Tundra Books. U.

1982—Hewitt, Garnet. (1981). *Ytek and the Arctic orchid*. (Ill. by Heather Woodall.) Toronto, Ont.: Douglas & McIntyre.

1981—Harris, Christie. (1980). *The trouble with princesses*. (Ill. by Douglas Tait.) Toronto, Ont.: McClelland & Stewart.

Book of the Year for Children. This award was first presented in 1947.

1991—Bedard, Michael. (1990). *Redwork*. Toronto, Ont.: Lester & Orpen Dennys (now available through Key Porter Books). U.

1990—Pearson, Kit. (1989). *The sky is falling*. Markham, Ont.: Penguin Books Canada. U.

1989—Doyle, Brian. (1988). *Easy avenue*. Toronto, Ont.: Groundwood Books (a division of Douglas & McIntyre).

1988—Pearson, Kit. (1987). *A handful of time*. Markham, Ont.: Puffin (an imprint of Penguin Books Canada). U.

1987—Lunn, Janet. (1986). *Shadow in Hawthorn Bay*. Toronto, Ont.: Lester & Orpen Dennys (now available through Key Porter Books). G, U.

1986—Taylor, Cora. (1985). *Julie*. Saskatoon, Sask.: Western Producer Prairie Books. G.

1985—Little, Jean. (1984). *Mama's going to buy you a mockingbird*. Markham, Ont.: Penguin Books Canada. G, U.

1984—Hudson, Jan. (1984). *Sweetgrass*. Edmonton, Alta.: Tree Frog Press. G, N, U.

1983—Doyle, Brian. (1982). *Up to low*. Toronto, Ont.: Douglas & McIntyre.

1982—Lunn, Janet. (1981). *The root cellar*. Toronto, Ont.: Lester & Orpen Dennys (now available through Key Porter Books). G, U.

1981—Kushner, Don. (1980). *The violin maker's gift*. Toronto, Ont.: Macmillan. U.

Great Britain

Kate Greenaway Medal. This award for illustration was first presented in 1956; two awards were made in 1982. The dates given in this case refer to the year of publication rather than the year the medal was awarded.

1990—Sheldon, Dyan. *The whales' song*. (Ill. by Gary Blythe.) London: Hutchinson (an imprint of Century Hutchinson). U.

1989—Foreman, Michael. *War boy: A country childhood*. London: Pavilion. U.

1988—Waddell, Martin. *Can't you sleep, little bear?* (Ill. by Barbara Firth.) London:

Walker Books.

1987—Hadith, Mwenye. *Crafty chameleon*. (Ill. by Adrienne Kennaway.) London: Hodder & Stoughton. U.

1986—French, Fiona. *Snow White in New York*. Oxford: Oxford University Press. U.

1985—Hastings, Selina. *Sir Gawain and the loathly lady*. (Ill. by Juan Wijngaard.) London: Walker Books. U.

1984—Longfellow, Henry Wadsworth. *Hiawatha's childhood*. (Ill. by Errol Le-Cain.) London: Faber & Faber.

1983—Browne, Anthony. *Gorilla*. London: Julia MacRae Books (a division of Walker Books). U.

1982—Carter, Angelo. *Sleeping Beauty and other fairy tales*. (Ill. by Michael Foreman.) London: Victor Gollancz. U; Piers, Helen. *Long Neck and Thunder Foot*. (Ill. by Michael Foreman.) London: Kestrel (an imprint of Penguin Books).

1981—Noyes, Alfred. (1981). *The Highwayman*. (Ill. by Charles Keeping.) Oxford: Oxford University Press. U.

1980—Blake, Quentin. (1980). *Mr. Magnolia*. London: Jonathan Cape.

Carnegie Medal. This award was established in 1937. The dates given here refer again to the year of publication.

1990—Cross, Gillian. *Wolf*. Oxford: Oxford University Press. U.

1989—Fine, Anne. *Goggle Eyes*. London: Hamish Hamilton. U.

1988—McCaughrean, Geraldine. *A pack of lies*. Oxford: Oxford University Press. U.

1987—Price, Susan. *The ghost drum*. London: Faber & Faber. U.

1986—Doherty, Berlie. *Granny was a buffer girl*. London: Methuen. U.

1985—Crossley-Holland, Kevin. *Storm*. London: William Heinemann. U.

1984—Mahy, Margaret. *The changeover: A supernatural romance*. London: J.M. Dent. U.

1983—Mark, Jan. *Handles*. London: Kestrel (an imprint of Penguin Books). U.

1982—Mahy, Margaret. *The haunting*. London: J.M. Dent. U.

1981—Westall, Robert. *The scarecrows*. London: Chatto & Windus. U.

1980—Dickinson, Peter. *City of gold*. London: Victor Gollancz.

New Zealand

Russell Clark Award. This award for illustration was established in 1978.

1991—Cartwright, Pauline. (1990). *Arthur and the dragon*. (Ill. by David Elliot.) Petone: Nelson. U.

1990—Gaskin, Chris. (1989). *A walk to the beach*. Auckland: Heinemann Reed.

1989—MacDonald, Caroline. (1988). *Joseph's boat*. (Ill. by Chris Gaskin.) Auckland: Hodder & Stoughton. A.

1988—Glover, Denis. (1987). *The magpies*. (Ill. by Dick Frizzell.) Auckland: Century Hutchinson.

1987—Kahukiwa, Robyn. (1986). *Taniwha*. Auckland: Penguin Books (NZ).

1986—Allen, Pamela. (1985). *A lion in the night*. Auckland: Hodder & Stoughton. G, U.

1985—Cowley, Joy. (1984). *The duck in the gun*. (Ill. by Robyn Belton.) Auckland: Shortland Educational Publications.

1984—Turner, Gwenda. (1983). *The tree witches*. Auckland: Penguin Books (NZ). A.

1983—no award.

1982—Bishop, Gavin. (1981). *Mrs. McGinity and the bizarre plant*. Auckland: Oxford University Press. G, U.

1981—no award.

Cover of *Agnes the Sheep*, winner of New Zealand's Esther Glen Award in 1991.

Esther Glen Award. This award was established in 1945.

1991—Taylor, William. (1990). *Agnes the sheep*. Auckland: Ashton Scholastic. U.

1990—Duder, Tessa. (1989). *Alex in winter*. Auckland: Oxford University Press. G.

1989—Lazenby, Jack. (1988). *The mangrove summer*. Auckland: Oxford University Press. U.

1988—Duder, Tessa. (1987). *Alex*. Auckland: Oxford University Press. G, N, U.

1987—no award.

1986—Gee, Maurice. (1985). *Motherstone*. Auckland: Oxford University Press. U.

1985—Mahy, Margaret. (1984). *The change-over: A supernatural romance*. London: J.M. Dent. G, U.

1984—Macdonald, Caroline. (1983). *Elephant rock*. Auckland: Hodder & Stoughton. A, G.

1983—Mahy, Margaret. (1982). *The haunting*. London: J.M. Dent. G, U.

1982—O'Brien, Katherine. (1981). *The year of the Yelvertons*. Auckland: Oxford University Press. A.

1981—no award.

United States

Randolph Caldecott Medal. This award for illustration was established in 1938.

1991—Macaulay, David. (1990). *Black and white*. Boston, MA: Houghton Mifflin.

1990—Young, Ed. (1989). *Lon Po Po: A red-riding hood story from China*. New York: Philomel (an imprint of the Putnam Berkley Group).

1989—Ackerman, Karen. (1988). *Song and dance man*. (Ill. by Stephen Gammell.) New York: Knopf (an imprint of Random House).

1988—Yolen, Jane. (1987). *Owl moon*. (Ill. by John Schoenherr.) New York: Philomel (an imprint of the Putnam Berkley Group).

1987—Yorinks, Arthur. (1986). *Hey, Al*. (Ill. by Richard Egielski.) New York: Farrar, Straus and Giroux.

1986—Van Allsburg, Chris. (1985). *The polar express*. Boston, MA: Houghton Mifflin. G.

1985—Hodges, Margaret. (1984). *Saint George and the dragon*. (Ill. by Trina Schart Hyman.) Boston, MA: Little, Brown. G.

1984—Provensen, Alice, and Provensen, Martin. (1983). *The glorious flight: Across the Channel with Louis Blériot*. New York: Viking (an imprint of Penguin USA). G.

1983—Cendrars, Blaise. (1982). *Shadow*. (Trans. and ill. by Marcia Brown.) New York: Scribner's (an imprint of Macmillan Publishing).

1982—Van Allsburg, Chris. (1981). *Jumanji*. Boston, MA: Houghton Mifflin. G.

1981—Lobel, Arnold. (1980). *Fables*. New York: Harper & Row (an imprint of Harper-Collins). G.

John Newbery Medal.   This award was first presented in 1922.

1991—Spinelli, Jerry. (1990). *Maniac Magee*. Boston, MA: Little, Brown.

1990—Lowry, Lois. (1989). *Number the stars*. Boston, MA: Houghton Mifflin. G.

1989—Fleischman, Paul. (1988). *Joyful noise: Poems for two voices*. New York: Harper & Row (an imprint of HarperCollins).

1988—Freedman, Russell. (1987). *Lincoln: A photobiography*. Boston, MA: Clarion (an imprint of Houghton Mifflin).

1987—Fleischman, Sid. (1986). *The whipping boy*. New York: Greenwillow (an imprint of William Morrow & Co.). G.

1986—MacLachlan, Patricia. (1985). *Sarah, plain and tall*. New York: Harper & Row (an imprint of HarperCollins). G.

1985—McKinley, Robin. (1984). *The hero and the crown*. New York: Greenwillow (an imprint of William Morrow & Co.). G.

1984—Cleary, Beverly. (1983). *Dear Mr. Henshaw*. New York: William Morrow & Co. A, G.

1983—Voigt, Cynthia. (1982). *Dicey's song*. New York: Atheneum (an imprint of Macmillan). G.

1982—Willard, Nancy. (1981). *A visit to William Blake's inn*. (Ill. by Alice Provensen and Martin Provensen.) San Diego, CA: Harcourt Brace Jovanovich.

1981—Paterson, Katherine. (1980). *Jacob have I loved*. New York: Thomas Y. Crowell (an imprint of HarperCollins). G.

SECTION THREE

This section focuses on some of the important issues that crop up once the decision to move to a literature-based program has been made. Chapter 10 discusses ideas to keep in mind when organizing the reading program and presents suggestions for structuring classroom activities, grouping, and assessment. A framework for establishing a reading/writing workshop is also included. Chapter 11 offers strategies and activities designed to encourage students to respond to literature in ways that help them learn and become active and involved in reading. At-risk readers require special guidance in responding to literature. Chapter 12 offers a model for encouraging critical response from at-risk readers throughout the elementary grades.

Thousands of good children's and young adult books are available for use in the classroom. This volume is full of suggestions for using specific books in particular ways, but there are many more books that are equally outstanding. Chapter 13 describes the many resources available to teachers to help them locate the best books for their students. Finally, chapter 14 discusses what to do when a book selection is criticized or a particular work becomes the target of attempted censorship. This sensitive issue is of particular concern to teachers who abandon bland—but uncontroversial—textbooks and basal readers in favor of more challenging and higher quality literature.

Putting It All Together

CHAPTER 10

The Reading/Writing Workshop
Key Components of the Reading Curriculum
Making the Move

Organizing a Literature-Based Reading Program

Dorothy S. Strickland

L iteracy programs in today's classrooms reflect a tremendous variety of approaches to literature-based instruction. As schools move toward literature-based approaches, many teachers attempt to retain the aspects of traditional programs that they view as effective or with which they are particularly comfortable. But for many teachers, feeling comfortable with an old approach has less to do with instructional issues than it does with concerns about management and organization. For example, neither heavy reliance on ability groups nor an emphasis on teacher-directed instruction is consistent with sound literature-based practices, yet these methods may persist even after an abundance of good literature has found its way into the classroom.

The marriage of preexisting, "comfortable" methods with new approaches sometimes produces an irreconcilable mismatch. After an exhausting and ineffectual effort to wed the new with the old, many teachers find themselves resorting to two parallel programs: "We do basals in the morning and literature in the afternoon." During one afternoon inservice workshop, a very earnest and obviously rather weary teacher aptly expressed her frustration: "I'm dancing as fast as I can." She, like so many conscientious and capable teachers, enthusiastically embraces the *idea* of using literature in the reading program but finds it difficult to rethink the way she structures classroom activities.

Today's teachers are not being asked simply to change or expand the type of materials they use to teach reading and writing; they are being asked to make fundamental changes in the manner in which literacy learning and teaching take place at school. For many, this change means shifting away from classrooms dominated by teacher-directed instruction,

prepackaged materials, and strict teacher control to classrooms characterized by variety and balance in the materials and methods used and where responsibility and control are shared by teacher and students.

Informed by current theories about language, literacy, and learning, teachers face a twofold challenge. First, they must decide on the key components worthy of inclusion in the curriculum. Second, they must decide how these components should be organized to support literacy learning. This chapter describes the rationale underlying a framework for organizing a literature-based curriculum, and provides suggestions to guide teachers in putting the framework into practice.

The Reading/Writing Workshop

One teacher I know began using a structured reading/writing workshop on Tuesdays and Thursdays as a means of "giving a literature-based approach a try." Maureen, the principal at Ron's school, had agreed to this departure from the regular fifth grade reading program provided that the skills were still covered. Ron admitted that Maureen's proviso did not exactly convey a sense of confidence in his new venture, but he was nonetheless excited by the prospect of spurring his unenthusiastic students to enjoy books as much as he did himself.

After a month of trying out some ideas we had shared in several staff-development workshops, Ron asked me to visit his class and observe him and his students at work. It was a few days before Halloween, and Ron had decided to target *The Ghost-Eye Tree* by Bill Martin Jr and John Archambault as the focal point of his workshop.

Ron started the workshop by having the whole group join him in rereading "Little Orphant Annie" by James Whitcomb Riley and "The Old Wife and the Ghost" by James Reeves. They were among several poems that Ron had introduced so far this year; he frequently started the reading/writing workshop by rereading one or two of them. According to Ron, poetry is perfect for numerous rereadings, and using familiar text before going on to a new selection provides a good warm-up to the workshop. Students in his class were encouraged to add personal favorites to their poetry folders and to write original poems to share with the group.

That day, Ron used the two "warm-up" poems as the basis for a strategy lesson in which students discussed the way the poets use language to appeal to the senses or to convey a certain mood. They found verses, lines, and specific words that evoked a particular image or feeling. They compared language and technique between the poems and poets, noting ideas for their own writing. Now Ron was ready to introduce *The Ghost-Eye Tree*.

Ron held up his copy of the book before the class, drawing his students' attention to the title and author and asking them to look at the cover and make predictions about the story. The ominous-looking illustration by Ted Rand depicts the moon peeking through the branches of an immense tree in which an owl lurks. A sinister-looking bat hovers in the background. Several spooky plots were predicted. Ron then read the book aloud, dramatizing the story of two children who are sent to fetch milk on a spooky evening and who must pass the dreaded ghost-eye tree on their way. The story is as much about the caring of an older sister for her brother (although she teases him most of the time) as it is about their "daring and scary" journey past the tree.

After reading the story, Ron asked the students to think about what they might say if they were asked to tell someone what the story was about. Next he asked them to share their ideas with a neighbor or a friend in the class. Finally, several students were called upon to share their thoughts with the whole group. In this way, Ron involved the whole class in the process of distilling the gist of the plot. While most of the students focused on the scary journey, several did talk about the relationship between the brother and sister. One very perceptive child said, "This story is about how a sister loves her little brother." Later Ron told me that he planned to revisit the story at the end of the week, when he would read it aloud once again and have the children observe how the authors and illustrator conveyed mood, setting, and the feelings of the characters.

After the discussion and a brief break came a planning time during which Ron and the students discussed workshop activities. Ron assigned some activities, while the students chose others. Ron noted the names of the students scheduled for one-to-one conferences with him. Then the class reviewed directions for working at a new center focused on their social studies unit. This led to a discussion of problems with the use of the new writing center: Mary Sue complained that Matt and Olin had spent too much time there the day before, preventing her from using the publishing materials. In less than two minutes the children generated an extraordinary number of good suggestions for self-regulation of the time spent in a center. Mary Sue agreed to put the suggestions on a chart. The entire planning time lasted only about five minutes, but in that brief period everyone gained a sense of his or her own responsibilities. This, Ron felt, was of immeasurable importance.

Figure 1
Framework for Organizing a Reading/Writing Workshop

Activity	Grouping	Time allotment*
Shared reading and writing	Whole group	10-15 minutes
Strategy lesson	Whole group	5-10 minutes
Planning time	Whole group	5-10 minutes
Activity time		60-75 minutes
Teacher assisted	One to one, small group	
Independent	Individual (reading or writing); individual or small group (center-based activities, projects, or teacher-assigned follow-up activities)	
Sharing time	Whole group	10-15 minutes

*Time allotments should be kept flexible.

During the remainder of the workshop, Ron worked with small groups and individuals. As part of a study of biographies, several children were creating timelines of significant events in the lives of people about whom they were reading. Three children were collaborating on a research project for social studies. Others were reading books they'd chosen themselves or writing on topics that interested them. Independent activities included both short-term tasks and the continuation of long-term projects. All had been discussed and agreed on during the planning time.

Ron allots 10 to 15 minutes at the end of the workshop for students to share their activities. This serves as an excellent oral language activity, and Ron finds that students gain a feeling of accomplishment when they share their work with others. In addition, a sense of community is fostered when students have this opportunity to learn about and comment on each other's work.

Figure 1 shows the general framework for organizing the reading/writing workshop Ron used in his class. Many teachers have found this outline helpful when they are setting out to replace instructional methods that depend on three ability groups or that focus on one large group. The framework may also be adjusted for use in pull-out programs and as a first step in moving toward a "seamless" day in which there are no fixed periods for instruction in specific areas. Ron told me that in his case the framework provided both him and his students with a predictable structure for planning. "The kids have a definite idea of what's going to happen during workshop, yet there's enough flexibility there to give us a lot of variety in the things we do. The neat thing is that I have a nice balance between direct instruction and independent work. Before this, I thought literature-based meant only independent reading."

Key Components of the Reading Curriculum

The most significant curriculum question for every teacher to consider is "What is most valuable for my students to know and do?" In the case of reading instruction, two words come to mind: variety and balance. Variety in the kinds of materials and activities provided and balance in the ways we engage students in those activities help ensure that every child has access to learning. As teachers gather print materials for use in their classrooms, they should try to include a variety and balance of fiction and nonfiction, picture books and chapter books, materials focused on units of study in the rest of the curriculum, magazines, computer programs, and the students' own writing. Once these materials are collected, teachers then face the challenge of achieving variety and balance in the ways they engage students with literature.

Teacher-Assisted and Independent Activities

Teacher-assisted activities are those in which instruction is largely teacher directed; with independent activities, students work either alone or collaboratively in small groups, without direct adult guidance. In the past, direct instruction dominated the teaching of reading. Teachers worked with students on a single reading selection at a time, exhausting its applications to every conceivable skill before moving on to the next selection. The only independent activity was seatwork—primarily countless workbook pages to complete—assigned by the teacher and designed to keep students busy so that work with small groups could be completed without interruption.

Today, both the nature of and the balance between teacher-directed and independent activities are changing, particularly in literature-based classrooms. Some examples follow.

Teacher-assisted reading and writing. This includes shared reading and writing activities and strategy lessons. Shared reading and writing activities are to some extent inspired by the work of Vygotsky (1962). They allow the teacher to demonstrate acts of literacy for students, who participate to whatever extent they can. In these activities, the teacher and students act together to do something that the students will eventually be expected to do alone. For example, during shared reading the teacher may read aloud to students, encouraging them to participate during and after the reading. After several shared experiences with the same book, students may "reenact" the reading on their own. Shared writing may involve chart work with a group, in which the teacher solicits help from students regarding the content to be included on the chart or the specific wording or spelling.

Strategy lessons, another teacher-assisted activity, are brief, highly focused units of instruction on a specific curriculum objective. These minilessons may deal with capitalization or the use of the comma, or with more abstract concepts such as foreshadowing or the use of descriptive language. Ideas for strategy lessons may present themselves when the class discovers gaps in what is needed to complete a particular task, or they may be prompted by a teacher's observations of students' attempts to try something new. When one teacher noticed that many of her students were placing random marks around the dialogue in their stories, she decided to do a strategy lesson on quotation marks. The children looked through familiar books to find examples of dialogue and discussed how it was punctuated. The purpose of the minilesson was not for students to master the topic, but simply for them to become more aware of something about which they were already interested.

Obviously content for strategy lessons may be drawn from the objectives suggested in a formal curriculum guide. The guide then becomes a monitoring device rather than a list of skills to be addressed sequentially. As one third grade teacher put it, "Our guide keeps me reminded of the things I need to focus on. For me, it's like checking up. I need to know that when I teach this way I'm still covering what the district wants."

Independent reading and writing. These sorts of activities are fundamental to a literature-based reading program. Although some of the reading and writing activities in a literature-based classroom may be assigned or "prompted" by the teacher, students need plenty of time for silent reading and independent writing on topics of their own choice. Opportunities for short-term and long-term independent work in activity centers and on projects must also be part of the daily program. Built into these independent activities, however, must be a system for providing teacher guidance when needed and feedback for students on their work. This tells the student that independent work is valued and is no less important than teacher-directed activities. In fact, it is independent activities that best foster ongoing literacy learning.

Even when independent work is assigned, some degree of choice should be built in. For example, one teacher asked her sixth graders to write a letter to the author of their choice. (One student's letter to Lucy Maud Montgomery, author of *Anne of Green Gables*, appears in Figure 2.) Although all of the students were engaged in the same process, each was encouraged to respond to the assignment in a personal way. Writing assignments can, of course, focus on responses to the literature students are reading; however, a significant amount of writing time should be set aside for students to create their own literature. Reading and writing to complete science and social studies projects should also be part of every child's daily activities.

Rereading.   There is a growing awareness of the value of rereading familiar stories and poems as either a teacher-assisted or an independent activity. Rereading helps students develop fluency and self-confidence as readers. Rather than studying a single selection at a time and then leaving it for good, children in literature-based programs are encouraged to read many texts and to return to them often for a variety of purposes. A child might choose independently to reread a book she has enjoyed previously. Another book or story might be reread as the focus of a whole group activity. Yet another selection might be used as a source for some social studies research.

Rereading can also be more formal in design. In partner reading, for example, two students take turns reading selections aloud to one another. In Readers Theatre students take on assigned roles from a book and reread the selection as a play (one student may serve as narrator, reading all the portions of the text that are not in dialogue form). In story theater, some students read while others act out the selection. Rereading is needed so that the readers can perform well and give the right instructions to the actors. To confirm predic-

Figure 2
A Sixth-Grader Writes to Her Favorite Author

Dear Mrs. Montgomery,

I am your biggest fan. I cherish the books you've written on Anne. Every book is like growing up with her. I have three books on Anne (the first three). I couldn't bring myself to read them but then I started and there was no end to them or the fun. I am on number four in the "Anne" series.

(I know you're dead, but I'm pretending you're not, just like Anne would have done.)

I have passed on the enjoyment of your books to my teacher, Mrs. Dillon, my schoolmates, and I'm still working on my younger sister. I hope to get your other books. You are my number one author, just like Anne is my number one character. I'm collecting all of your books. Anne is just so real I can't stop reading about her.

When I read your books I travel into another world with Anne and we are very best friends.

I wish you were alive. How much would loved to meet the creator of loving, caring, irresistable, Anne. I'm considered a different child by my peers. I've heard I act like a baby and an adult but I'm only twelve.

I'd have loved to have lunch or chat with you. (Although I doubt there is any chance of that.) I forgot to tell you about myself. My parents are divorced. I live with my father and sister Deborah, she is a year younger than me. Thank you for giving the world Anne.

Your faithful friend,
Laura

P.S. I just love Davy.

tions, to identify the most exciting, scariest, or funniest part of a book, or to develop expression in reading dialogue, teachers might direct students to reread selected parts of a text. In a read along, students read silently while listening to a tape recording of the selection or to a fluent reader reading aloud. With choral reading, students read aloud together, usually with the teacher as lead reader, while with echo reading, students "echo" a fluent reader's rendition of a selection, usually one sentence at a time. Students might also reread to plan a play or puppet production of a text.

Flexible Grouping

Many teachers still look to ability grouping as the primary means of tailoring instruction to different students' needs. The practice works this way: At the beginning of the school year, two or three groups are formed on the basis of students' ability levels. These groups remain virtually unchanged throughout the year. As the range of materials in the classroom and the interests of the students begin to develop and expand, however, so does the need for different kinds of collaborations and group interactions. For that reason, teachers in literature-based programs tend to engage in flexible grouping. The literature-based classroom makes use of whole group and one-to-one instruction as well as a variety of small groups that frequently change in composition.

Whole group instruction. This traditional type of grouping has a very important role in the literature-based classroom. As shown in Figure 1, a reading/writing workshop may begin and end with whole group activities. These activities can include shared reading and writing, reading aloud by the teacher, response activities, and strategy lessons. Whole group instruction ensures that all

students have some common experiences, including knowledge of a common repertoire of literature that can form the basis of strategy lessons. It offers every child equal access to some portion of the literacy activities in the classroom, and it provides an opportunity to spin off into unit work of all types.

One second grade teacher uses fiction, nonfiction, and poetry related to science and social studies as the basis for much of the shared reading and writing in her classroom, thus providing the base for a host of related activities. According to this teacher, "When we're heavy into dinosaurs or a weather unit, I always integrate it into our workshop. It saves time and makes sense to the children."

Small group instruction. Working in smaller groups has the advantage of allowing teachers and students to collaborate in a more intimate manner than is possible with one large group. In small groups, teachers can gear instruction to the needs, interests, and abilities of particular students. Literature-response groups, research groups, interest groups, strategy groups, and collaborative groups are all typical in literature-based classrooms. Single-selection grouping makes use of all of these types of groups when students are studying the same text.

The literature-response group, in which students share ideas about the material they are reading, is one of the most popular forms of small group instruction in literature-based classrooms. These groups may be teacher or student led; either way, they provide excellent support for reading comprehension. If students are reading the same book, the teacher may give a prompt for them to keep in mind as they read. Students' responses to the prompt act as a springboard for later group discussion. Responses may be written in journals or simply talked over.

If each student is reading a different book, more general prompts may be used to get the discussion going. For example, if the students are all reading fiction, they can be asked to describe their favorite character and then share specific passages that show how the author revealed what the character is like. Students reading nonfiction may want to share one or two facts they have learned from their reading. Some prompts should require students to compare and contrast different books, authors, and illustrators, as well as to reflect on their own experiences in light of those depicted in literature. Discussions such as these help students move beyond the literal meaning of a specific book to interpret text within the context of both the literary and the real world.

Research groups, in which students work collaboratively, are useful vehicles for exploring specific areas of a larger unit of study. The composition of these groups can change from project to project. The group activity can culminate in producing a finished work, such as a collaboratively written informational book. Such a book—complete with a table of contents, a dedication, and chapters and illustrations prepared by different members of the group—may become part of an oral presentation to the entire class and later be displayed in the class library.

Interest groups may be formed around topics, genres, or authors that appeal to certain groups of children. As with research groups, these should be heterogeneous and their activities should be short term, lasting only a few weeks. Interest groups may be organized by the teacher or grow spontaneously out of the common interest of a few students. In one second grade class, the students formed a Vera B. Williams Club. Their teacher had met the author at a conference at a nearby university. When she returned with several au-tographed Williams books, the children were eager to have them read aloud. Over the next few weeks four girls formed a small group, in which they took turns reading and rereading Williams's books almost daily during independent reading time. They also wrote to the author and borrowed phrasing and ideas from her books for their own writing.

With strategy groups, teachers group children to focus on a specific skill or strategy, sometimes as a follow-up to teaching that skill or strategy to the whole class. In some cases the purpose may be to reinforce the strategy for those who need additional instruction. For others, the teacher may use small group work to extend the strategy to more advanced applications. A strategy group may include as few as two or three students, and may meet only once or twice.

Collaborative groups allow students to act as both teachers and learners as they work together to achieve a common goal. Students may work in pairs or small groups to respond to literature, conduct research on various topics, work in activity centers, or solve problems and share findings about something that has been presented to the whole group. In order to keep these groups working productively, teachers use a variety of techniques to ensure that everyone knows who should be doing what at each stage.

One fourth grade teacher introduces group work to her students in a slow, deliberate manner early in the year. She models strategies that she wants small groups to emulate when they work independently later on. This teacher feels that showing rather than telling goes a long way toward helping youngsters learn how to function in small groups: "When I urge children to frame questions and call on others to answer them or to summarize our whole group discussion, I am providing practice for activities I hope children will ultimately do on their own." Sometimes she calls on four or five children to model group processes while the remainder of the class sits in a circle around them and watches them work. "I let them take turns modeling for the others," she says. "I use the same approach to demonstrate how to work at centers, make use of our classroom library, and work collaboratively on independent projects." Taking time to model, discuss, and evaluate work behavior can go a long way toward ensuring a productive, well-disciplined classroom.

Single-selection flexible grouping, like strategy grouping, makes use of whole group *and* small group instruction. After a particular selection has been taught to the entire group, instruction can be continued with small groups while others work independently. This allows teachers to use a selection or group of selections as the basis for themed work with the entire class, while providing extra instruction for those who need help. The small groups in this type of arrangement may include research groups and other types of response groups as well.

One-to-one instruction.   This type of instruction often takes the form of teacher-pupil conferences about the student's reading or writing. Such conferences are important not only because they personalize instruction but also because they allow teachers to monitor the progress of individual students. A typical reading conference begins with questions and discussion about a book the child is reading independently. Since teachers cannot be familiar with every book a child might select, some general questions may be used to get the discussion started: Why did you select this book? How does it compare with other books by this author? How does it compare with other stories of the same type? What is the best part so far? Next the child selects a brief portion of the book to read aloud. The teacher should record his or her impressions about the conference in a special reading conference notebook. Figure 3 shows a page from a third grade teacher's notebook.

Figure 3
Sample Entry in a Reading Conference Notebook

Student's name ___Billy___

Date	Book title & author	Comments
4/6	Henry and Mudge + the Happy Cat Cynthia Rylant	3rd book in Mudge series. Growing in fluency, confidence. Still overly dependent on phonics.

Responses to Literature

Lack of variety in the way we ask children to respond to literature can lead to boredom and perhaps to a dislike of reading. Children generally enjoy doing story maps, for example, but requiring one for every story will induce some well-deserved groans after a while. Many of the rereading strategies discussed previously are good, varied methods of getting children to respond to literature. After reading a selection aloud to students, some teachers simply ask them to think about some aspect of the reading and then share their ideas with a neighbor and perhaps with the entire group. This kind of response involves everyone and can be done at any point during the reading.

More elaborate means of generating responses may accompany the study of a novel. One sixth grade teacher has his class study at least four novels each year. Two of the novels are selected on the basis of social studies and science themes typically taught at the sixth grade level. The other two are selected on the basis of the teacher's preferences and recommendations from previous students.

Before introducing *My Brother Sam Is Dead* by James and Christopher Collier to his students, this teacher read through each chapter, noting the various points that seemed to offer opportunities for specific instruction. He then introduced the book, giving some background information about the authors and the Revolutionary War period in U.S. history in which the book takes place. Next he directed students to write an entry in their response journals on what they thought the book might be about. After reading the first chapter aloud, the teacher discussed it with his students and had them return to their journals to revise their initial entries. As subsequent chapters were assigned, he sometimes offered prompts to the students about things they might consider as they read. The students met regularly to share their responses in small groups and as a class.

As this class moves through a book, the students respond to assigned chapters in various ways. Sometimes they write in journals about any aspect of the chapter they wish. Sometimes they are asked to focus on a particular character or episode. They may be asked to link this book or its author with others they have read or with their content area lessons; or they may focus on some literary element, such as metaphorical language or plot structure. In addition to writing in their response journals, students may be asked to share some idea related to the text with a friend or family member. Some books relate to other books, poems, or music, and the teacher may ask students to explore these links. Offering a variety of means of responding to literature not only helps to keep the reading interesting, it also allows students with different talents and learning approaches to find multiple ways to strengthen their understanding and their enjoyment.

Informal Assessment

Assessment in literature-based classrooms can take many forms. Teachers can keep a variety of running records (Clay, 1985), checklists, and anecdotal records as they observe children's literacy development. A simple checklist used during one-to-one conferences can yield valuable information about students' ability to apply reading strategies. Conferences may also be tape-recorded. The recordings, along with written comments, provide excellent documentation of each student's reading progress over time.

A typical checklist for evaluating oral reading focuses on the reader's comprehension of the text and includes such items as these:

- Reads familiar material fluently.

- Reads with appropriate expression.

- Makes corrections to preserve meaning.

- Observes punctuation to construct meaning.

- Takes risks in pronunciation.

- When confronting unfamiliar words—
  skips the word, continues to read;
  rereads the sentence;
  uses context clues;
  uses picture clues;
  attempts to sound out;
  asks another person
  (Fairfax County Office of Curriculum Services, 1987, p. 45; reproduced by permission).

Teachers can make use of checklists to monitor students during group instruction as well. Lists of items related to aspects of reading comprehension and to attitudes about reading can be generated and used while students are responding to stories read aloud or while they are sharing their responses to books they have read independently (Strickland et al., 1989).

Making the Move

Teachers, administrators, and students are enthusiastic about new approaches to the use of literature in the reading program. Literature-based programs offer a greater degree of flexibility and autonomy to teachers and students. For many teachers, however, the move toward more holistic approaches requires adopting a new theoretical paradigm for making daily decisions about teaching and learning. This can be particularly perplexing as it relates to organizing and managing the instructional day. I hope this chapter has provided a framework and some specific instructional suggestions that teachers, administrators, and students can use to put literature-based programs effectively in place.

References

Clay, M. (1985). *The early detection of reading difficulties*. Portsmouth, NH: Heinemann.

Fairfax County Office of Curriculum Services. (1987). *Suggestions for assessment/evaluation in the integrated language arts classroom*. Fairfax County, VA: Author.

Strickland, D.S., Dillon, R.M., Funkhouser, L., Glick, M., & Rogers, C. (1989). Classroom dialogue during literature response groups. *Language Arts, 66*, 192-200.

Vygotsky, L. (1962). *Thought and language*. Cambridge, MA: MIT Press.

Children's Books

Collier, J.L., & Collier, C. (1974). *My brother Sam is dead*. New York: Four Winds.

Martin, Bill, Jr, & Archambault, J. (1985). *The ghost-eye tree*. (Ill. by T. Rand.) New York: Henry Holt.

CHAPTER 11

Responding to Literature: Activities for Exploring Books

Linda DeGroff
Lee Galda

Working within the framework of a literature-based curriculum is not easy—at least it's not easy to do right. Babbitt speaks eloquently about some of the dangers inherent in the rush to implement literature-based curricula in her article "Protecting Children's Literature" (1990). She acknowledges the value of using fiction rather than basal texts to teach reading, but voices her concern that some teachers may be treating works of fiction as if they were basals. Real stories are being saddled with "a related workbook with sentences to complete, quizzes, questions to think about, and all kinds of suggested projects." She worries that "this will make a dry and tedious thing out of fiction" (p. 697).

Using trade books in the same way we have used basals works against the very idea we are trying to promote. Trade books have become part of the curriculum because we hope they will interest children and help them become literate in the full sense of the word. Given this goal, it is important to let the trade books be as interesting as they can be. It is important not to ruin the power of trade books by turning them into nothing more than material for exercises, mere sources of information on topics or for teaching moral lessons.

We know that when we read, we activate our own personal schemata. However, the stance we take when reading informational material is fundamentally different from the stance we take when reading fiction. As explained by Rosenblatt (1982), when we read informational text, our primary purpose is efferent—to carry away information that we can do something with. When we read fiction or poetry, our primary purpose is aesthetic—to live for a while in the spell of a good book, to have a virtual experience with the text, to feel pleasure in its words and rhythm and in the images and emotions it evokes as we read. We do damage if we ask our students to read a work of fiction or poetry for information, to find facts. It is damaging because fiction and poetry are intended to be read aesthetically. So workbook-like exercises and preset questions and projects, most of which force readers into an efferent stance, work against our goal of providing children with pleasurable experiences with literature. Some speculate, in fact, that a literature-workbook-quiz-project cycle may be worse than the basals.

What happens when readers and books meet is fragile and complex. Reader-response theory and research, as well as reports from teachers about the way children read in their classrooms, attest to the unpredictability, complexity, and power of the act of reading. By reading, readers turn literature into their own stories and poems and derive information that is meaningful for them. By reading, readers create meaning for themselves, and that meaning is not always the same for all readers.

Rosenblatt, one of the first theorists to describe the active role readers play in creating meaning, argues that a literary work exists only in the live circuit set up between the reader and the text (1976, 1978). Readers infuse intellectual and emotional meaning into what they read; the meaning they create is shaped by their experiences. Because no two people have had exactly the same experiences, no two readings are exactly the same. The meaning of a text will even change with each reading by one individual: We construct new meanings each time we read a book because time and new experiences have made us different people.

We can, however, reach some measure of consensus about the meaning of a text. This consensus is possible because our experiences overlap to some extent and we share certain understandings of word denotations. At the same time, we all contribute unique understandings and constructions of meaning. In a classroom grounded in collaborative learning and a belief in the worth of each student, this combination of consensual meaning and individual significance is a natural and important part of reading and responding to literature.

Because of the fragile and unique nature of individual response, our curricula should focus not on the literature or the topics or skills that we are seeking to cover, but on the response, on the mind of the reader as it meets the books. When we consider students' responses as the heart of the reading curriculum, we give value to their unique experiences, prejudices, personal tastes, and understandings. We include their responses not only to the world of the book, but to their personal worlds as well. And we can't prescribe or predict what those responses will be.

A response-centered curriculum provides numerous opportunities for students to read and respond to literature, both fiction and nonfiction. It is one in which teachers and librarians value the diversity of what children have to say about a book and understand the importance of peers in shaping an individual's reading and response. The talk that surrounds reading helps readers clarify and expand their understandings about texts and their strategies for reading. And teachers and librarians working in this sort of curriculum know that children need time to read and respond to text, and to explore their own responses. The response of the individual must come first. Activities designed to develop children as readers and responders and to move them from pleasure to understanding to deeper appreciation can come later.

It is in this spirit that we offer some examples of planned activities—intended to be introduced after reading and individual response have occurred—that will help students come to know how literary texts work. It is our conviction that by building on the initial individual pleasure and understanding that young readers bring to books, we can help them appreciate the author's craft. This, in turn, can increase the potential for pleasure and understanding that they will bring to the next book they read.

Responding to Style

Children grow as language users when they become aware of, learn to appreciate, and begin to experiment with a range of styles in their own reading and writing. To help children grow we draw their attention to authors' choices of such things as topic, genre, and language. The following activity, designed for the early elementary grades, guides readers in drawing comparisons among texts and illustrations in books by several authors, all of whom address a common idea. Next, in an activity for the intermediate grades, we look at how readers might compare different authors' works from a single genre. We conclude with an activity for the upper elementary grades that suggests how students might explore style in an in-depth study of the works of a single author.

Single Topic, Different Authors

This activity is designed to help children in the primary grades notice how authors treat the same topics or ideas in their own ways. *Mouse Paint* by Ellen Stoll Walsh, *Planting a Rainbow* by Lois Ehlert, and *Growing Colors* by Bruce McMillan are all concerned with color. (This is only one possible theme to explore; any group of books about a single con-

Figure 1
A Comparison of Three Books

	Mouse Paint	*Planting a Rainbow*	*Growing Colors*
Type of Illustration	collage	paint	photographs
Objects Illustrated	mice and paint	plants (flowers)	fruits and vegetables
Colors	white, red, blue, yellow, orange, green, purple	red, orange, yellow, green, blue, purple	red, orange, yellow, green, blue, purple, tan, brown, white, black
What We Learn	You learn about mixing colors. The mice hide from the cat so it's like a story.	You learn about different flowers.	You learn about things to eat.

cept or theme—friendship, family, dinosaurs, or the sea, for example—could be explored to equal advantage.) Comparing books such as these three helps children notice similarities and differences in other books they read and hear. Comparisons also help them understand that books are linked to other books.

Procedure.   Over a day or two, read and explore these three books with your students, encouraging them to look at the books independently or in small groups. Begin the activity by taking the books, a piece of chart paper divided into two columns labeled "Like" and "Different," and markers with you into the reading corner. Reread the books if you think the children don't have them firmly in mind. Then start a discussion by asking "How are these books like each other?" Someone will certainly mention that they all deal with color and are themselves brightly colored. After listing the similarities generated by the students in the "Like" column, ask for differences (which are often given spontaneously) and list these in the "Different" column. You can then organize the children's ideas in a chart that reflects points of comparison across the texts. It may look something like the chart in Figure 1.

The Style of Poetry

The purpose of the following activity is to help students recognize distinctive elements of an individual writer's style. *Chocolate Dreams* by Arnold Adoff, *The Way Things Are and Other Poems* by Myra Cohn Livingston, *The New Kid on the Block* by Jack Pre-

Bonbons act as
cheerleaders in
Chocolate Dreams.

lutsky, *Where the Sidewalk Ends* by Shel Silverstein, and *All the Small Poems* by Valerie Worth are collections of poetry suitable for the intermediate grades. (Other genres also lend themselves to this kind of activity. In the primary grades, you could, for example, compare the various picture storybooks by Steven Kellogg, Cynthia Rylant, Maurice Sendak, or William Steig. In the upper grades, you might compare works of historical fiction and biography by writers such as Russell Freedman, Jean Fritz, Scott O'Dell, or Elizabeth Speare.)

Procedure. Over a short period of time read aloud from each of these poetry books and encourage your students to look through these and other books by the same authors.

When your students have had ample time to explore the poems of these authors, break your class into five small groups. Give each group one book (or a number of books by the same author) and ask the students to spend about ten minutes taking turns reading aloud their favorite poems to the group. Then give them a list of questions like this one:

- What topic(s) does this author usually write about?

- Are this author's poems usually humorous or serious?

- Are this author's poems usually rhymed or unrhymed?

- Do this author's poems usually have a regular rhythm or does the rhythm vary?

- Are this author's poems usually long or short?

- Do this author's poems usually tell a story or describe something?

- How do you usually feel after reading this author's poems?

Students should discuss the questions as a group, using specific poems to come to an agreement on a collective answer for each question. When they have their answers, each group should present to the whole class a concise description of the work of their particular poet. They can then post the information in a written display along with some representative poems.

Follow-up activities can include a "Name that Poet" game in which you read aloud a poem and ask students to identify the poet. You can also challenge each group to find poems by their author that do not conform to the pattern they have described. These poems can be included as "stumpers" in the Name that Poet game.

A Writer of Many Genres

This activity is designed to help upper elementary students recognize variations of style within any one author's work. For example, you can use *I Am Phoenix*, *Joyful Noise*, *Graven Images*, *Saturnalia*, and *Rear-View Mirrors*—books with very different subjects and styles, all by Paul Fleischman. (Fleischman has also written a number of other books that could be substituted for these.) Other authors whose work includes books from different genres include Jean Craighead George, Virginia Hamilton, Kathryn Lasky, Lois Lowry, Katherine Paterson, and Jane Yolen.

Procedure. Read aloud from *I Am Phoenix* and *Joyful Noise*, Fleischman's poetry collections. Next, have students choral read a few of these poems. This type of reading, for which these poems are designed, will help students gain a "feel" for the language. Now discuss the form and quality of sound evident in Fleischman's poems and record on chart paper the characteristics that students notice.

Figure 2
Works of Paul Fleischman

	I Am Phoenix	*Joyful Noise*	*Graven Images*	*Saturnalia*
Genre	poetry	poetry	short stories	historical fiction
Themes/ Subjects	birds	insects	idolatry	masters and servants; hatred; Puritan Boston
Special Qualities	musical, two-voice construction	musical, two-voice construction	supernatural	entwining stories

Comments: Both volumes of poetry and *Saturnalia* have a musical quality in their structure. Music is important in *Saturnalia*. *Saturnalia* and two stories in *Graven Images* are set in Colonial times in the U.S. and examine both wicked and humorous aspects of people. Neither volume of poetry is about people. All of the books are full of interesting, unusual words.

After discussing Fleischman as a poet, read aloud over a period of three days the three stories in *Graven Images*. Discuss characters, setting, theme, and genre, again noting on chart paper the characteristics that students identify. Next read *Saturnalia*, a novel set in Boston in the 17th century. Discuss the novel, encouraging your students to comment on its setting, characters, and structure.

At this point your students will be able to chart similarities and differences in the works of Paul Fleischman. Students can summarize their findings with comments listed at the bottom of the chart. The chart might look something like the one in Figure 2.

Some students might like to go on to read *Rear-View Mirrors*, a work of contemporary realistic fiction for young adults (or another of Fleischman's books), noting similarities among this novel and the books read in class.

Responding to Character

Children are drawn to books with vivid and memorable characters. When children respond to characters, they notice such things as the characters' traits, how they act and react to events, and how they resolve conflicts. The following activities demonstrate how you might explore character by graphing the impact of events on a character, by writing poetry that responds to character traits and behaviors, and by charting the growth of a character who is in conflict with the environment.

Graphing a Book

The following graphing activity is designed to help students in the intermediate grades recall memorable events in E.B. White's *Charlotte's Web*, organize them into sequence, and evaluate the effect of each event on one of the main characters, Wilbur the pig. This activity is suitable for any book full of adventure and with a main character whose fortunes rise and fall with events. For example, you might try this activity with primary students if you are reading picture storybooks such as *The Tale of Peter Rabbit* by Beatrix Potter, *Ira Sleeps Over* by Bernard Waber, or *Sylvester and the Magic Pebble* by William Steig. (Note:

This activity is based on an idea from Johnson & Louis, 1987.)

Procedure. After reading *Charlotte's Web*, ask students to recall memorable events. List these on the chalkboard. Next ask students to tell which event happened first, second, and so forth. Write the corresponding numerals in front of each event and recopy the events in sequence on the bottom of a piece of chart paper.

Wilbur, who really is some pig, meets a special spider in *Charlotte's Web*.

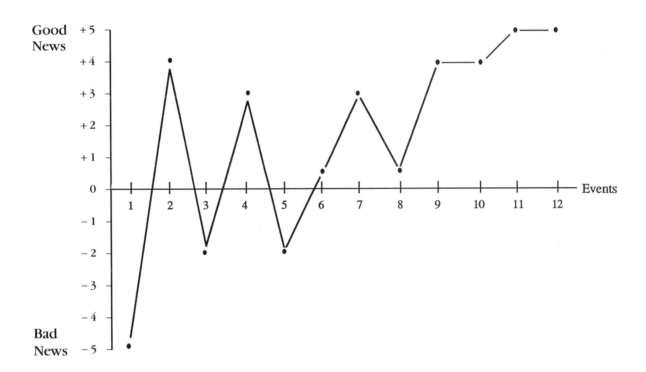

Figure 3
The Rise and Fall of Wilbur's Fortunes

Events in Plot

1. Mr. Arable gets the ax.
2. Mr. Arable gives Wilbur to Fern.
3. Goose helps Wilbur escape.
4. Wilbur hears a voice in the night.
5. Sheep notices Wilbur is gaining weight.
6. Wilbur tries to spin web.
7. Charlotte notices that people are gullible.
8. Avery breaks the goose egg.
9. Charlotte writes "Some Pig!"
10. Wilbur wins a special award.
11. Templeton bites Wilbur's tail.
12. Wilbur meets Joy, Aranea, and Nellie.

DeGroff & Galda

Now sketch out two axes of a graph on the chart paper. The horizontal one will represent the events, while the vertical will indicate the impact of each event on Wilbur. Have children evaluate the effect of each event. Was it good news or bad news for Wilbur? Place a point on the graph where the event number and the good news – bad news rating coincide. Now connect the points to form a graph. The completed graph might resemble the one in Figure 3.

Individual students or small groups might like to prepare their own graphs for the fortunes of characters in other books.

Character Poems

The next activity is intended to encourage students to respond to favorite characters by creating poems based on those characters' names. Each line of the "name poem" begins with a letter from a character's name and is followed by a word, phrase, or sentence that reveals a students' thoughts on that character's physical traits, actions, or feelings. Students may enjoy responding to people in works of nonfiction as well as fictional characters.

Procedure. Introduce students to this activity by sharing with them some name poems you've written yourself. Here are three examples—for Wilbur from *Charlotte's Web*, Winnie from Natalie Babbitt's *Tuck Everlasting*, and Gilly from Katherine Paterson's *The Great Gilly Hopkins*—to get you started:

Wilbur
_____

Whiny,
Imitating,
Lovable,
But
Unpredictable
Runt.

Winnie
_____

Wondering, then wandering
Into the wood
Nearby.
Never guessing
Its secret about for-
Ever.

Gilly
_____

Giving up fear and hate
Is hard when you've had
Little
Love. But
You did.

Now have students recall some of their own favorite characters from books they have read. List these on the chalkboard to provide the class with some names to select from. They can, of course, think up other names later on. Students can then participate in writing poems in a variety of ways. Several students who want to write on the same character may be more comfortable and productive collaborating on a poem; others may prefer working independently. To help students get started, suggest that they brainstorm words and phrases that describe the chosen character, that are associated with memorable events from the book, or that describe the setting or minor characters. After allowing time for drafting, revising, and editing, celebrate the final products by placing the poems on display.

Encourage students to respond to new characters they meet throughout the year by writing name poems for them as well.

Conflict in Survival Tales

Survival tales, often read by upper grade students, show a character in conflict with the environment. The conflict (or series of conflicts) is resolved as the character discovers ways of coping with the outside world of nature. At the same time, the character comes to important discoveries about the inner world of the self.

The "comparison chart" activity that follows shows one way to explore conflict with the environment while also examining the character's development, behavior, and attitudes. The description focuses on Gary Paulsen's *Hatchet*, but comparison charts would work with characters from many other survival tales. *Homecoming* by Cynthia Voigt, *Julie of the Wolves* by Jean Craighead George, *The Sign of the Beaver* by Elizabeth George Speare, or *Z for Zachariah* by Robert O'Brien would all be appropriate choices.

Procedure. Draw three columns—headed "Conflict or Problem," "Outer Discovery," and "Inner Discovery"—on a large sheet of paper. Tell students that they will be keeping track of the problems or conflicts that Brian faces as you read the book aloud or while they read in small groups or independently. In addition, they will be noting how these problems are solved and how Brian's feelings and attitudes change.

After each reading session, work with students as they record their observations. The example in Figure 4 shows observations that might be recorded after reading Chapter 5. Note that because there is not always a direct relationship between conflict and discoveries, some cells in the chart will be empty—at least at the outset.

As the chart fills, ask students to consider the pattern in Brian's development. Is there a steady, positive progression, or are there lapses and regressions? Brian's development, like that of most characters in survival tales, is marked by temporary retreats into depression and panic, but students should be able to see quite easily that the overall trend is toward strength and wisdom.

Figure 4
Charting Brian's Development

Conflict or Problem	Outer Discovery	Inner Discovery
Thirsty	Learns that the lake water is safe to drink, but too much makes him ill.	Feels alone and has nothing.
Hungry		Thinks positively.
	Takes stock of possessions	"You are your most valuable asset."
Needs shelter	Becomes aware of creatures in the woods.	Must help himself.

Responding to Structure

In literature we find certain recurring structures. Children who are aware of these structures are able to use their knowledge to predict events in stories and explore relationships among facts and concepts in informational books. In the following activities we suggest ways in which teachers can help students become aware of the rising, falling, cyclical, and episodic nature of plot structures; explore organization in their own lives and relate it to events in informational books; and notice how authors make use of comparison as a way of organizing and presenting scientific facts.

A Variety of Story Maps

The three story-mapping activities that follow are designed to help children in the primary grades develop basic understandings of plot. By studying plot, children learn to identify patterns that appear over and over again in the books they read. With older students, plot maps can be drawn to focus on key events in particular chapters or to discover the shapes of whole books. You might try mapping the rise to climax and quick resolution in *The Great Gilly Hopkins* by Katherine Paterson, the cyclical return-to-home structure in *The Book of Three* by Lloyd Alexander, or the episodic story structures in Beverly Cleary's Ramona books or Laura Ingalls Wilder's Little House books.

Procedure. Read aloud *The Tub People* by Pam Conrad, *Who's Sick Today?* by Lynne Cherry, and *Will's Mammoth* by Rafe Martin and allow children to exhaust their spontaneous responses to the books. Once they are very familiar with the books, ask the children to recall important events in one of the stories,

starting from the beginning. Write their ideas on chart paper or the chalkboard, adding any major events that the children leave out.

Now show the children how the events can be organized into a map that gives the "shape" of the story. A story map for *The Tub People* might take the shape of a mountain with a gradual incline to a peak and then a sharp decline. This would reflect the mounting tension as one of the Tub People gets trapped in the drain and the quick resolution when he's rescued. The story map can help point out shifts in setting, too. In this case, the story starts in the tub and the plot line takes the characters to a different setting (the windowsill) at the end.

A story map for *Will's Mammoth*, which begins and ends in the same place, might take the form of a circle. Compare this map with the one for *The Tub People*. Help children notice how the map of *The Tub People* reflects the different settings at the beginning and end of the story while that of *Will's Mammoth* is cyclical.

Some books have episodic structures with a series of equally important events. *Who's Sick Today?* uses a question-and-answer structure that is of an episodic nature. A story map might list the questions and corresponding answers, showing that all the events have equal significance and can be arranged only by the order in which they occur in the story.

Versatile Charts

Charting activities can be used in the primary grades to help children see organization in their personal experiences and to relate this knowledge to the ways ideas are organized in books. The activity that follows concerns *Farming* by Gail Gibbons, but children can

Figure 5
Activities of a Farm Family

	Outside	Inside
Spring	Put cows out to pasture. Plant vegetable garden. Finish making maple syrup. Lug water to the chicken house. Fertilize, plow, harrow, and plant fields.	Clean stalls. Care for baby chicks. Tend new baby animals. Milk cows in morning and evening.
Summer	Gather vegetables. Collect honey. Mow, rake, and bale hay.	Can and freeze vegetables. Collect eggs each day. Have vet give calves checkups. Milk cows twice a day. Put hay in loft.
Fall	After chores, go to school. Pack eggs for delivery. Harvest remaining fruits and vegetables. Harvest cornfields. Fill silo with corn. Pack hayloft.	Sell apples at farm stand. Put canned goods on shelves. Sell animals at market. Sell milk.
Winter	Plow roads. Lug water to the chicken house.	Repair and clean machinery. Milk cows. Tend animals in barn. Cook vegetables. Do bookkeeping and plan next year's crops. Go to bed early.

also create similar charts for books structured according to seasons, months, or days of the week. Books such as *First Comes Spring* by Anne Rockwell, *The Little House* by Virginia Lee Burton, *The Very Hungry Caterpillar* by Eric Carle, and *Chicken Soup with Rice* by Maurice Sendak would be appropriate.

Procedure. Prepare two charts on large paper. Print the seasons of the year on the left side of each chart and "Outside" and "Inside" across the top.

Review the seasons of the year with the class. Ask children to think of things they do outside and inside the house during each season. Some things, especially those done inside the house, can be done during any season; these things are perfectly acceptable to include. Write the children's responses about their own experiences on one chart.

Now read *Farming* aloud. Ask the children to notice what the farm family does outside and inside the house during each season as you read. Use the second chart to record children's observations of events on the farm. The chart will look something like the one in Figure 5.

Have the children compare the experiences listed on the two charts. They should notice that some events change with the seasons and others happen around the year.

The charts can be saved so that later comparisons with other personal experiences and books can be made. You could also consider working with children to develop similar charts to help them write reports or narratives about personal experiences.

Comparing Information

Forming comparisons is one way that authors can organize their writing. When we read informational books with students, we should draw their attention to this form of organization. Being conscious of comparison helps both comprehension and writing.

The following activity is designed to help students in the intermediate grades explore *Animal Fact/Animal Fable* by Seymour Simon and *The News about Dinosaurs* by Patricia Lauber, two books that compare myth with fact and old information with new. This

Figure 6
A Comparison Chart about Dinosaurs

Old Ideas	The News Is
Scientists have discovered all the dinosaurs.	New kinds of dinosaurs are being found all the time.
Dinosaurs were slow, clumsy walkers.	Dinosaurs were quick and nimble walkers.
The brontosaurus was a newly discovered species of dinosaur.	The "brontosaurus" is really the head and body of two different dinosaurs.

activity may be extended to the study of comparisons in fiction and poetry.

Procedure. After reading *Animal Fact/ Animal Fable*, prepare a chart with columns labeled "Fable" and "Fact." Work with students to help them sort information from the book into the appropriate columns. A similar chart can be developed for *The News about Dinosaurs*, which compares outdated thinking with current understanding about dinosaurs. The chart might look like the one in Figure 6.

Draw students' attention to other books or sections of books that are organized around comparisons. Students can also be encouraged to create comparison charts as they organize for writing reports, personal narratives, or even poetry.

Juggling in the Classroom

Teaching a literature-based curriculum requires the timing, sensitivity, and agility of juggling. Pleasure, individual response, and the study of literature each must enter the act at the right time, be supported, and be moved along in appropriate directions by teachers and librarians—the ultimate jugglers. As we said at the start, it isn't easy; but we are sure it is worth it.

References
Babbitt, N. (1990). Protecting children's literature. *The Horn Book Magazine, 66*(6), 696-703.

Johnson, T.D., & Louis, D.R. (1987). *Literacy through literature*. Portsmouth, NH: Heinemann.

Rosenblatt, L.M. (1976). *Literature as exploration*. New York: Noble & Noble.

Rosenblatt, L.M. (1978). *The reader, the text, the poem: The transactional theory of the literary work*. Carbondale, IL: Southern Illinois University Press.

Rosenblatt, L.M. (1982). The literary transaction: Evocation and response. In C.S. Huck, J. Hickman, & F. Zidonis (Eds.), *Theory into practice: Children's literature, 21*(4), 268-277.

Children's Books
Adoff, A. (1989). *Chocolate dreams*. (Ill. by T. MacCombie.) New York: Lothrop, Lee & Shepard.

Alexander, L. (1964). *The book of three*. New York: Henry Holt.

Babbitt, N. (1975). *Tuck everlasting*. New York: Farrar, Straus & Giroux.

Burton, V.L. (1942). *The little house*. Boston, MA: Houghton Mifflin.

Carle, E. (1969). *The very hungry caterpillar*. New York: Philomel.

Cherry, L. (1988). *Who's sick today?* New York: Dutton.

Conrad, P. (1989). *The tub people*. (Ill. by R. Egielski.) New York: HarperCollins.

Ehlert, L. (1988). *Planting a rainbow*. San Diego, CA: Harcourt Brace Jovanovich.

Fleischman, P. (1982). *Graven images*. New York: HarperCollins.

Fleischman, P. (1985). *I am Phoenix*. New York: HarperCollins.

Fleischman, P. (1986). *Rear-view mirrors*. New York: HarperCollins.

Fleischman, P. (1988). *Joyful noise: Poems for two voices*. (Ill. by E. Beddows.) New York: HarperCollins.

Fleischman, P. (1990). *Saturnalia*. New York: HarperCollins.

George, J. (1972). *Julie of the wolves*. New York: HarperCollins.

Gibbons, G. (1988). *Farming*. New York: Holiday House.

Lauber, P. (1989). *The news about dinosaurs*. New York: Bradbury.

Livingston, M.C. (1974). *The way things are and other poems*. New York: Atheneum.

Martin, R. (1989). *Will's mammoth*. (Ill. by S. Gammell.) New York: Putnam.

McMillan, B. (1988). *Growing colors*. New York: Lothrop, Lee & Shepard.

O'Brien, R.C. (1975). *Z for Zachariah*. New York: Atheneum.

Paterson, K. (1978). *The great Gilly Hopkins*. New York: Crowell.

Paulsen, G. (1987). *Hatchet*. New York: Bradbury.

Potter, B. (1901). *The tale of Peter Rabbit*. London: Warne.

Prelutsky, J. (1984). *The new kid on the block*. New York: Greenwillow.

Rockwell, A. (1985). *First comes spring*. New York: Crowell.

Sendak, M. (1962). *Chicken soup with rice*. New York: HarperCollins.

Silverstein, S. (1974). *Where the sidewalk ends*. New York: HarperCollins.

Simon, S. (1979). *Animal fact/animal fable*. New York: Crown.

Speare, E.G. (1983). *The sign of the beaver*. Boston, MA: Houghton Mifflin.

Steig, W. (1969). *Sylvester and the magic pebble*. New York: Windmill.

Voigt, C. (1981). *Homecoming*. New York: Atheneum.

Waber, B. (1972). *Ira sleeps over*. Boston, MA: Houghton Mifflin.

Walsh, E.S. (1989). *Mouse paint*. San Diego, CA: Harcourt Brace Jovanovich.

White, E.B. (1952). *Charlotte's web*. (Ill. by G. Williams.) New York: HarperCollins.

Worth, V. (1987). *All the small poems*. New York: Farrar, Straus & Giroux.

CHAPTER 12

Guiding Principles
The Response to Literature Model
Helping Students Feel the Story

Using Literature with Readers at Risk

Roselmina Indrisano
Jeanne R. Paratore

n 1978 in the preface to *The Reader, the Text, the Poem: The Transactional Theory of the Literary Work*, Louise Rosenblatt wrote, ''A text, once it leaves its author's hands, is simply paper and ink until a reader evokes from it a literary work—sometimes, even, a literary work of art'' (p. ix). In the years that have followed, other researchers and theoreticians, inspired by Rosenblatt's work, have added their insights to the growing body of knowledge about the essential role of the reader in literary response. But while teachers whose students perform at average or higher levels have recently come to appreciate their own influence in guiding students' responses to literature, teachers of disabled readers rarely take advantage of this influence. Research indicates that at-risk readers spend as little as half as much time reading text in class as do their more able peers—and even less time than that in discussion and critical response (Allington, 1983).

In this chapter, we present a model of literary response to assist teachers of students who are challenged by reading and writing. The emphasis on developing prior knowledge, joined to the use of graphic organizers, makes this instructional model appropriate for various types of learners. It is particularly effective for those who experience difficulty in understanding and organizing complex text. This plan is designed to provide students with more opportunities to read longer texts and to guide them in responding to literature. With this model, we hope to expose more children at all levels to the joy of literature.

Guiding Principles

Squire (1990), in studying responses to literature, examined more than 300 investigations in this field conducted over the past 50 years. His conclusions can be summarized according to their emphasis on the reader or the teacher.

The reader:

- Engaging in transactions with the writer is the primary goal of reading and responding to literature.
- Readers and reader responses, including emotional responses, are affected by prior knowledge, past experience, and developmental differences.
- Responses vary with the reader, genre, and mode of presentation.

The teacher:

- Teachers can enhance the points of connection between the reader and the text.
- Reading aloud—particularly poetry and drama—enhances responses.
- Language is critical to response; learning comes from collaboration with others through talking, reflecting, or sharing after reading or writing.
- Literary works of high quality are more likely to evoke response.
- Programs should explicitly teach the processes involved in comprehending and responding.
- The ways students are taught to respond to literature will affect the ways they read literature long after instruction has ended.

In working to develop instructional practices for at-risk children grounded in research on reader response, we concentrated on three types of responses that enhance the literary experience: (1) aesthetic, (2) strategic, and (3) generative. Although here we discuss the three types individually in linear fashion, they are all, in fact, interrelated and occur in an overlapping, recursive way during reading.

The *aesthetic* response is an affective reaction to the text in general. This type of response is limited only by the reader's capacity to understand and relate to the text. As Squire (1990) notes, it is affected by the reader's interests, purposes for reading, emotions, experiences, and background knowledge. The aesthetic response comes from the readers themselves with minimal teacher guidance, and may be generated by the teacher's reading the text to students or by the students' own reading. Note that recent research in the affective domain acknowledges the contribution of both cognition and metacognition to the emotional component of aesthetic response (Schunk, 1985; Winne & Marx, 1989). The evidence suggests that development of cognitive and metacognitive awareness may enhance readers' motivation as well as their attitude toward learning. Such development can occur through explicit strategy instruction.

The *strategic* response is cognitive or metacognitive and occurs in relation to a specific aspect of the text, perhaps its genre or the reasons for reading. While this stage focuses primarily on text comprehension, the development of strategy awareness should ultimately enhance both the aesthetic and the generative responses to literature as well. At-risk readers often require help with this type of response to a text. Teachers can help learners connect with the writer of the text in a number of ways. Such intervention should be guided by Scardamalia and Bereiter's (1983) notion of "procedural facilitation": teachers should structure and organize tasks for the students but should leave them to do the productive thinking. Cooperative grouping is particularly effective with learners at risk (Slavin, Karweit, & Madden, 1989). Paired learning, a form of cooperative grouping, allows students to enjoy the sounds of the language created by the writer through shared reading and rereading. Scaffolding pairs the at-risk learner with the teacher or a more able peer to accomplish a task that the reader is unable to complete independently.

The *generative* response may be aesthetic, cognitive, or metacognitive. It provides an opportunity for the reader to go beyond the aesthetic and strategic responses to create an extension of the literary experience, usually through discussion, writing, or dramatization. Here the reader may "even [evoke] a literary work of art" (Rosenblatt, 1978, p. ix). The now well-established concepts of the reader-writer as a meaning maker (Wells, 1986; Wittrock, 1984) and of the relationship between reading, writing, and thinking (McGinley & Tierney, 1988; Tierney & Pearson, 1983; Wittrock) support the practices recommended for developing the generative response.

Keeping these three types of literary response in mind, we have been working to develop a particular course of instruction. Our proposed instructional model links investigations in literary response to those in effective practices for at-risk learners (Slavin, Karweit, & Madden, 1989) in several ways. First, by viewing comprehension as the foundation for response (but not synonymous with it), the model provides a framework for instruction in cognitive and metacognitive processes that enhances comprehension while providing opportunities and encouragement for students to have personal responses to texts. Second, it acknowledges the teacher's role in drawing out the points of connection between readers and texts and encourages intervention to elicit

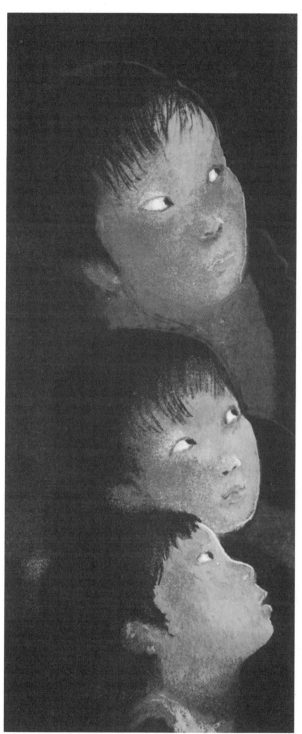

a strategic response after students have had an opportunity for individual response. This practice allows readers to bring to the text their own prior knowledge, past experiences, emotions, and developmental differences. Third, the model recognizes the power of re-reading or rethinking. Finally, it recognizes the importance of shared learning and promotes collaboration between teachers and students and between students and their peers. In all phases of the model, the emphasis is on guiding and extending the literary experience.

The Response to Literature Model

In this section, our "multiple response" instructional model is applied to some favorite fiction and nonfiction books for children. The suggestions may be used with at-risk readers after they have either listened to the book read aloud or read the text independently.

Lon Po Po

In *Lon Po Po*, a Caldecott Medal winner, Ed Young has translated and illustrated a Chinese version of the Red Riding Hood story. This book combines exquisite art with prose in a way that evokes reader response.

Aesthetic response. Teachers can help prompt an initial response by asking students to talk about how the book made them feel and what thoughts it provoked. Students may be encouraged to go back and browse through

Shang, Tao, and Paotze
plot to trick the wolf in
*Lon Po Po: A Red-Riding
Hood Story from China.*

the book as they think about and describe their first reactions to it. Teachers could ask students to support their feelings or thoughts by describing or pointing out specific passages or illustrations that contributed to the response. Interaction between students can be promoted by inviting others in the class to respond to each student's ideas. For example, teachers could ask whether anyone else had similar reactions or thoughts or suggest that students question each other further and compare and contrast their ideas.

Students may react to the beauty of the illustrations in *Lon Po Po*, the humor and cleverness of the prose, or the similarities and differences between this and the western version of Red Riding Hood. Depending on background knowledge, some students might tell of times or events when they encountered a scary situation or when they solved a problem; others might engage in metacognitive thinking, responding to the elements of the fairy tale genre.

Strategic response. As described previously, a strategic response usually requires teacher or expert intervention to guide and challenge the at-risk student in cognitive or metacognitive processing. Story mapping is one effective strategy for extending students' understanding of *Lon Po Po*. Students are asked to reread the tale and think about the major story elements:

- What was the setting for this story?
- What problem did the characters have?
- How did they solve their problem?
- What was the consequence?

Students may be given an example of a story map to help focus their attention on the essential parts of the story. (A story map for *Lon Po Po* appears in Figure 1.) Students who have particular difficulty recalling or organizing information may use the map as a note-taking guide, recording their ideas during, rather than after, rereading.

Figure 1
Story Map for *Lon Po Po*

Characters:	Shang, Tao, Paotze, wolf
Setting:	house and tree
Problem:	The wolf wanted to eat the children.
Resolution:	The children climbed a gingko-nut tree and tricked the wolf. They told him the nuts were magical and delicious and that if he climbed into a basket they would pull him up to reach the nuts. Three times he climbed in, and each time the children dropped him.
Consequence:	The third time the wolf was dropped, he died. The children returned to the house and fell peacefully asleep.

Figure 2
Extended Story Map:
A Comparison of Red Riding Hood Tales

	Lon Po Po (Ed Young)	*Little Red Riding Hood* (Paul Galdone)
Characters:	Shang, Tao, Paotze, wolf	Little Red Riding Hood, wolf, Grandmother, woodsman
Setting:	house and tree	woods and Grandmother's cottage
Problem:	The wolf wanted to eat the children.	The wolf ate Grandmother, tricked Little Red Riding Hood by pretending to be Grandmother, and ate her, too.
Resolution:	The children climbed a gingko-nut tree and tricked the wolf. They told him the nuts were magical and delicious and that if he climbed into a basket they would pull him up to reach the nuts. Three times he climbed in, and each time the children dropped him.	A woodsman coming by the house heard snoring, went inside, and found the wolf. He cut the wolf open and found the girl and her grandmother. They filled the wolf with stones.
Consequence:	The third time the wolf was dropped, he died. The children returned to the house and fell peacefully asleep.	They lived happily ever after.

Generative response. The generative response involves students' creative thought. For example, with *Lon Po Po*, readers might begin by pointing out the similarities and differences between it and other versions of the Red Riding Hood story. To prompt students' memories, the teacher should have on hand other versions—Paul Galdone's book and Trina Schart Hyman's retelling of the Brothers Grimm story are both good ones—for students to browse through, reread, and review. To facilitate the thinking process, the story map shown in Figure 1 can be extended to include the elements of another version. Working in cooperative groups or pairs, students record the elements of two versions of a tale. (An example comparing Ed Young's and Paul Galdone's versions appears in Figure 2.) Students can then use the completed map to help them compose a brief group report of how the tales are alike and different. Group leaders can present the report to the whole class, and the teacher can then guide students into a class discussion. Finally, students (in pairs or in groups) may be asked to compose their own version of Little Red Riding Hood.

Jumanji

In this book, another Caldecott winner, Chris Van Allsburg engages the reader by crossing and interweaving the lines of reality and fantasy. The text is complemented with rich, detailed pencil drawings.

Aesthetic response. Aesthetic response can be prompted with the same strategies presented for use with *Lon Po Po*. Students' initial reaction to *Jumanji* might focus on the striking illustrations, particularly on Van Allsburg's use of size and shading to evoke mood and reaction, or on the traits and actions of the adults and children in the story. Other students may focus on the dialogue or the events themselves, discussing how they would respond to such a situation.

Strategic response. This is an ideal text for exploring the use of reality and fantasy in storytelling. Read aloud, or ask students to reread silently, the first four pages of text, and ask students to focus their attention on the

The black-and-white drawings in *Jumanji*, done in pencil and Conté dust, are full of depth and detail.

first fantastic event, the appearance of the lion. What makes this event believable? How does the development of the main characters cause the reader to believe what is happening? What makes the reader share Judy's horror? Discuss students' responses with them, engaging in a think-aloud if necessary to direct attention to unobserved parts of the text or illustrations. Ask students to continue rereading the story in pairs. At appropriate points in the text, have them discuss with each other the elements of fantasy and reality. Prompts may be used to structure their discussion: How does the author weave fantasy and reality together? How does the joining of fantasy and reality influence readers' response to the text?

Generative response. Have students reread the last page of the story. In pairs, ask them to create the next episode, weaving elements of reality and fantasy into their story. Provide an opportunity for pairs to share their episodes with the rest of the class.

Desert Giant: The World of the Saguaro Cactus

This fact-filled book by Barbara Bash introduces the reader not only to the saguaro cactus, but also to the beauty and ecology of the desert environment.

Aesthetic response. Ask questions to prompt students' aesthetic responses to the text. Students' initial reactions might focus on specific new information (like the importance of the saguaro cactus to the desert community) or on the quality and effectiveness of the illustrations. Some readers might demonstrate awareness of text structure, commenting on elements that make particular sections understandable (e.g., the use of chronology in ordering ideas) or interesting (e.g., the close

This nonfiction book describes not only the saguaro cactus but also the complex world the cactus helps support.

Figure 3
Graphic Organizer for *Desert Giant*

How It Looks	*How It Grows*	*How It Is Used*
• can grow as tall as 50 feet	• begins under the canopy of a larger tree or "nurse plant"	• male woodpeckers make holes in the cactus for their mates' eggs
• can weigh several tons	• after 50 years it produces its first flowers	• elf owls and hawks live in them
• has sharp spines	• after 75 years, arms start to appear	• bats, doves, bees, and butterflies eat its flowers
• has accordion-like pleats that expand when it rains to store water	• at 150 years, it towers over the desert	• thrashers, lizards, and ants eat its fruit
	• can live for 200 years	• fruit used for jams, candy, and wine
		• hardened parts of dead cactus can be used as food containers
		• termites feed on dead cactus
		• snakes, geckos, and spiders use the dead stalks as a home

relationship between the illustrations and the text on each page; the emphasis on how the saguaro affects animals and people).

Strategic response. Graphic organizers are particularly suited for use with this type of text. These descriptive or main idea/supporting detail maps help readers focus attention on, organize, and recall their reading of expository text. Explain to students that when reading texts that contain considerable information, the use of a visual display can aid recall. Demonstrate how to record information on the map after rereading the beginning four or five pages together. Then have students form pairs to complete the rereading and mapping of information. They may choose to complete the map during or after reading. An example of a completed graphic organizer based on *Desert Giant* appears in Figure 3.

Generative response. Ask students to imagine they are living in the desert for a week. Have pairs of students review their graphic organizers and use the information as background for creating an observation log of what they see in that setting. Remind them that the time of day and the time of year during which they choose to observe will influence what they see. Provide a time when pairs can discuss and share their observations with the class.

The Land I Lost: Adventures of a Boy in Vietnam

This book is an exciting autobiographical account of a young boy's experiences and memories, written by Huynh Quang Nhuong. Since the setting for these short stories will be unfamiliar to many students, the book's introduction should be explored in depth to help build background knowledge and facilitate understanding and response. The following ac-tivities are designed to be used after reading the introduction but before reading the rest of the book.

Aesthetic response. Elicit aesthetic response to the book's introduction by asking students how it made them think and feel. In their responses, students are likely to note the contrast between their lives and the life the author describes.

Strategic response. Explain to students that the experiences and memories described

Figure 4
Story Chart for Building Background Knowledge
with *The Land I Lost*

Where People Lived

- in hamlets of about 50 houses along rivers or mountainsides
- houses were made of bamboo and coco-nut leaves
- houses were surrounded by a deep trench to protect them from animals or thieves
- no shops or marketplaces in the hamlet

What People Feared

- tigers (stole cattle)
- wild boars (attacked everything in sight)
- crocodiles
- horse snakes (crushed animals or people)

What People Ate

- vegetables (sweet potatoes, Indian mus-tard, eggplant, tomatoes, hot peppers, corn)
- rice
- meat (animals were hunted)

What Adults Did

- men farmed, hunted
- some men were educated to do things like teaching
- women managed the households, helped in the fields, and nursed husbands' injuries

What Children Did

- worked at an early age
- girls worked in the kitchen, weeded gar-dens, gathered eggs, watered cattle
- boys herded water buffalo, fished, and hunted
- some boys went to school

in this book are likely to be more meaningful and interesting for them if they understand the setting for the stories. Present a chart such as the one shown in Figure 4 and explain to students that each heading represents a major element of the book's setting. Select one heading and discuss the supporting details that could be listed under it. If necessary, demonstrate how a reader can look back through the text for specific information. After filling in information for one heading with the whole class, have the students form small groups or cooperative pairs to complete the map, rereading or looking back as necessary. When the maps are completed, have group leaders share the ideas they included under each heading and discuss the way the author's life and country differ from their own.

Generative response. Here the generative response is used to set the stage for understanding and responding to the stories that follow. Encourage students to use their charts and the discussion about the introduction to form an image of Vietnam, which they can then keep in mind as they read and respond to the author's memories and adventures. Some students might wish to paint or draw the image before reading the stories.

Helping Students Feel the Story

Our proposed model for enhancing at-risk readers' responses to literature is designed to move instruction away from the frequently used question-answer approach that relies almost exclusively on student-teacher interaction. Our model is, instead, discussion based. It not only encourages but requires reader-text and student-student interaction. The strategies we've suggested here are intended to promote more thoughtful, personal responses to fiction and nonfiction text by first encouraging free, unstructured reactions and then focusing students' thinking about what they have read. By waiting until after the first reading to teach specific strategies or focus attention in a particular direction, the model conveys the idea that reading can be done for recreation and not just to complete school assignments. Later strategic reading and rereading are introduced to show how reading can be structured to meet specific goals or complete defined tasks. In addition, the model promotes cognitive and metacognitive engagement by encouraging students to integrate their ideas through creative and shared responses.

One third grader in a class that had used the model for about six weeks commented, ''I like it. The third time I read it, I really feel the story!'' As Squire (1990) has noted, however, the ultimate test won't happen until long after instruction has ended. We hope, though, that this young student will continue feeling stories for a lifetime.

References

Allington, R.L. (1983). The reading instruction provided readers of differing ability. *Elementary School Journal, 83*, 548-559.

McGinley, W., & Tierney, R.J. (1988). *Reading and writing as ways of knowing and learning*. Urbana, IL: University of Illinois, Center for the Study of Reading.

Rosenblatt, L.M. (1978). *The reader, the text, the poem: The transactional theory of the literary work*. Carbondale, IL: Southern Illinois University Press.

Scardamalia, M., & Bereiter, C. (1983). Child as coinvestigator: Helping children gain insight into their own mental processes. In S.G. Paris, G.M. Olson, & H.W. Stevenson (Eds.), *Learning and motivation in the classroom*. Hillsdale, NJ: Erlbaum.

Schunk, D.H. (1985). Self-efficacy and classroom learning. *Psychology in the Schools, 22*, 208-223.

Slavin, R., Karweit, N.L., & Madden, N.A. (1989). *Effective strategies for students at risk*. Needham Heights, MA: Allyn & Bacon.

Squire, J.R. (1990). *Fifty years of research on response to literature*. Boston, MA: Boston University Press.

Tierney, R.J., & Pearson, P.D. (1983). *Toward a composing model of reading*. Urbana, IL: University of Illinois, Center for the Study of Reading.

Wells, G. (1986). *The meaning makers: Children learning language and using language to learn*. Portsmouth, NH: Heinemann.

Winne, P.H., & Marx, R.W. (1989). A cognitive-processing analysis of motivation within classroom tasks. In C. Ames & R. Ames (Eds.), *Research on motivation in education: Vol. 3. Goals and cognition*. San Diego, CA: Academic.

Wittrock, M.C. (1984). Writing and the teaching of reading. In J.M. Jensen (Ed.), *Composing and comprehending*. Urbana, IL: ERIC/RCS.

Children's Books

Bash, B. (1989). *Desert giant: The world of the saguaro cactus*. Boston, MA: Little, Brown.

Galdone, P. (1974). *Little Red Riding Hood*. New York: McGraw-Hill.

Grimm, Jacob & Wilhelm. (1983). *Little Red Riding Hood*. (Retold and ill. by T.S. Hyman.) New York: Holiday House.

Huynh, N.Q. (1982). *The land I lost: Adventures of a boy in Vietnam*. New York: HarperCollins.

Van Allsburg, C. (1981). *Jumanji*. Boston, MA: Houghton Mifflin.

Young, E. (1989). *Lon Po Po: A red-riding hood story from China*. New York: Philomel.

CHAPTER 13

Reference Books
Review Sources and Booklists
Materials from Publishers
Using the Resources

Resources to Identify
Children's Books

Arlene M. Pillar

Editor's note: Arlene Pillar died shortly after completing
this chapter, her last piece of professional writing. I have
updated some of the sources she cited in her original
manuscript.

Arlene's contributions to our field are noteworthy. She is
missed as a colleague, coauthor, and friend.

BC, February 1992

During my years as a consultant to school districts developing programs for integrating children's literature into the reading curriculum, I met some outstanding administrators and classroom teachers. Three in particular come to mind.

Beverly uses trade books with her second grade class in many creative ways. She is always on the lookout for new and exciting stories to read aloud to her students or to recommend for their personal reading. She browses in the public and school libraries; she listens to the children's recommendations and reads aloud books they bring to class; she attends professional conferences to learn about recent publications; she scans review journals in the library and staffroom; and she has begun to build a library of her own. Beverly's students learn to read by using both their basal readers and the trade books she finds for them. If Beverly knows that her students will be reading a story in their basals about someone who has acted silly, for example, she will bring related picture books to class—perhaps Kathryn Hewitt's *The Three Sillies*, Anne Rockwell's *The Three Sillies and 10 Other Stories to Read Aloud*, and Jan Ormerod's *Silly Goose*. Sometimes Beverly builds a language experience activity from this complementary literature lesson. After discussing ways in which her students have been silly and listing these on a flip chart, she encourages them to write stories of their own.

Naomi is a reading specialist who teaches fifth and sixth grade reading-disabled students. She depends solely on what she calls "fine literature" to educate the youngsters in her charge. She is committed to showing them that reading opens the door to the wonderful realistic and fantastic tales that have been woven through the ages. She is dedicated to her craft; she reads all the books she recommends to her students. One reason Naomi does this is to avoid the risk of "turning kids off" by recommending inappropriate books. "It takes a great deal of time," she says, "but how can I possibly tell a student that a particular book is wonderful if I haven't read it? My enthusiasm is contagious only when it is genuine. I love reading children's books. I don't see this as a job; it's a joy." Naomi looks for books in the same places Beverly does. She also takes university courses in children's literature.

Carol is a middle school librarian whose expertise in children's books has been built over years of commitment to her profession. She serves as a resource for the students in her school and for many of her colleagues. For example, if a sixth grade teacher asks for a read-aloud book that is not too long and that will capture his students' imagination with vivid imagery, Carol knows from her own broad reading that John Bellairs's *The Chessmen of Doom* is just what that teacher needs. She discovered Bellairs's book by reading it herself after seeing a positive review in a professional journal. Carol frequently reads reviews, but reading (or at least skimming) the book itself is always a necessary step. "It's impossible to read every single book that comes in; however, if I don't at least skim them, how do I know the joys they hold? My endorsements are always authentic."

Most teachers are so busy with the everyday demands of teaching that they do not have time to read as extensively as these three individuals. Perhaps it is because many teachers think that including fine literature in the reading program will be additional work that they shrink from the task. Let me assure you that you need not find it overwhelming. A wide variety of resources are available for teachers who decide to enhance their curricula with the best trade books published.

Teachers not only need to read what they recommend, they need to listen to their students, too. We learn from our students when we listen as they speak enthusiastically about books they have read. Further, we know that they will increasingly take responsibility for their own learning if they choose their own reading matter. Remember, though, that students who want the latest Natalie Babbitt or Katherine Paterson or Gary Paulsen books need to know how to use library resources or reference books to locate them. Teachers, too, may need some guidance in finding and using the resources that can lead them to the best books available for their students.

What follows is a comprehensive list of resources for teachers. It consists of descriptions of various types of reference books, sources of book reviews, booklists, and promotional material available from publishers.

Reference Books

General Bibliographies

Bibliographies, which may be either general or quite focused, are simply lists of books, usually organized alphabetically. They seem to be proliferating faster than yeast in warm water. In essence, a library's card catalog is a bibliography organized by title, author, and subject for books in that library's collection; for other books it is necessary to consult a broader bibliography. A comprehensive one is *Children's Books in Print*, an annually published listing of everything in print. It is organized in two volumes: one according to author, title, and illustrator; the other according to subject under the separate title *Subject Guide to Children's Books in Print*. In 1991-1992 there were 6,630 categories in the sub-ject index and 73,051 children's books listed in its companion volume. *The Elementary School Library Collection: A Guide to Books and Other Media* is more helpful as a selection tool; it contains detailed annotations of reference books, nonfiction, fiction, easy-to-read books, periodicals, and professional collections, as selected by qualified librarians. The *ESLC* also suggests which books are most valuable for elementary school collections by means of a three-point rating system. Several fine appendixes and listings of audiovisual materials (videocassettes, 16mm films, microcomputer programs) are incorporated into the sections describing books on the same subject. *Children's Catalog* is another selective listing of fiction, nonfiction, short stories, and easy-to-read books, organized by author, title, and subject. Choices are made by children's librarians.

Another reference, *A to Zoo: Subject Access to Children's Picture Books*, lists nearly 10,000 fiction and nonfiction picture books for preschool through second grade, arranged by subject and indexed by author, title, and illustrator. ABC books, cumulative tales, and wordless books are included. *The Elementary School Paperback Collection* is an equally thorough reference, with annotations of 4,000 paperbacks for young readers arranged by interest categories. *Best Books for Children*, revised every three years, gives annotations of 12,000 books for preschool through sixth grade. The entries are listed under 500 subheadings and only books that have received three or more positive reviews are included. The *Bibliography of Books for Children* contains more than 1,500 annotations, arranged by subject and age level for new titles and classics. In addition, this book has a guide to magazines and newspapers and a section on reference books. A more modest

Bibliography of General Bibliographies

Listed below are publication data for the general bibliographies to children's books described in this section, arranged alphabetically by title. This information should help you locate these resources easily.

A to Zoo: Subject Access to Children's Picture Books (3rd ed.), by Carolyn W. Lima and John A. Lima. New York: Bowker, 1989.

Best Books for Children: Preschool Through the Middle Grades (4th ed.), by John T. Gillespie and Corinne J. Naden. New York: Bowker, 1990.

Bibliography of Books for Children. Wheaton, MD: Association for Childhood Education International, 1989.

Children's Books in Print. New York: Bowker, updated annually. (See also the companion to this resource, *Subject Guide to Children's Books in Print*.)

Children's Catalog (16th ed.), edited by Juliet Yaakov. Bronx, NY: H.W. Wilson Co., 1991.

The Elementary School Library Collection: A Guide to Books and Other Media (18th ed.), edited by Lois Winkel. Williamsport, PA: Brodart, 1992.

The Elementary School Paperback Collection, by John T. Gillespie. Chicago, IL: American Library Association, 1985.

Paperback Books for Children: A Selected List Through Age Thirteen. New York: Bank Street College, Child Study Children's Book Committee, 1988.

Subject Guide to Children's Books in Print. New York: Bowker, updated annually. (See also the companion to this resource, *Children's Books in Print*.)

---

booklet of carefully made recommendations is *Paperback Books for Children: A Selected List Through Age Thirteen*. Using guidelines developed over 50 years of reviewing, the Child Study Children's Book Committee at Bank Street College, which put together this booklet, has included brief annotations of books arranged by age and interest.

Specialized Bibliographies

Many bibliographies of children's books are more focused than the general references just discussed. For example, a number of resources give recommendations of books aimed at younger readers. *First Readers: An Annotated Bibliography of Books for Children Beginning to Read* lists approximately 1,500 fiction and nonfiction titles with annotations and recommendations for professionals and parents. *Mother Goose Comes First* is an annotated guide to more than 700 books, records, and cassettes for preschool children. *Good Books to Grow on: A Guide to Building Your Child's Library from Birth to Age Five* and *Children's Literature from A to Z: A Guide for Parents and Teachers* are fine resources for recommendations of books intended for very young readers. *Books Kids Will Sit Still For* provides brief descriptions of over 1,000 read-aloud books. The author gives hundreds of ways to use books to enrich children's learning and has included a section titled "Fifty Ways to Celebrate Books."

Locating the Specialized Bibliographies

Listed below is the information you will need to locate the specialized bibliographies described in this section.

Books for Children to Read Alone: A Guide for Parents and Librarians, by George Wilson and Joyce Moss. New York: Bowker, 1988.

Books Kids Will Sit Still For, by Judy Freeman. Hagerstown, MD: Alleyside, 1984.

Children's Books: Awards & Prizes, 1985. New York: Children's Book Council, 1985.

Children's Books of International Interest (3rd ed.), edited by Barbara Elleman. Chicago, IL: American Library Association, 1985.

Children's Literature Awards and Winners (2nd ed.), compiled by Dolores Blythe Jones. Detroit, MI: Gale, 1988.

Children's Literature from A to Z: A Guide for Parents and Teachers, by Jon C. Stott. New York: McGraw-Hill, 1984.

Dictionary of American Children's Fiction, 1960-1984: Recent Books of Recognized Merit, by Althea K. Helbig and Agnes Regan Perkins. Westport, CT: Greenwood, 1986.

Easy Reading: Book Series and Periodicals for Less Able Readers (2nd ed.), by Randall J. Ryder, Bonnie B. Graves, and Michael F. Graves. Newark, DE: International Reading Association, 1989.

First Readers: An Annotated Bibliography of Books for Children Beginning to Read, by Barbara Barstow and Judith Riggle. New York: Bowker, 1989.

Good Books to Grow on: A Guide to Building Your Child's Library from Birth to Age Five, by Andrea E. Cascardi. New York: Warner, 1985.

Mother Goose Comes First, by Lois Winkel and Sue Kimmel. New York: Henry Holt, 1990.

The Newbery and Caldecott Awards: A Guide to the Medal and Honor Books, by the Association for Library Service to Children. Chicago, IL: American Library Association, updated annually.

Promoting World Understanding Through Literature, K-8, by Mary C. Austin and Esther C. Jenkins. Littleton, CO: Libraries Unlimited, 1983.

Reading for the Love of It: Best Books for Young Readers, by Michele Landsberg. Englewood Cliffs, NJ: Prentice Hall, 1987.

Resources for Middle-Grade Reluctant Readers: A Guide for Librarians, by Marianne Laino Pilla. Littleton, CO: Libraries Unlimited, 1987.

Sequences: An Annotated Guide to Children's Fiction in Series, by Susan Roman. Chicago, IL: American Library Association, 1985.

Books for Children to Read Alone: A Guide for Parents and Librarians is arranged by readability level (from 1.0 to 3.9) as determined by the Fry and Spache scales. Each entry is described by genre (wordless books, adventure, humor, concept books, or historical fiction) and subject; the entry for *The Snowman* by Raymond Briggs, for example, is "genre—fantasy; subject—dreams, snow."

A fine guide to series books is *Sequences: An Annotated Guide to Children's Fiction in Series*. This selective list for grade 3 through junior high is organized alphabetically by author (about 125 authors are included). The indexes are to main characters, book titles, and series titles. This reference includes both sequels—books about established characters in new settings—and sequences—books that develop character and plot across several titles.

Easy Reading: Book Series and Periodicals for Less Able Readers reviews 44 series and 15 periodicals for grades 4 through 12. It includes reading and interest levels. *Resources for Middle-Grade Reluctant Readers* describes and gives reading levels for high/low (high interest materials with easy vocabulary) books and magazines to use with grades 4 to 6. This book goes beyond annotations to address planning programs for disabled readers, who make up 15 percent of children in the United States.

International bibliographies are also available. A good one is *Reading for the Love of It: Best Books for Young Readers*, a comprehensive guide to 400 works of fiction from around the world. The entries are arranged alphabetically according to ages and reading levels and include each book's country of origin. All of the books included address issues of censorship or sexual, racial, or social stereotypes.

Multiculturalism and international understanding are issues that are on the minds of all thoughtful parents and educators. A number of resources are available to help you find books that describe or originate from different cultures. *Children's Books of International Interest* describes more than 350 books that "incorporate universal themes or depict the American way of life." *Promoting World Understanding Through Literature, K-8* addresses planning a multicultural literature program and discusses books about Hispanics, African Americans, and Native Americans. The authors stress the need to promote knowledge about and understanding of all the cultures represented in the United States.

If you're looking for a near sure-fire way to locate the very best in children's literature, you can't go wrong with the many listings of award-winning books. (Chapter 9 by Sylvia Hutchinson and Ira Aaron in this volume lists some of the award winners from five English-speaking countries.) The *Dictionary of American Children's Fiction, 1960-1984: Recent Books of Recognized Merit* lists only books that have won significant awards—for example, those on *The Horn Book*'s "Fanfare List." The 1,550-plus entries include Western winners of the Spur Award and mysteries that have won the Edgar Allan Poe Award. *The Newbery and Caldecott Awards: A Guide to the Medal and Honor Books* is a handy guide to the winners of and runners-up for those U.S. prizes. It is updated annually and includes indexes of authors, illustrators, and titles. The 1991 edition has brief descriptions of every book honored since the awards' inception and an illustration from each of the most recent winners. *Children's Books: Awards & Prizes* is a comprehensive directory of 125 major U.S., British, and international book awards. Each entry includes a brief description of the award and a chronological list of winning titles. *Children's Literature Awards and Win-*

ners covers 211 awards and identifies 5,000 books. It also provides useful title and author/ illustrator indexes.

Subject Bibliographies

Also available are a number of fine resources for locating books of a particular type or genre, or those that are well suited to certain readers.

Fantasy Literature for Children and Young Adults gives annotations of 3,300 fantasy novels and story collections—from allegorical fantasy to witchcraft and sorcery—for grades 3 through 12. Brief biographies of 600 authors and selected articles and interviews are also included. *Worlds Within: Children's Fantasy from the Middle Ages to Today*, though not a bibliography, is an intriguing history of fantasy in which the literature discussed is linked to the times in which it was written.

The Museum of Science and Industry Basic List of Children's Science Books has 17 main subdivisions, from animals and astronomy to plant life and technology/engineering, in addition to a listing of children's science magazines. Books are organized by title under each heading. *Science and Technology in Fact and Fiction: A Guide to Children's Books* addresses books about space, aeronautics, computers, and robotics.

Books in Spanish for Children and Young Adults discusses books about the lifestyles, folklore, heroes, and history of Hispanic cultures. *Juvenile Judaica: The Jewish Values Bookfinder* includes annotations of both popular fiction and nonfiction.

A number of bibliographies are geared to certain groups of young readers. *Growing Pains: Helping Children Deal with Everyday Problems Through Reading* is a guide to pic-

ture books that focus on the dilemmas of the growing years. The authors are a children's librarian and a pediatric nurse. *The Single-Parent Family in Children's Books* gives annotations of 600 fiction and nonfiction works intended for preschool through young adult readers. *Girls Are People Too! A Bibliography of Nontraditional Female Roles in Children's Books* discusses books that show women and men working together as equals or that depict women as leaders. The book includes an appendix of firsts: a chronological list of noteworthy events and personalities in the history of women. *A Guide to Non-Sexist Children's Books* cites 600-plus titles in a list organized by the stages in a child's life and depicting characters who solve problems independently and who are not categorized by sex roles.

More Notes for a Different Drummer and *Books for the Gifted Child* consider books about the physically challenged and the gifted, respectively. Volume 2 of *Books for the Gifted Child* is an updated edition in the "Serving Special Needs" series. It has introductory chapters on identifying gifted children and understanding their needs. Two additional volumes in the series are *Books to Help Children Cope with Separation and Loss*, which considers real-life situations such as losing a friend or moving to a new neighborhood, and *Accept Me As I Am: Best Books of Juvenile Nonfiction on Impairments and Disabilities*, which lists about 350 books, including biographies and autobiographies.

Indexes

Indexes, like bibliographies, can help teachers and librarians locate information about particular kinds of works. For example, the *Index to Fairy Tales, 1978-1986* helps lo-

Finding the Subject Bibliographies

Here is the information you'll need to locate the bibliographies mentioned in this section.

Accept Me As I Am: Best Books of Juvenile Nonfiction on Impairments and Disabilities, by Joan Brest Friedberg. New York: Bowker, 1985.

Books for the Gifted Child, by Barbara Baskin and Karen Harris. New York: Bowker, 1980.

Books for the Gifted Child: Volume 2, by Paula Hauser and Gail A. Nelson. New York: Bowker, 1988.

Books in Spanish for Children and Young Adults: An Annotated Guide, by Isabel Schon. Metuchen, NJ: Scarecrow, 1985.

Books to Help Children Cope with Separation and Loss (vol. 3), by Joanne E. Bernstein and Masha K. Rudman. New York: Bowker, 1988.

Fantasy Literature for Children and Young Adults: An Annotated Bibliography (3rd ed.), by Ruth Nadelman Lynn. New York: Bowker, 1989.

Girls Are People Too! A Bibliography of Nontraditional Female Roles in Children's Books, by Joan E. Newman. Metuchen, NJ: Libraries Unlimited, 1987.

Growing Pains: Helping Children Deal with Everyday Problems Through Reading, by Maureen Cuddigan and Mary Beth Hanson. Chicago, IL: American Library Association, 1988.

A Guide to Non-Sexist Children's Books (vol. II, 1976-1985), edited by Denise Wilms and Ilene Cooper. Chicago, IL: Academy, 1987.

Juvenile Judaica: The Jewish Values Bookfinder, edited by Marcia W. Posner. New York: The Association of Jewish Libraries, 1985.

More Notes for a Different Drummer: A Guide to Juvenile Fiction Portraying the Disabled, by Barbara Baskin and Karen Harris. New York: Bowker, 1984.

The Museum of Science and Industry Basic List of Children's Science Books, compiled by Bernice Richter and Duane Wenzel. Chicago, IL: American Library Association, 1988.

Science and Technology in Fact and Fiction: A Guide to Children's Books, by DayAnn Kennedy, Stella Spangler, and MaryAnn Vanderwerf. New York: Bowker, 1990.

The Single-Parent Family in Children's Books: An Annotated Bibliography (2nd ed.), by Catherine Townsend Horner. Metuchen, NJ: Scarecrow, 1988.

Worlds Within: Children's Fantasy from the Middle Ages to Today, by Sheila Egoff. Chicago, IL: American Library Association, 1988.

Locating the Indexes

Publication information for the indexes mentioned in this section is listed below.

Index to Collective Biographies for Young Readers, edited by Karen Breen. New York: Bowker, 1988.

Index to Fairy Tales, 1978-1986: Including Folklore, Legends, & Myths in Collection, by Norma Olin Ireland and Joseph W. Sprug. Metuchen, NJ: Scarecrow, 1989.

Index to Poetry for Children and Young People: 1982-87, compiled by Meredith Blackburn III. New York: Wilson, 1989.

cate specific tales in collections. Arranged by title and subject, it analyzes 262 collections, has 2,000 subject headings, extensive cross-references, and headings for folklore and mythology for adult readers. The *Index to Poetry for Children and Young People, 1982-87*, part of a multivolume reference series, lists thousands of poems according to title, subject, author, and first line. The *Index to Collective Biographies for Young Readers* has entries for more than 10,000 notable people, from presidents to race-car drivers, representing the contents of about 1,100 collective biographies. The index is organized by biography, occupation or field, and title of collective work.

Biographical Dictionaries and Encyclopedias

These resources contain information about children's authors and illustrators and may be either quite general or more limited in scope.

Each volume of *Illustrators of Children's Books* includes critical essays for the new entries and updated information on the entries in previous volumes. *Black Authors and Illustrators of Children's Books* is a biographical dictionary current through 1986. *Behind the Covers: Interviews with Authors and Illustra-tors of Books for Children and Young Adults* contains 21 interviews, preceded by biographical information and complete bibliographies of those interviewed.

The more than 50 volumes of *Something about the Author* are appropriate reading for students and teachers alike. Early figures in the field of children's books—such as John Newbery and L. Frank Baum—are included. The series covers more than 6,000 people and gives a thorough account of each life in sections titled "Personal," "Career," and "Writing." If the author's work has been reworked in another medium, this information is included in "Adaptations." "For More Information" presents other books, reviews, and articles in which the person appears. Most interesting of all is "Sidelights," which contains direct remarks from the authors themselves. Extensive lists of works and many graphics, portraits, and illustrations make this series very appealing.

Authors & Artists for Young Adults is about particular favorites of junior and senior high school students. It includes novelists, poets, illustrators, cartoonists, and lyricists. *Children's Authors and Illustrators*, an index to biographical dictionaries, covers 25,000 authors and illustrators of children's books. In the *Something about the Author Autobiogra-*

phy Series, personal essays are complemented by a list of the authors' works and many illustrations. Two volumes in the Dictionary of Literary Biography series—volume 52, *American Writers for Children since 1960: Fiction*, and volume 61, *American Writers for Children since 1960: Poets, Illustrators, and Nonfiction Authors*—are also useful resources. They are filled with illustrations, photographs of events in authors' lives, and replicas of handwritten manuscripts and galley proofs, in addition to listings of biographical essays.

Handbooks

The strength of handbooks is that they present considerable information on a single subject in a very accessible form. One popular one is *The New Read-Aloud Handbook*. The author tells parents and teachers how to encourage children to want to read, and ultimately how to turn them into book lovers. *For Reading Out Loud! A Guide to Sharing Books with Children* and *Choosing Books for Children: A Commonsense Guide* are two other fine guides for tracking down good books to share with children.

Primaryplots: A Book Talk Guide for Use with Readers Ages 4-8 is designed to help teachers introduce readers to wonderful literature. Each of the 150 titles, summarized by plot and theme, is grouped under headings, such as ''Enjoying Family and Friends'' and ''Developing a Positive Self-Image.'' The author includes discussion ideas and enrichment activities. *Eyeopeners! How to Choose and Use Children's Books about Real People, Places, and Things* addresses choosing and using nonfiction with a ''Total Literature Connection'' to works of fiction.

Guide to the Biographical Dictionaries and Encyclopedias

Listed below are publication data for the biographical resources described in this section.

American Writers for Children Since 1960 (vol. 52: Fiction, and vol. 61: Poets, Illustrators, and Nonfiction Authors), edited by Glenn Estes. Detroit, MI: Gale, 1986, 1987.

Authors & Artists for Young Adults (vol. 2), edited by Agnes Garrett and Helga P. McCue. Detroit, MI: Gale, 1989.

Behind the Covers: Interviews with Authors and Illustrators of Books for Children and Young Adults (vol. II), by Jim Roginski. Littleton, CO: Libraries Unlimited, 1989.

Black Authors and Illustrators of Children's Books: A Biographical Dictionary, by Barbara Rollock. New York: Garland, 1988.

Children's Authors and Illustrators (4th ed.), edited by Joyce Nakamura. Detroit, MI: Gale, 1987.

Illustrators of Children's Books (multivolume set organized chronologically), edited by Lee Kingman et al. Boston, MA: The Horn Book, updated periodically.

Something about the Author Autobiography Series (vol. 8), edited by Joyce Nakamura. Detroit, MI: Gale, 1989.

Something about the Author: Facts and Pictures about Contemporary Authors and Illustrators of Books for Young People (multivolume set), edited by Anne Commire. Detroit, MI: Gale, updated periodically.

How to Find the Handbooks

Below is the information you'll need to locate the handbooks described in this section.

Choosing Books for Children: A Commonsense Guide, by Betsy Hearne. New York: Delacorte, 1981.

Eyeopeners! How to Choose and Use Children's Books about Real People, Places, and Things, by Beverly Kobrin. New York: Penguin, 1989.

The Family Story-Telling Handbook, by Anne Pellowski. New York: Macmillan, 1987.

For Reading Out Loud! A Guide to Sharing Books with Children, by Margaret Mary Kimmel and Elizabeth Segel. New York: Delacorte, 1983.

Her Way: A Guide to Biographies of Women for Young People (2nd ed.), edited by Mary-Ellen K. Siegel. Chicago, IL: American Library Association, 1984.

The New Read-Aloud Handbook, by Jim Trelease. New York: Penguin, 1989.

Primaryplots: A Book Talk Guide for Use with Readers Ages 4-8, by Rebecca L. Thomas. New York: Bowker, 1989.

Shadow and Substance: Afro-American Experience in Contemporary Children's Fiction, by Rudine Sims. Urbana, IL: National Council of Teachers of English, 1982.

Storytelling: Art and Technique (2nd ed.), by Augusta Baker and Ellin Greene. New York: Bowker, 1987.

The Story Vine, by Anne Pellowski. New York: Macmillan, 1984.

Shadow and Substance: Afro-American Experience in Contemporary Children's Fiction surveys 150 books for preschool through grade 8. In a chapter entitled "The Image-Makers," the author profiles major African-American writers. This valuable book helps teachers and librarians make informed decisions regarding recent literature. Another reference, *Her Way: A Guide to Biographies of Women for Young People*, is a rich resource of biographies of 1,100 historical and contemporary women. The books included are free of race and sex bias.

Two storytellers wrote *Storytelling: Art and Technique*, a manual for the novice on how to select, prepare, and tell stories. The book includes appendixes on inservice education and sources for the storyteller, as well as a glossary. *The Story Vine* and *The Family Story-Telling Handbook* are sources of stories from around the world and ways to use them creatively in schools, libraries, and homes.

Professional Books

Each year there is a new textbook about children's literature for those who want to learn a great deal about the field. *Literature and the Child* is filled with teaching ideas and activities for using books in the elementary classroom and curriculum webs on topics such as "Animals" (primary), "Endangered Species" (intermediate), and "Space Exploration" (advanced). In addition, this comprehensive textbook includes an informative timeline titled "Touchstones in the History of Children's Literature" and a special feature for each genre, called "Landmark Books," which

Locating the Professional Books

Publication information on the books mentioned in this section follows.

The Best in Children's Books, by Zena Sutherland. Chicago, IL: University of Chicago Press, 1986.

Booktalk: Occasional Writing on Literature and Children, by Aidan Chambers. New York: HarperCollins, 1985.

Caldecott & Co.: Notes on Books & Pictures, by Maurice Sendak. New York: Farrar, Straus & Giroux, 1988.

Canadian Books for Children: A Guide to Authors and Illustrators, by Jon C. Stott and Raymond E. Jones. Toronto, Ont.: Harcourt Brace Jovanovich Canada, 1988.

Canadian Books for Young People/Livres canadiens pour la jeunesse (4th ed.), by Andre Gagnon and Anne Gagnon. Toronto, Ont.: University of Toronto Press, 1988.

Children and Books (8th ed.), by Zena Sutherland. New York: HarperCollins, 1991.

Children and Their Books: A Celebration of the Work of Iona and Peter Opie, by Gillian Avery and Julia Briggs, Oxford, UK: Oxford University Press, 1989.

Children's Literature in the Classroom: Weaving Charlotte's Web, edited by Janet Hickman and Bernice E. Cullinan. Needham Heights, MA: Christopher-Gordon, 1989.

Children's Literature in the Elementary School (4th ed.), by Charlotte S. Huck, Susan Hepler, and Janet Hickman. Fort Worth, TX: Holt, Rinehart & Winston, 1987.

Engines of Instruction, Mischief & Magic, by Mary V. Jackson. Lincoln, NB: University of Nebraska Press, 1989.

Innocence and Experience: Essays and Conversations on Children's Literature, compiled by Barbara G. Harrison and Gregory Maguire. New York: Lothrop, Lee & Shepard, 1987.

The Language of the Night: Essays on Fantasy and Science Fiction, by Ursula K. LeGuin. New York: The Women's Press, 1989.

Literature and the Child (2nd ed.), by Bernice E. Cullinan. Orlando, FL: Harcourt Brace Jovanovich, 1989.

Modern Canadian Children's Books, by Judith Saltman. Don Mills, Ont.: Oxford University Press, 1987.

The Spying Heart: More Thoughts on Reading and Writing Books for Children, by Katherine Paterson. New York: Dutton, 1989.

Stepping away from Tradition: Children's Books of the Twenties and Thirties, edited by Sybille A. Jagusch. Washington, DC: Library of Congress, 1988.

The World Treasury of Children's Literature (vols. 1-3), selected by Clifton Fadiman. Boston, MA: Little, Brown, 1984-85.

lists titles that are essential reading. *Children's Literature in the Classroom: Weaving Charlotte's Web* is an inspirational tribute to the work of Charlotte S. Huck. The book, which focuses on how to plan and implement a literature-based program, lists more than 300 books in its bibliography. Other popular texts are *Children's Literature in the Elementary School, Children and Books*, and *The Best in Children's Books*.

For an interpretive history of children's literature in England, try *Engines of Instruction, Mischief, & Magic* which covers the field from its beginnings to 1839. Also from England comes *Children and Their Books: A Celebration of the Work of Iona and Peter Opie*.

A number of fine reference works present information about the growing body of Canadian literature for young readers. These include *Canadian Books for Children: A Guide to Authors and Illustrators, Canadian Books for Young People/Livres canadiens pour la jeunesse*, and *Modern Canadian Children's Books*.

The three volumes of *The World Treasury of Children's Literature* should be on every teacher's desk and in every parent's library. In it are poems, stories, and excerpts from novels—the best of the old and the new—to delight adults and children alike. The essay "For Grown-ups Only" should be essential reading for all interested adults.

Books by writers writing about their craft are a great source of inspiration for teachers. Some of the best include Katherine Paterson's *The Spying Heart: More Thoughts on Reading and Writing Books for Children*, Maurice Sendak's *Caldecott & Co.: Notes on Books & Pictures*, Ursula LeGuin's *The Language of the Night: Essays on Fantasy and Science Fiction*, and Aidan Chambers's *Booktalk: Occasional Writing on Literature and Children*.

Innocence and Experience: Essays and Conversations on Children's Literature is a compilation that touches on all aspects of children's books. *Stepping Away from Tradition: Children's Books of the Twenties and Thirties* includes a most informative remembrance by Mildred Batchelder entitled ''The Leadership Network in Children's Librarianship.''

Review Sources and Booklists

Thoughtful reviewers can offer sound recommendations on books that might be appropriate for the students in your class. The *Children's Book Review Index* (edited by Barbara Beach and published by Gale) tells teachers where to locate specific book reviews from more than 470 periodicals. An annual listing, it contains over 18,000 review citations covering more than 10,000 books for children through age ten. (The reviews themselves are not provided.)

Among the many review sources available to teachers are the American Library Association's *Booklinks, Booklist*, and *Journal of Youth Services in Libraries*, the *Bulletin of the Center for Children's Books* from the University of Chicago Graduate Library School, *The Horn Book Magazine*, the International Board on Books for Young People's *Bookbird*, Beverly Kobrin's *The Kobrin Letter, Publishers Weekly* and the *School Library Journal* (both from Bowker), *The New Advocate* (from Christopher-Gordon), and Ohio State University's *The Web*. Each of these resources has a different format and serves a different function. *Booklist*, for example, is quite comprehensive and includes media evaluations, while *Booklinks* features articles on strategies for using books with children; IBBY's *Bookbird* includes recommendations of books with "international interest" as well as articles on children's literature; *The Kobrin Letter* reviews nonfiction for children; in December, the *School Library Journal* runs a "Best Books of the Year" feature; *The New Advocate* focuses on creating, reading, and appreciating children's literature and has tips for the classroom; and *The Web*, which is organized thematically, includes a "web" of related books and activities in each issue.

Some large collections of reviews are also available. *Popular Reading for Children II: A Collection of Booklist Columns* (from 1980 to 1985) is a good aid for identifying topics of interest to students in grades 2 to 9. *The Horn Book Guide* is a comprehensive semiannual selection guide that includes reviews of the most recent hardcover trade books. Fiction titles are organized by age categories; nonfiction is organized under Dewey decimal system headings. There are author, illustrator, subject, and title indexes.

Booklists are just that: lists of books organized by topic, grade, or award. These lists are generally prepared in pamphlet or booklet form and may or may not be annotated. Booklists do not provide as much information as do reviews, nor are they as comprehensive as bibliographies. Nevertheless, they are handy resources for locating noteworthy titles.

Recommended Readings in Literature: Kindergarten Through Grade 8, from the California State Department of Education, recommends 1,010 titles to help teachers plan their literature programs. Both classic and contemporary works are listed, as are titles for children whose first language is not English. Books relating to specific ethnic or cultural groups are identified by letter symbols.

Numerous lists appear in the ALA's *Booklist*, including "Children's Editors' Choice" and the annual "Notable Children's Books." The Children's Book Council (CBC) in New York produces several brief booklists in conjunction with other organizations: "Outstanding Science Trade Books for Children," produced with the National Science Teachers Association; "Notable Children's Trade Books in the Field of Social Studies," produced with the National Council for the Social Studies; and "Children's Choices," produced with IRA. "100 Favorite Paperbacks 1989" (Kimmel & Pillar) is also available from CBC. IRA also publishes "Young Adults' Choices" and "Teachers' Choices."

Dianne Monson, with the National Council of Teachers of English Elementary Booklist Committee, edited *Adventuring with Books: A Booklist for Pre-K – Grade 6*. It lists almost 1,700 children's books of high literary and artistic quality published between 1981 and 1984. Another booklist for teachers is *The Black Experience in Children's Books*, from the New York Public Library, which includes annotations of nearly 850 titles for children from preschool to grade 6. The book includes sections on Africa and the Caribbean. The Westchester Library System has produced *Compartiendo La Magia Del Mundo*, a selected booklist in Spanish.

The Horn Book Magazine has produced "Children's Classics: A Book List for Parents," a 20-page pamphlet that lists favorite titles for babies through young adults, and "Newbery and Caldecott Medal Books, 1976-1985." Margaret N. Coughlan of the Children's Literature Center of the Library of Congress compiles the annual annotated list "Books for Children." Recommendations are for children from preschool to junior high.

The computer program *BookBrain* functions like an extensive booklist. Its three databases include several thousand cleverly annotated fiction titles and are organized for grades 1 to 3, 4 to 6, and 7 to 9. The lively descriptions appeal to teachers and students alike. The software, created by Elizabeth A. Hass and available from Oryx Press in both IBM and Apple II versions, comes with a 64-page manual with full bibliographic information for all books listed.

Materials from Publishers

Publishers, particularly the larger ones, will send newsletters and other promotional materials about their books on request. Librarians and teachers can write and ask that their names be added to the mailing list.

One newsletter from Lothrop, Lee & Shepard Books in New York included an interview with long-time collaborators Elizabeth James and Carol Barkin, a list of Lothrop books that had received state, regional, and other awards, descriptions of promotional materials available at no charge, details of tours planned for authors and illustrators, and annotations of new books. One issue of Scholastic's "Book Talk" included an editorial on multicultural books, a profile of author Robert Westall, a section titled "On the Road with Scholastic Authors," a piece by Jim Murphy on what led him to write a book about wolves, and details of movie tie-ins.

Publishers' catalogs frequently include biographical data about authors and illustrators in addition to listing books, prices, and ordering information. Occasionally catalogs include subject indexes for books, as well as the usual title and author indexes. Holiday House's information sheet for Russell Freedman provides a profile of the award-winning author and describes forthcoming and past books with words and pictures. Penguin USA's bro-

chure "All about Dahl" is filled with information about the late author Roald Dahl and his answers to questions such as these: Where does a writer get his ideas? What sort of person must one be to become an author? Which is harder—writing for children or writing for adults?

Also of interest, although not really as resources for locating books, are the many teaching aids available from publishers. Putnam & Grossett offers a resource guide for Jean Fritz's American history books (and a free, full-color chronological time chart of events described in these books). Simon & Schuster's *Teacher's Guide to Books by Bill Wallace* and Ballantine/Fawcett's teacher's guides to novels by Cynthia Voigt and Bette Greene are available free to teachers. These guides include teaching suggestions and ideas for activities that help students extend their understanding of the texts to the arts, writing, and other curriculum areas.

HarperCollins has produced activity cards for the Let's-Read-and-Find-Out science series. The cards include well-developed questions and activities labeled "for very young readers," "for older students," and "may need supervision."

Using the Resources

At first glance, the number of resources described here appears overwhelming. If approached systematically, however, using these resources effectively won't be difficult and should quickly yield valuable information.

Teachers will want to start with resources that make sense for their students' needs, interests, and concerns. After determining certain general information about your students (their abilities in reading, their likes and dislikes, and so on), the resources to consult will be narrowed down. You will soon decide which resources are best for you. One teacher chose *The Horn Book Guide, Booklinks*, and *The Elementary School Library Collection* as the three resources she valued most; your own favorites will be determined by your circumstances, your students, and the availability of professional materials in your school or district. Each resource takes us to a selection of children's books and gives us choices about the books to add to our school libraries and classroom collections. We should also listen to what our students have to say about books we may never get to read for ourselves.

Once the resources have been selected, they need to be used. Membership in professional organizations can help here by keeping you informed about current practices and policies as well as innovations. Often these organizations publish professional materials on a variety of aspects of teaching and educational research.

The American Library Association (50 East Huron Street, Chicago IL 60611, USA) oversees the Newbery and Caldecott awards for excellence in writing and illustration, respectively. In addition, the ALA has an extensive publications program and produces new books on children's literature regularly.

The International Reading Association (800 Barksdale Road, PO Box 8139, Newark DE 19714-8139, USA) publishes *The Reading Teacher*, which includes a regular review column of children's books, and the *Journal of Reading*, which includes reviews of young adult literature. IRA also publishes numerous books on the use of children's literature in the classroom and sponsors conventions of interest to those in the field.

The National Council of Teachers of English (1111 Kenyon Road, Urbana IL 61801, USA) includes the Children's Literature Assembly (CLA) and the Assembly on Literature for Adolescents (ALAN) within its larger framework. During national conventions of NCTE these two assemblies present programs on using trade books in the classroom. CLA publishes *The Bulletin* and ALAN produces *The ALAN Review*. NCTE's *Language Arts* carries a book review column in each issue.

The United States Board on Books for Young People (write to USBBY care of the International Reading Association) is a national section of the International Board on Books for Young People. Its twice yearly newsletters feature articles about international and U.S. children's literature.

The Children's Book Council (PO Box 706, New York NY 19276-0706, USA) is a professional association of children's book publishers. Although individuals cannot join the CBC, for a one-time fee they can be added to the mailing list to receive the pamphlet *Features* and other information about children's books and their creators.

Maybe the best thing to do as we step toward making fine children's literature part of our reading programs, however, would be to remember Emily Dickinson's lines:

There is no frigate like a book
To take us lands away....

CHAPTER 14

The California Reading Initiative
Different Faces of Censorship
What Should Educators Do?

The Censorship Challenge

Francie Alexander

What do Huckleberry Finn, Holden Caulfield, and Little Red Riding Hood have in common? These fictional characters have all been expelled from classrooms at one time or another. This chapter reports on the nature of various censorship disputes and suggests strategies for dealing with such controversies. I focus here on issues that were an unintended consequence of the California Reading Initiative, but debates about censorship have affected efforts to establish literature-based programs across the United States and in many other countries.

The California Reading Initiative

In 1987 California began implementing an exciting initiative designed to improve reading instruction and connect students to good books. The *English-Language Arts Framework for California Public Schools, Kindergarten Through Grade Twelve* (California Department of Education, 1987) set an ambitious agenda for exposing all students to good literature. According to this document, "If the end of an English-language arts program is developing a literate, thinking society, then surely the means to that end must be devising for students meaningful encounters with the most effective sources of human expression" (p. 6). To establish this means to the desired end, most school districts in the state have made a certain core of literary works the centerpiece of new, updated English and language arts programs. Many of these titles were selected from lists developed by teachers, librarians, school administrators, professors, and community representatives and published by the California Department of Education. As of spring 1992 there were lists of recom-

mended readings for elementary and middle school, high school, and history and social science, as well as a bibliography of books in Spanish; lists for science and preschoolers were being prepared. All the lists are regularly updated. The names of the lists now available appear in Figure 1.

The adoption of new English-language arts materials was an important element in California's overall reform strategy. These new texts reflected the approach of using literature in the classroom. Publishers' desire to have their products adopted by the state for use in kindergarten to grade 8 led many to replace the unfocused narratives of the previously adopted texts and basals with literary works that had not been abridged.

Teachers have been most enthusiastic about getting literature into the textbooks. California Literature Project teachers wrote in *CLP Teacher-Leaders Speak Out: The Inside Story about the New K-8 Textbooks in English-Language Arts and What to Do about Them* (1988) that "teachers throughout California are finding that literature, a major component in the curriculum reform in English-language arts, engages both the hearts and minds of their students. Therefore, the recent statewide adoption of instructional materials has been awaited eagerly as a way to afford a range of literature in more classrooms, available for all students" (p. 5).

Preliminary results of the California Reading Initiative are encouraging. Scores on state-developed English-language arts tests at grades 8 and 12 show steady student progress. Students in California make a good showing in comparison with students in the rest of the United States on literacy indicators released by the National Assessment of Educational Progress (NAEP) in the report *Learning to Read in Our Nation's Schools* (Langer et al., 1990).

Figure 1
Booklists from the California Reading Initiative

All of the following lists are available from the California Department of Education, Sacramento, California.

Annotated Recommended Readings in Literature, Kindergarten Through Grade Eight (1988).

Literature for History-Social Science, Kindergarten Through Grade Eight (1991).

Recommended Literature, Grades Nine Through Twelve (1990).

Recommended Readings in Spanish Literature, Kindergarten Through Grade Eight (1991).

As of this writing, booklists of recommended readings for preschoolers and of science-related literature for kindergarten through grade eight were being prepared.

Data collected by the California Assessment Program (CAP) indicate that fewer eighth graders in California than in the national sample have difficulty reading their literature textbooks. Furthermore, California's eighth graders reported more reading for pleasure than did their counterparts in the national sample. This is no small accomplishment since—as pointed out by the U.S. Secretary of Education—approximately 91 percent of children's time is spent away from school. Through the California Reading Initiative, parents and communities are promoting more out-of-school reading activities, and students seem to be benefiting from the new approach to reading instruction. However, the cooperation between school and community can break down when it comes to selecting textbooks and library books.

Different Faces of Censorship

In *Literature and the Child*, Cullinan (1989) defines censorship as "the removal or banning of books, films, or magazines that are harmful or unacceptable according to the view of the censor" (p. 676). Major censorship controversies have erupted in California, and in the rest of the United States, over a new generation of literature-based readers (kindergarten to grade 8) and core works (kindergarten to grade 12) that are an integral part of English-language arts programs. These texts were intended to replace the vapid, but uncontroversial, material contained in the "Dick and Jane" variety of basal readers and heavily abridged anthologies. The stilted language and boring stories contained in these materials failed to engage readers and encourage critical thinking. However, the professional judgment of teachers and school administrators in California was questioned as they went about the task of choosing and using new materials.

In examining censorship issues, it is important to distinguish between selection and suppression. Not all materials are appropriate for student use in a classroom setting, and selections must be made on the basis of informed judgment. Educators trying to

The Many Faces of Censorship in U.S. Schools

Censorship of books takes many forms. In the United States, most challenges are aimed at schools and libraries. Some are simply cause for amusement, like the notorious case of *Making It with Mademoiselle* (a book whose presence in one library generated outraged calls for its removal until it was discovered to be a collection of sewing patterns). Others are more serious, challenging both teachers' authority to decide what belongs in the classroom and students' right to learn.

Below are a few examples of the thousands of censorship cases reported each year.

Americans All, a history textbook, was rejected by the Alabama state textbook committee in 1986 after it came under attack from usually opposing corners: feminists objected to some of the book's language, while conservatives complained that the book "lavished praise on blacks, women, labor unions, and Democrats."

The school board in Island Trees, New York, removed 11 books from library shelves in 1982, including *A Hero Ain't Nothing But a Sandwich* (labeled "anti-American" because in the book a teacher tells a student that George Washington owned slaves). The case went to the U.S. Supreme Court, which ruled that it is unconstitutional for school boards to remove books from the library "simply because they dislike the ideas contained in those books."

Maurice Sendak's *In the Night Kitchen* has been pulled from school libraries in several U.S. states because in it a little boy appears naked. In one case, the book was returned to the shelves after the librarian drew shorts on the boy.

Aleksandr Solzhenitsyn's *One Day in the Life of Ivan Denisovich* has been removed from the shelves of a number of high school libraries in the United States because of objectionable language. Ironically, this book was barred from publication for political reasons in Solzhenitsyn's native Soviet Union, and eventually (with his other writing) led to the author's expulsion from the country.

The *American Heritage Dictionary* has been removed from school libraries in Anchorage (Alaska), Folsom (California), Cedar Lake (Indiana), and Eldon (Missouri) because of "objectionable language."

James and Christopher Collier's *My Brother Sam Is Dead,* a 1974 Newbery Honor Book, has faced challenges in several school districts because of profanity. It was removed from the curriculum in New Richmond, Ohio, in 1989 because of several objectionable words and because it did not represent "acceptable ethical standards for fifth graders."

In an ironic case, Nat Hentoff's *The Day They Came to Arrest the Book*—which discusses censorship—faced a call for removal from schools in Charlottesville, Virginia, in 1990 for being "inflammatory" in its questioning of authoritarian roles.

implement literature-based programs face the challenge of seeing members of the outside community attempt to suppress carefully selected high-quality materials that have educational merit. Attempting to satisfy all potential critics puts educators in an almost impossible position, since the criticisms of the would-be censors are often so broad as to be applicable to most literary works written for children and young adults.

The next sections of this chapter outline the criticisms most frequently leveled at materials that are targets of attempted censorship.

This Text Is Too Negative

A charge of negativity is often made by critics who want to suppress any themes, plots, or characters that they feel are too dark or do not provide an upbeat point of view. This criticism is used particularly to assail any story that mentions or deals with death. For example, Katherine Paterson's award-winning book about friendship and loss, *Bridge to Terabithia*, is often criticized because of the death of one of the lead characters. Even A.A. Milne's poem "Happiness" (which is included in Harcourt Brace Jovanovich's *Impressions* basal reading series) has been attacked because it does not include the word *happiness*. Wearing a rain hat and boots on a rainy day is apparently too depressing an image for some critics.

According to the California Department of Education's *English-Language Arts Framework* (1987), using literary works in the classroom has the potential "to capture the breadth of human experience" (p. 7). This simply cannot be accomplished if difficult and potentially dark or negative themes are excluded from classroom study.

The California document goes on to describe themes such as the struggle between conscience and laws or social mores. This struggle, while occasionally negative, is clearly an important issue for children to consider if they are to become responsible adults. It is beautifully depicted in Mark Twain's *The Adventures of Huckleberry Finn*, and Huck himself—in a reincarnation imagined by writer Daniel J. Boorstin (1991)—sums it up this way: "What I done, the professors like to explain, was spit on conventional morality to follow my heart, which is what true morality's all about, they says." Huck also says, "Well, if I'm to tell the whole truth, I reckon I should put in here that we is still banned from some classrooms." Certainly, the removal of Twain's classic from some classrooms and libraries is an event far darker and more ominous than the exposure of students to negative behavior.

That Book Conflicts with My Religion

Public schools have been silent for a long time on the subject of religion. Lately, however, calls for change have come from a broad cross-section of the population, who feel that schools should teach *about* religion. Books and stories with religious themes are no longer avoided, and the role of religion in current and past events is discussed in history and social studies textbooks. It must be remembered, though, that there are still many who would impose on schools a strict silence in the area of teaching about religion. There are also those who object to the treatment of religion in particular materials. Still others have difficulty with teaching about religion without promoting any one religion over another. This is clearly a sensitive and complicated area, and one where teachers and administrators must exercise caution and their best professional judgment.

An interesting offshoot of the issue of teaching about religion is the belief of some would-be censors that stories that include witches or aspects of fantasy or the supernatural promote witchcraft and the occult. This puts books like Richard Baum's *The Wizard of Oz* in jeopardy—even the Good Witch of the North is a problem for some. A recent report for the Educational Congress of California, *Curriculum Challenges in California* (Adler, 1990), notes that witchcraft is one of the topics most frequently cited as offensive by would-be censors. Some critics examined one book so carefully that they discovered Satan lurking in an illustration—but only after photocopying the page, turning it upside down, and looking at the illustration in the mirror.

If all books with witches were removed from classrooms, students would not have the opportunity to read classics as diverse as *Snow White* and *Macbeth*. On the broader issue of including religion, important cultural and literary works—like the Bible—would have to be excluded from English classes if the proponents of "no religion in schools" or "only the religion I adhere to" prevail.

These Materials Are Subversive

A book or story that contains any demonstration of lack of respect for authority can be subject to challenge by censors. Many important works of classic and contemporary children's literature that appeal to the reader's imagination match this description, however.

Lurie (1990) describes the "subversive" nature of children's literature in *Don't Tell the Grown-Ups*. She points out the disobedient behavior and challenges to authority of characters from such well-known works as Kenneth Grahame's *The Wind in the Willows* (Toad is described as "foolish, rash and boastful as well as incorrigibly criminal") and Beatrix Potter's *Peter Rabbit*. Indeed, Peter is the original rascally rabbit. One suspects that the reader identifies more with his pranks, however, than with the obedience of Flopsy and Mopsy; it is Peter who is the memorable character. Most readers would settle for camomile tea over pie if this were the cost of sharing in his adventures!

Lurie points out further how parental authority is undermined in P.L. Travers's *Mary Poppins* and James Barrie's *Peter Pan*. She concludes that "most of the great works of juvenile literature are subversive in one way or another: they express ideas and emotions not generally approved of or even recognized at the time; they make fun of honored figures and piously held beliefs and they view social pretenses with clear-eyed directness, remarking—as in Andersen's famous tale—that the emperor has no clothes" (p. 4).

What adult critics of "subversive" children's literature fail to realize, however, is that such works can often help children develop desirable attitudes and behaviors. Books that question authority encourage readers to think about issues and to come up with their own well-reasoned opinions. Children who read such books and who are taught about them in a sensitive and sensible way may be helped in their development as creative, independent, critical, and innovative thinkers.

There's Bad Language in This Book

Any book in which a character swears, takes the name of the Lord in vain, or uses opprobrious language is vulnerable to this charge. Holden Caulfield is the character whose mouth critics would most frequently like to wash out with soap. Holden himself is outraged when he finds profanity written in the stairwell of his sister's school but, as he learns, you cannot erase all "bad" language. Holden also gives voice to the fears and confusion adolescents face—which is why J.D. Salinger's *The Catcher in the Rye* is read in so many high school classes.

It must be remembered that language inappropriate for use by students and teachers can be used effectively in literature to assist in creating a memorable and believable character. In most cases, the language is a device for getting at a higher truth, as it is in *The Catcher in the Rye*. In a classroom setting, students are trying to get at the meaning of the story and come to an understanding of the character, not to dwell on the language he or she uses. In the case of Holden, young readers realize that he swears to cover up his disillusionment and to provoke a reaction. It is this realization that is important.

This Material Is Simply Disagreeable or Inappropriate

Many controversial issues are vigorously debated in a democracy. Dr. Seuss's *The Lorax*, for example, has been criticized as being too proenvironmental and insensitive to the legitimate concerns of the logging industry. Other critics want all books about zoos and all cookbooks that include recipes with meat or meat products removed because of their beliefs about animal rights.

It is certainly true that some books are in conflict with the sincerely held views of some segments of the population. Student reading would be seriously curtailed, however, if every

political, social, and ethical point of view held in our pluralistic society had to be catered to in the selection of texts. Rather than supressing books because they tackle controversial issues, teachers can use these books to explore issues with students.

What Should Educators Do?

The elimination of all books with controversial content would indeed have a chilling effect on academic freedom and on students' access to ideas. Certain professional organizations, such as the International Reading Association and the American Library Association, strongly oppose censorship and attempts to restrict student access to quality material. (A list of organizations involved in opposing censorship and promoting intellectual freedom in the United States, along with information about the resources they provide, appears in Figure 2.) In testimony before the Idaho State Board of Education, the executive director of the International Reading Association asserted that "school programs and materials may come under attack by individuals or groups with narrow interests. Even though it is recognized that one purpose of reading is to learn about diversity in the world, the individuals or groups would at times deny students the right to read about other cultures, customs, and beliefs. Often materials and reading programs are eliminated or drastically modified as a result of noninstructional considerations" (Mitchell, 1991).

The following five-step strategy for selecting textbooks and library books may prevent some censorship efforts. It is designed to support the professional judgment of trained

Figure 2
Education Organizations with Resources on Censorship Issues

American Library Association (ALA)
Freedom to Read Foundation *or* Office for Intellectual Freedom
50 E. Huron St.
Chicago IL 60611
(tel. 800-545-2433, 312-280-4224, *or* 312-280-4220)

> Resources include *Censorship and Selection: Issues and Answers for Schools* (published with the American Association of School Administrators); *Intellectual Freedom Manual* (3rd ed.); "Censorship in the Schools" (brochure); *Newsletter on Intellectual Freedom* (bimonthly); "Freedom to Read" statement; "Intellectual Freedom" statement; Banned Books exhibit; Banned Books Week materials.

International Reading Association (IRA)
Public Information Office
800 Barksdale Rd.
PO Box 8139
Newark DE 19714-8139
(tel. 302-731-1600, ext. 215)

> Resources include text of the executive director's testimony to the Idaho State Board of Education (January 1991); "The Dangers of Censoring Textbooks and Reading Program Materials" (statement); "Censorship" statement; "On Textbook and Reading Program Censorship" (resolution); "On Opposing Abridgement or Adaptation as a Form of Censorship" (resolution); "Selection of Reading Materials" (resolution); "Availability of Reading Materials" (resolution).

National Council of Teachers of English (NCTE)
1111 Kenyon Rd.
Urbana IL 61801
(tel. 217-328-3870)

> Resources include *Dealing with Censorship* (2nd ed.); "Censorship: Don't Let It Become an Issue in Your Schools" (pamphlet); "The Students' Right to Know" (booklet); "The Students' Right to Read" (pamphlet); "Procedure for Handling Challenges Against Intellectual Freedom"; "Report on Basal Readers: A Statement of the NCTE Commission on Reading."

A number of other groups and associations are involved in opposing censorship and may be able to offer specific resources and materials of interest on these issues. These organizations include the American Booksellers Association, the American Civil Liberties Union, the Association of American Publishers, the Association for Supervision and Curriculum Development, the First Amendment Congress, International P.E.N., the Modern Language Association, the National Association of Elementary School Principals, the National Association of Secondary School Principals, the National Coalition Against Censorship, the National Education Association, and People for the American Way.

teachers, librarians, and school administrators when selections are challenged. As Edwards (1986) wrote, "Controversy is something educators must live with; schools have always been society's battlegrounds. What is needed is not an end to conflict, but clearer goals, firmer convictions, and stronger defenses." The five-step strategy outline can help educators handle these unavoidable controversies in a thoughtful manner.

1. **Establish clear educational standards**. The curriculum should determine what instructional materials are ultimately selected. In California this is accomplished by seeking a broad professional consensus on curriculum frameworks and model curriculum standards. Local school districts then use the frameworks and standards in developing their curricula. This establishment of clear educational standards puts the emphasis on instructional considerations in the selection process.

2. **Develop standard procedures for selecting materials**. Most educators oppose censorship, but not selection; clearly, not all materials belong in classrooms. Well-defined procedures that rely heavily on teacher input and involvement are important to making thoughtful decisions about what to include in the curriculum and what to leave out. These procedures should include the development of criteria for selecting both textbooks and library books.

3. **Involve parents in the process**. Parents and teachers can be most effective in helping children when working together on common objectives. The selection procedures established should provide parents and other interested community members with the opportunity to review and comment about the materials under consideration. A public display of the materials should be arranged for this purpose. Once materials are selected, many parents enjoy participating in "book talks" with teachers about the texts their children will be using.

4. **Establish procedures to follow when challenges are made**. Confrontational situations are easier to defuse when procedures with which to respond to challenges have been prepared and widely disseminated. A recent California study found that 23 percent of reporting districts had not adopted policies for dealing with challenges. It is more difficult to resolve conflict when the steps for doing so are not in place.

5. **Teach and model tolerance and respect**. The most disturbing aspect of recent censorship controversies in California has been that when some critics wanted to suppress certain materials that the majority of parents supported, disagreements have degenerated into rude and threatening behavior. One California teacher sent out more than 100 letters to alert parents to the presence of four-letter words in *The Catcher in the Rye*, a book the class would be reading (Keller-Gage, 1990). Five parents requested that their children read one of the alternative books that were offered. Finally a complaint about the

book was made to the local school board and it was removed from the supplemental reading list. In another California district, one controversy over school reading materials became so heated that tires were slashed, homes were defaced, and teachers were threatened. Some children were directed to boycott the books in class—ironic in light of one common charge that the material undermined respect for authority.

It is obvious that adult role models usually have more of an impact on children's behavior than books do. Freedom of speech must be celebrated and respected; critics should have a forum for making their opinions known. Tolerance is valued and necessary in a pluralistic society and must be practiced by both sides when censorship disputes arise.

It would do well for all of us to remember that children are influenced by many factors. Unfortunately, most children spend more out-of-class time on mind-numbing activities like playing video games and watching television than on reading. Given the pervasiveness of these sorts of influences, alternatives in the form of high-quality literary works could be extremely beneficial in connecting and informing our young people politically, ethically, and socially. Some of these works will be controversial but are nonetheless of social and educational value. Do not, however, overestimate the influence of any one book; instead, students should be encouraged to read widely.

Here's an example of an extreme overreaction. Trina Schart Hyman's *Little Red Riding Hood*, a widely acclaimed rendering of

the familiar story by The Brothers Grimm, has been banned in some classrooms because Little Red is depicted bringing wine to her grandmother. At the end of the tale, Grandma is drinking the wine and seems to feel better. Well-meaning concern was expressed that young readers might associate wine with good health and high spirits. But this is surely an adult interpretation, not that of a first grader who probably associates Grandma's improvement to relief from having escaped the wolf. Indeed, if it is that easy to influence a child, why do we have to provide antidrinking messages to students so frequently?

As educators and parents we should take care not to underestimate our children and ourselves. As Shelley Keller-Gage (1990), the teacher in *The Catcher in the Rye* dispute, wrote, "I wish those who will censor books had more faith in their children, in their teachers, and in their own parenting."

References

Adler, L. (1990, October). *Curriculum challenges in California*. Fullerton, CA: California State University – Fullerton.

Boorstin, D.J. (1991, April 22). History's hidden turning points. *U.S. News and World Report*.

California Department of Education. (1987). *English-language arts framework for California public schools, kindergarten through grade twelve*. Sacramento, CA: Author.

California Literature Project. (1988). CLP *teacher-leaders speak out: The inside story about the new K-8 textbooks for English-language arts and what to do about them*. San Diego, CA: Author.

Cullinan, B.E. (1989). *Literature and the child* (2nd ed.). Orlando, FL: Harcourt Brace Jovanovich.

Edwards, J. (1986, Spring). *Virginia English bulletin*.

Keller-Gage, S. (1990, March 13). Full circle: "The catcher in the rye." *Family Circle*.

Langer, J.A., Applebee, A.N., Mullis, I.V.S., & Foertsch, M.A. (1990). *Learning to read in our nation's schools: Instruction and achievement in 1988 at grades 4, 8, and 12.* Princeton, NJ: National Assessment of Educational Progress, Educational Testing Service.

Lurie, A. (1990). *Don't tell the grown-ups.* Boston, MA: Little, Brown.

Mitchell, P.K., Jr. (1991, January 23). Testimony of the International Reading Association in opposition to the proposed censorship of the reading textbook series Impressions to the Idaho State Board of Education, Boise, ID.

Children's Books

Baum, F.L. (1982). *The Wizard of Oz.* New York: Henry Holt.

Grimm, J., & W. (1983). *Little Red Riding Hood.* (Retold and ill. by T.S. Hyman.) Boston, MA: Houghton Mifflin.

Paterson, K. (1977). *Bridge to Terabithia.* New York: Crowell.

Seuss, Dr. (1971). *The Lorax.* New York: Random House.

Twain, M. (1967). *The adventures of Huckleberry Finn.* New York: Bobbs-Merrill.

This chapter was written by the author in her private capacity. No official support or endorsement by the U.S. Department of Education is intended or should be inferred.

A Letter to Bee Cullinan

Afterword

Bill Martin Jr

Bee, you asked me what I think about when I write books for children, so I'll tell you as best I know. The things I believe about language have become so much a part of the way I think and write that it's hard for me to sort them out and talk about them separately. I guess I've become integrated, sort of like the curriculum.

But there's a place to start—because I don't *write* books, I *talk* them. Of course, words do get set down on paper at some point but that's not where I begin. My writing process is talking; I talk a story through many times to see if I'm saying what I mean. I need to hear what I have to say.

Over 25 years ago I worked on the teacher's edition of *Sounds of Language* (Holt, Rinehart & Winston, 1964), and I said some things in that book that I still believe today: One of the miracles of language is its way of working in chunks of meaning. For example, an experienced reader doesn't move through a sentence by reading each word separately; instead a reader learns to see—and sense—groups of words that best create meaning. When a sentence is written across a column or a page, the reader must do the work of seeing the words in clusters that release their meaning.

Children's intuition about language leads them through a written sentence the way they would speak it. I suppose I was beginning to understand these things when I wrote,

''Brown Bear,
Brown Bear,
What do you see?''

''I see a redbird
looking at me.''

Children quickly figure out natural language patterns and use them to make sense of print. This is also how they learned to talk. They listened to talk on all sides of them, began to experiment and figure out how talk works, and then made talk work for them. They do the same with reading and writing.

I know you love to hear me tell about how I wrote *Brown Bear, Brown Bear* on the Port Washington line of the Long Island Railroad, because that's the same train you take into New York City. It's true, I got on the train at Plandome station, the first stop after Port Washington (where you get on), and 33 minutes later, when we arrived at Penn Station, I had completed *Brown Bear*; I had the entire story worked out in my head. No one else could share the joy I was feeling about the story until I got to my office; in fact, the person in the seat beside me on the train had glared at me a few times because I muttered the lines aloud to get the rhythm of the language just right. *Brown Bear* was a sort of watershed for me. I saw what children were able to do with that story and I became more courageous in creating rhythmic, highly patterned stories.

I was beginning to learn that each of us has a linguistic storehouse into which we deposit patterns for stories and poems and sentences and words. When language patterns enter through the ear they remain available for a lifetime of reading, writing, listening, and speaking. My own language storehouse was given a pretty good boost by my teacher Miss Davis. I told about her in *Children's Literature in the Reading Program*, the book a group of us wrote for Ron Mitchell:

> A blessed thing happened to me as a child. I had a teacher who read to me. Of course she was reading to all other children in the classroom, but I believed she was reading *just to me* because I was a nonreader.

Since then, I've learned that good readers look at a page of print and trigger patterns that have been stored in their linguistic treasuries. These patterns range all the way from the plot structure an author has used in a story to the rhyme scheme that holds a poem together to the placement of an adjective in front of a noun to the rhythmical structure of a line of prose or poetry to the *-ed* ending of a word. Children are able to figure out a lot of new vocabulary because of the similarity between new structures and structures already in their linguistic storehouses.

A poor reader, on the other hand, looks at a page and can trigger no patterns to help unlock the print. This person may not have been read to or talked with very much and therefore may not have had a lot of story and poem and sentence and word patterns deposited in his or her linguistic storehouse. A child's lack of triggering can also occur if the spoken language patterns he or she has heard are not the kind encountered in print. Shirley Brice Heath talks about this in *Ways with Words* (Cambridge University Press, 1983). She showed us that children's home language sometimes doesn't match their school language; this creates problems for the child.

So you can see why I think reading stories and poems aloud is so important. In the preschool and school years children are filling their storehouses of language possibilities. Sometimes when we read aloud the children are listening, sometimes they are chiming in, sometimes they are reading in chorus, sometimes the boys and girls read in dialogue, sometimes they are joining in by memory, sometimes we and the children are reading aloud together—with the children following the print in their books so their eyes can see what their ears hear their tongues say. It doesn't matter how it's done, just as long as children hear those miraculous language patterns over and over.

There is no better way for children to learn to appreciate and use language than for them to have broad experiences that attune their ears and tongues—and later their eyes—to the rhythms, melodies, and sounds of language. This makes it possible for children to build bridges between the linguistic facts of their worlds and the linguistic facts of the printed page. That's why I pay so much attention to the rhythms, melodies, and sounds of language in writing. I want the books to attune the ear and tongue first, then the eye. If words come trippingly from the tongue and fall pleasantly on the ear, they'll be easier on the eye—or should I say, "in the eye."

Do you remember the day I stopped by your class at New York University and we read a story together? You started to show the students the pictures after we'd finished the first page of reading aloud, but I said, "No, the visual part is another experience. We're just going to depend on listening this time. Let them savor the words." I really do value the work of great artists like Ted Rand, Eric Carle, and others who have illustrated so many of my books, but words must first carry the show alone. The words create pictures in the head. The words must sound like a real person talking and say something a real person would say.

John Archambault and I have created a number of books that are totally talk centered. *The Ghost-Eye Tree* grew out of a session in which John and I were telling each other the scariest ghost stories we knew; *Here Are My Hands* is a highly patterned word poem about body parts that we learned when we were in kindergarten; *Knots on a Counting Rope* is a conversation we developed between a child and his grandfather. John has a marvelous ear for the sound and rhythm of language. He did a tape with Ray Charles not long ago, and on it he talks about how we came to write *Chicka*

Chicka Boom Boom:

> It all started with a cheer I heard from a teacher. It goes something like this: Chicka chicka whole potato, half past alligator, bim bam bolligator. Give three cheers for the dippy dappy happy sappy readers. Are we happy? Well I guess. Readers. Readers. Yes, yes, yes....
>
> I said, "Would you write it down for me?" and he started to write down c-h-i-c-k, but then he said, "No, no, it was not chick-ka, it was chig-ga." But guess what stuck in my head? It was the chicka chicka. So for days—weeks—I started walking around saying "chicka chicka boom boom...." Even my son, who was six months old at the time, started going "boom boom, boom boom...."

So *Chicka Chicka Boom Boom* came together because the words sounded so good —not just to me and John, but to a six-month-old baby, too.

Well, Bee dear, you see how important the rhythm of language is to me. You see how important it is for children to own the basic language structures so they can give wings to what they want to say. I'm delighted when children borrow a literary structure and adorn it with their own thoughts and their own language. That means they have already deposited the basic pattern in their linguistic storehouses and it is now available for a lifetime of use in reading and writing and literary appreciation.

Can you imagine what will happen to children who during their elementary school reading experiences feel the flow and depth of life-lifting language every day? And if each teacher's literature-based reading program fulfills all of its expectations, you and I and every concerned human being who is dedicated to helping children learn will have developed a camaraderie that will change the course of language instruction in our schools. We will have succeeded in making language truly available to children in terms of their human needs. This possibility brings me great joy.

ILLUSTRATION ACKNOWLEDGMENTS

page xviii: From *Amazing Grace* by Mary Hoffman, illustrated by Caroline Binch. Copyright ©1991 by Caroline Binch for illustrations. Used by permission of Dial Books for Young Readers, a division of Penguin USA, Inc.

page 5: Illustration copyright 1970 by Arnold Lobel from *Frog and Toad Are Friends*, published by Harper & Row. Reprinted by permission of HarperCollins Publishers.

page 8: Illustration from *Five Little Monkeys Jumping on the Bed* by Eileen Christelow. Copyright ©1989 by Eileen Christelow. Reprinted by permission of Clarion Books, a Houghton Mifflin Company imprint. All rights reserved.

page 9: Illustration by Jan Brett reprinted by permission of G.P. Putnam's Sons from *Goldilocks and the Three Bears*, copyright ©1987 by Jan Brett.

pages 17 & 18: Illustrations by Gerald Smith from *Let Me Be the Boss* by Brod Bagert. Reprinted by permission of the publisher, Wordsong, an imprint of Boyds Mills Press.

page 30: Jacket painting by Ruth Sanderson from *Good-bye, Chicken Little*, copyright 1979 by Betsy Byars, published by Harper & Row. Reprinted by permission of HarperCollins Publishers.

page 33: Illustration copyright 1984 by Marc Simont from Bette Bao Lord's *In the Year of the Boar and Jackie Robinson*, published by Harper & Row. Reprinted by permission of HarperCollins Publishers.

page 36: From *Lyddie* by Katherine Paterson, jacket illustration by Debbi Chabrian. Copyright ©1991 by Katherine Paterson. Used by permission of Lodestar Books, an affiliate of Dutton Children's Books, a division of Penguin USA Inc.

page 43: Illustration copyright 1981 by Aliki Brandenberg from *Digging Up Dinosaurs*, a Harper Trophy Book published by Thomas Y. Crowell. Reprinted by permission of HarperCollins Publishers.

page 45: From *Christopher Columbus: Voyager to the Unknown* by Nancy Smiler Levinson. Copyright ©1990 by Nancy Smiler Levinson. Used by permission of Lodestar Books, an affiliate of Dutton Children's Books, a division of Penguin USA Inc.

page 52: Illustration from *Lulu and the Flying Babies* by Posy Simmonds. Copyright ©1988 by Posy Simmonds. Reprinted by permission of Alfred A. Knopf, Inc.

page 56: Jacket illustration by Mike Wimmer reprinted by permission of G.P. Putnam's Sons from *The Great Little Madison* by Jean Fritz, jacket illustration copyright ©1989 by Mike Wimmer.

page 65: Illustration by Tomie dePaola reprinted by permission of G.P. Putnam's Sons from *The Art Lesson*, text and illustrations copyright ©1989 by Tomie dePaola.

page 68: Illustration from *The Popcorn Book*, copyright ©1978 by Tomie dePaola. Reprinted by permission of Holiday House.

page 74: Cover illustration by Lois Ehlert from *Chicka Chicka Boom Boom* by Bill Martin Jr and John Archambault, copyright 1989. Reprinted by permission of the publisher, Simon and Schuster Books for Young Readers, New York, New York 10020.

page 82: Jacket illustration from Walter Dean Myers's *The Mouse Rap*. Jacket art copyright 1990 by Andy Bacha, jacket copyright 1990 by Harper & Row, Publishers, Inc. Reprinted by permission of HarperCollins Publishers.

page 89: Jacket illustration by Ronald Himler for *Dragonwings*, copyright 1975 by Laurence Yep, published by Harper & Row. Reprinted by permission of HarperCollins Publishers.

page 97: Illustration from *War Boy: A Country Childhood* by Michael Foreman. Copyright ©1989 by Michael Foreman. By permission of Little, Brown and Company (for the U.S.) and Pavilion Books (for the U.K. and Canada).

page 100: Cover photograph by Carol Palmer from *Maniac Magee* by Jerry Spinelli. Copyright ©1990 by Jerry Spinelli. By permission of Little, Brown and

Company (for the U.S. and Canada) and the author's agent, the Ray Lincoln Literary Agency (for Australia, New Zealand, and the U.K.).

page 106: Jacket art for William Taylor's *Agnes the Sheep* copyright ©1991 by David Gaadt. Reproduced by permission of the publisher, Ashton Scholastic Limited, Auckland, New Zealand.

page 126: Illustration from *Chocolate Dreams* by Arnold Adoff, illustrated by Turi MacCombie. Illustrations copyright ©1989 by Turi MacCombie. Reprinted by permission of Lothrop, Lee & Shepard Books, a division of William Morrow & Company, Inc.

page 129: Illustration by Garth Williams from *Charlotte's Web* by E.B. White, copyright 1952. Reprinted by permission of HarperCollins Publishers.

page 141: Illustration by Ed Young reprinted by permission of Philomel Books from *Lon Po Po*, copyright ©1989 by Ed Young.

page 144: Illustration from *Jumanji* by Chris Van Allsburg. Copyright ©1981 by Chris Van Allsburg. Reprinted by permission of Houghton Mifflin Company. All rights reserved.

page 145: Jacket from *Desert Giant: The World of the Saguaro Cactus* by Barbara Bash. Copyright ©1989 by Barbara Bash. By permission of Little, Brown and Company.

Children's Book Authors and Illustrators

Note: Authors and illustrators (or photographers) are listed together in one index. If an illustrator is not also the author of the book listed, his or her name is followed by "(Ill.)" to indicate that the book is also indexed under an author's name.

Children's Book Titles

Title Index